100

Quality Health Care
Worldwide
1888-1988

THE ABBOTT ALMANAC:

100 YEARS OF COMMITMENT TO QUALITY HEALTH CARE

BENJAMIN

Credits
The original manuscript for this book was prepared by William D. Pratt, a 31-year Abbott employee who served as vice president, public affairs, from 1972 to 1982. The editing of the manuscript involved many employees and retirees. Abbott archivist Ronald G. Wiegand verified all Abbott facts and collected the Abbott photographs. Miriam Trangsrud Welty, director of public affairs, served as project manager. The Benjamin Company, Inc., served as editor and publisher, verifying facts in the world section, obtaining world photographs with the help of Diane Hamilton, photo researcher, and providing art direction.

Contents

February 4, 1987

Chairman Robert A. Schoellhorn
Abbott Laboratories
Abbott Park, Illinois 60064

Dear Chairman Schoellhorn:

I thought you might be interested in hearing about the long and fruitful relationship my family has had with Abbott Laboratories. We may be rather modest stockholders, but each year we become more amazed as we watch the growth of Abbott and its stock, considering our humble beginnings!

At the turn of the century, my grandparents Bruce and Edna Birmingham lived in the Ravenswood area of Chicago. Not far from their home, Dr. Abbott began his business in the carriage house of his home. My grandmother knew Dr. Abbott very well through the Ravenswood bank where she worked. The Abbotts also happened to go to the same church, Ravenswood Methodist, and their daughter later became the Sunday School teacher of my mother, Betty Birmingham Moorehead. My mother went on to be a Sunday School teacher for Dr. Abbott's grandchildren!

In 1934 and 1935 my grandfather purchased a total of 6⅓ shares of Abbott stock for $330.50. From these few shares, our family has been able to do a great deal. Of course it has split, and split, and split, so much so that we can hardly calculate the total of shares that are or have been spread around the family. First, it helped finance my mother's education. When my parents were married in 1942, they were given Abbott stock which, among other things, helped finance their first car. Through continual splits, they were able to give each of their four children a sizable amount of stock to help finance their college educations. The Abbott stock has made it possible for us to pursue careers in the health-care and human services fields. We continue to watch the Abbott stock with great interest and are already planning for its legacy to help our children through college.

Whenever we see an Abbott product or drive by Abbott Laboratories on our way north, we always feel like we are a part of Abbott Laboratories. Taking the good fortune of the past and looking toward the bright future we are sure Abbott has, we look forward to many more years as an "Abbott family."

Most sincerely,
Becky Moorehead Hoag
Batavia, Illinois

6

Foreword

That letter on the facing page from shareholder Becky Hoag — and other letters like it from shareholders small and large whose families have been a part of Abbott Laboratories for many of its 100 years — can't help but make us stop and reflect on the great legacy left us by our founder, Dr. Wallace Calvin Abbott. The company he created has touched the lives of millions of shareholders, employees, health-care providers, and patients across America and around the world. Dr. Abbott's vision and the company's subsequent success reflect our ongoing commitment to provide quality health care at an affordable cost.

As we celebrate our Centennial and begin our second century, we reaffirm this commitment to the principles that have guided Abbott through its first 100 years. Inherent in that pledge is our recognition that, despite the technological advances that have radically altered the face of health care today, the story of Abbott remains a story of *people*. And whether it's the physician in Florence, the patient in Pittsburgh, the researcher at his lab bench in North Chicago, or the "modest stockholder" in Batavia, Illinois, we look forward to another 100 distinguished years of serving the needs of all the members of the "Abbott family."

Robert A. Schoellhorn

ROBERT A. SCHOELLHORN
CHAIRMAN AND
CHIEF EXECUTIVE OFFICER

Abbott Park, Illinois
January 1988

Introduction

It was the year a minister's son from New Jersey passed along the keys to the White House to the dapper grandson of the "hero of Tippecanoe" . . . the year America was devastated by a series of natural disasters ranging from fires down south to blizzards up north . . . the year Jack the Ripper shook up England and Kaiser Wilhelm took over Germany.

It was the year a Vermont farmer's son-cum-fledgling physician set out in "a very modest way" to launch a venture that would have a long-term impact on the world of medicine.

In 1888, when Dr. Wallace Calvin Abbott turned his energies to the task of manufacturing a new kind of pill, the state of medical practice was sorely in need of reform. To the 19th-century physician, patient care consisted mainly of primitive procedures and crude medicinals based on fluids extracted from herbs and plants. Dr. Abbott was convinced a better treatment *had* to be possible. And inspired by the theories of Belgian-born surgeon Adolphe Burggraeve, he set out to find that better way.

In the tiny kitchen of his cramped apartment quarters in the Ravenswood section of Chicago, the young doctor began to produce medicinal granules based on the "active principles" or "alkaloids" of drug plants. His granules proved to be more accurate and soluble than the "nauseous mixtures" currently in vogue. First-year sales totaled $2,000 — testament to the acceptance of those accurate granules by fellow physicians.

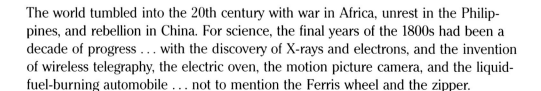

The world tumbled into the 20th century with war in Africa, unrest in the Philippines, and rebellion in China. For science, the final years of the 1800s had been a decade of progress . . . with the discovery of X-rays and electrons, and the invention of wireless telegraphy, the electric oven, the motion picture camera, and the liquid-fuel-burning automobile . . . not to mention the Ferris wheel and the zipper.

Progress also characterized the decade at the newly incorporated Abbott Alkaloidal Company. Sales passed the $100,000 mark in 1898, and by 1900 readers of Abbott catalogs could choose from nearly 350 alkaloidal granules and tablets, as well as an assortment of gelatin capsules, elastic bandages, abdominal belts, syringes, aspirators, and a variety of alkaloidal literature. Over the next 15 years, Abbott would weather its first downturn in sales, a disastrous fire, and a sobering U.S. depression to achieve, in 1915, retail sales totaling nearly $600,000.

It was the year U.S. common stock prices reached an all-time high in September . . . only to crash on Tuesday, October 29, with the greatest one-day loss in Wall Street history, an infamous record that would stand for 58 years.

By ironic coincidence, 1929 was also the year Abbott chose to make its first public offering of stock, at $32 per share on the Chicago Stock Exchange. By 1986, 100 shares of that first issue would become 80,256 shares, with a market value of about $4 million.

The seeds for that phenomenal growth were planted during World War I, when America's entry into the war raging in Europe signaled an end to the German patent monopoly in synthetic chemical and medicinal products. Abbott was well positioned to take advantage of the inherent opportunities. Under the guidance of Dr. Alfred Burdick, research emphasis had shifted from alkaloids to synthetics, a new direction reflected in 1915 in the company's new name, Abbott Laboratories. By war's end, it was clear that Abbott had taken a significant step toward becoming a full-fledged, research-driven pharmaceutical firm.

With growth came an urgent need for expanded production facilities. In 1925, all company operations were moved 30 miles to the north, from Ravenswood to a 26-acre tract of land in the city of North Chicago. Dr. Abbott inaugurated the project, but upon his death in 1921, its fulfillment was left to Dr. Burdick, the founder's successor as president.

A long decline in U.S. stock prices in 1930 marked the beginning of the Great Depression that would engulf much of the world. Three years later, Franklin D. Roosevelt began an unprecedented three-term U.S. presidency, while Adolph Hitler swept into office in Germany. The first rumblings of war could be heard with Hitler's 1935 denunciation of the Versailles Treaty — and in 1941, the Japanese bombing of Pearl Harbor compelled America's entry into what had become a worldwide maelstrom. By war's end, nearly 45 million people had died, most of them civilians.

Despite depression, recession, and a slow recovery, the years leading up to World War II were marked by exciting advances at Abbott: three major acquisitions under the leadership of Dr. Burdick . . . product diversification and innovation with the development of *Nembutal*, the classic drug for sedation; *Pentothal*, destined to become the world's largest-selling intravenous anesthetic; and commercial breakthroughs in the field of nutritionals . . . rapid expansion of the international division under Dr. Burdick's successor S. DeWitt Clough and future Abbott President Rolly Cain . . . and dedication of a $500,000 state-of-the-art research center at the North Chicago plant on the occasion of the company's 50th anniversary.

Among Abbott's many contributions during the war were its production of dried blood plasma for the armed forces . . . pioneering research in the commercial output of penicillin . . . production of the battlefield anesthetic *Pentothal*, Halazone tablets for water purification, and *Sterilope* Envelopes for sterilizing wounds . . . and the sponsoring of paintings by important artists for a series of War Bond posters distributed by the Treasury Department.

The fifties and sixties saw the Cold War heat up to the boiling point and civil discord plague the U.S. America managed to extract its forces from Korea only to be drawn ever deeper into the quagmire of Vietnam. The U.S.S.R. won the race into space, but the Soviet Union blinked first in its showdown with the U.S. over missile bases. And violence rocked the nation in a series of assassinations, civil rights demonstrations, and antiwar protests.

Meanwhile at Abbott, the course was steady and the direction, ever upward. By the late 1960s, a metamorphosis was complete — a "new" Abbott had emerged, evolving from a traditional ethical pharmaceutical house to a diversified company with products that embraced a broad spectrum of health care including pharmaceuticals, hospital products, consumer health products, and infant and medical nutritionals. Sales passed the $100 million mark in 1957, $200 million in 1964, and $300 million in 1967. Behind this spectacular climb lay product innovations like the antibiotic **10**   *Erythrocin* . . . industry-leading research in radioactive pharmaceuticals . . . and continuing diversification through acquisition. Another harbinger of growth: the purchase in 1961 of 420 acres of land five miles southwest of the North Chicago plant — future site of Abbott Park, world headquarters of the flourishing firm.

From the constitutional crisis of Watergate to the 444-day ordeal of American hostages in Iran ... from the final cessation of war in Vietnam to continuing terrorism and violence in the Middle East ... from the hoopla of America's bicentennial celebration to the horror of the *Challenger* explosion ... from Corazon Aquino's electoral victory to the record stock market plunge of 1987 ... the world has traveled a long and often perplexing path through the past two decades. Along the way, one bright beacon has shined encouragement: research in the field of health care has continued to solve seemingly insurmountable problems, and the people of the world have continued to benefit from outstanding advances in medical therapy.

Dr. Wallace Calvin Abbott would scarcely recognize the diverse, global health-care enterprise that over the past century has sprung from the seeds of his inspiration. Today, the company the young doctor founded comprises some 37,000 employees in 41 countries — researching, developing, producing, and distributing a multitude of health-care products for the benefit of the citizens of 130 nations.

Most of those products have come from the research efforts of the past two decades. Many — the *Ausria* diagnostic test, the *VP* clinical analyzer, and the *TDx* drug monitoring system among them — are important offspring of the world-leading diagnostics division created in 1973. One promising new drug approved in 1985, *Lupron*, is doubly significant as the first product to be marketed by TAP, the joint venture between Abbott and Japan's Takeda Chemical Industries. And all new products reflect Chairman Robert A. Schoellhorn's commitment to an emphasis on high-quality, cost-effective patient care — a long-term strategy that has proven itself by making Abbott one of the most diversified and profitable companies in the health-care industry.

In 1987, Abbott reported sales of more than $4 billion — a number impressive in its own right, staggering when compared to the $2,000 first-year sales total of Dr. Abbott's new enterprise in 1888. Between those two figures lies a century of service, innovation, and managed growth. The company has prospered by recognizing and meeting the needs of patients and health-care providers throughout the world. For that reason, this Centennial volume presents the story of Abbott against the greater

11

backdrop of world affairs. The pages that follow will entertain as they inform . . . and through this narrative, the reader will gain an insight into the people and the principles that have guided Abbott Laboratories through 100 years of growth, innovation, and commitment to excellence in health care.

ABBOTT LABORATORIES — SALES WORLDWIDE

YEAR	SALES	YEAR	SALES	YEAR	SALES
1888	$ 2,000	1923	$ 2,154,000	1958	$ 116,598,000
1889	4,500	1924	2,164,000	1959	122,602,000
1890	8,000	1925	2,226,000	1960	125,968,000
1891	11,000	1926	2,379,000	1961	129,850,000
1892	14,000	1927	2,531,000	1962	144,127,000
1893	21,000	1928	3,357,000	1963	158,648,000
1894	29,000	1929	3,502,000	1964	212,586,000
1895	43,000	1930	4,309,000	1965	236,802,000
1896	64,000	1931	4,054,000	1966	265,804,000
1897	86,000	1932	3,622,000	1967	303,341,000
1898	100,000	1933	4,066,000	1968	350,955,000
1899	120,000	1934	5,193,000	1969	403,877,000
1900	125,000	1935	6,118,000	1970	457,503,000
1901	133,000	1936	7,768,000	1971	458,105,000
1902	146,000	1937	9,510,000	1972	521,818,000
1903	162,000	1938	9,727,000	1973	620,398,000
1904	185,000	1939	11,485,000	1974	765,415,000
1905	200,000	1940	12,981,000	1975	940,660,000
1906	240,000	1941	16,744,000	1976	1,084,856,000
1907	290,000	1942	20,005,000	1977	1,244,976,000
1908	360,000	1943	33,265,000	1978	1,445,017,000
1909	445,000	1944	38,428,000	1979	1,683,168,000
1910	546,000	1945	37,930,000	1980	2,038,155,000
1911	600,000	1946	54,210,000	1981	2,342,524,000
1912	538,000	1947	59,621,000	1982	2,602,447,000
1913	587,000	1948	66,931,000	1983	2,927,873,000
1914	617,000	1949	67,552,000	1984	3,103,962,000
1915	594,000	1950	73,506,000	1985	3,360,273,000
1916	664,000	1951	84,366,000	1986	3,807,634,000
1917	904,000	1952	85,528,000	1987	+4,000,000,000 (est.)
1918	1,259,000	1953	88,142,000		
1919	1,486,000	1954	88,106,000		
1920	1,663,000	1955	91,707,000		
1921	1,453,000	1956	96,789,000		
1922	1,651,000	1957	111,271,000		

12

THE
ABBOTT
ALMANAC

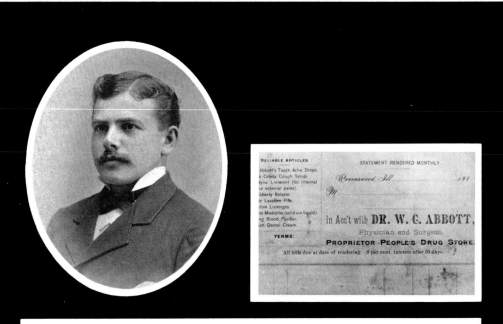

14

🌐 Grover Cleveland is president of the United States, but not for long. He'll lose in November to Indiana's Benjamin Harrison — even though Cleveland will win the popular vote by 5.5 million to Harrison's 5.4 million. Other major news across the U.S. is the string of holocausts: Mount Vernon, Illinois, virtually wiped out by a late winter cyclone . . . 400 lives lost in New York City when a freak 36-hour March blizzard paralyzes the city . . . a summer and fall epidemic of yellow fever in Jacksonville, Florida, with 4,500 cases and 400 deaths . . . and 85 people killed over the Christmas holidays in Mississippi steamboat fires.

In London, Jack the Ripper is in the midst of his series of unsolved murders of women. Germany's Emperor William I dies and is succeeded by his son Frederick III — who in turn dies after ruling only 99 days, passing the scepter to *his* son William II, the "Kaiser." An act of Parliament frees all the slaves in Brazil, opening up the labor market to 1.25 million immigrants, chiefly from Italy and Portugal.

Back in the States, sports fans along the East Coast glory when New York wins the National League pennant as Tim Keefe sets a major league record with 19 straight victories. DeWolf Hopper celebrates by offering the first public recital of "Casey at the Bat" at New York's Wallack Theatre.

Little does the world know, or care, that out in the Chicago suburb of Ravenswood, a small-time doctor and druggist is about to launch an idea new to the practice of medicine . . .

TOP LEFT: *In the parting words of young Dr. Abbott's favorite medical school professor, Dr. Victor C. Vaughn: "Go anywhere, Abbott. You will succeed wherever you go." This photograph of Wallace Calvin Abbott was taken during his student days at the University of Michigan.* TOP RIGHT: *This early copy of a monthly statement from Dr. Abbott gives customers a look at the "Reliable Articles" available at the People's Drug Store.* BOTTOM: *Swearing in ceremony for Benjamin Harrison, elected this year as the 23d president of the U.S.*

ⓐ Dr. Wallace Calvin Abbott, with a new bride and in debt for $1,000 for his purchase of a medical practice and drugstore in Ravenswood, Illinois, is not the likeliest candidate to startle the world of therapeutics this year. Between pedaling furiously to house calls on his Beckley-Ralston bicycle and building up the trade at his "People's Drug Store," Dr. Abbott is a very inquisitive and exceptionally dissatisfied physician.

The uncertainties of fluid-extract medication in particular bother him. A better way seems to be a new idea developed by a Belgian-born surgeon named Adolphe Burggraeve. That idea centers on using the "active principles" of drug plants. As such, it involves a radical departure from using entire plants or their crude water or alcoholic extracts. The large doses, the nauseating taste, the readiness with which they spoil and spill, and the uncertainty of action of fluid-extract types of medications are all good reasons to look for something better.

To do this, Dr. Burggraeve uses the only part of drug plants that really has any remedial action. The active part, or "alkaloid," can be compressed into a tiny granule or pill, and can be taken without distress or discomfort by anyone, even a baby. Another advantage of the active-principle method, or *dosimetry,* is that it allows the physician to give small, frequent *doses* of the pure, isolated alkaloid, just until the desired effect is observed.

Dr. Abbott becomes a disciple of the active-principle theory and soon begins to buy granules of varying strengths. Many, however, are not soluble enough. They disintegrate too slowly. So, in characteristically direct style, Dr. Abbott begins to manufacture his own granules . . . in the kitchen of the small apartment behind the People's Drug Store.

His total sales: $2,000. And thus the beginning.

15

The world gets a new lease on laughter this year with the birth of Charlie Chaplin. And it is immeasurably impoverished with the birth of Adolf Hitler. North and South Dakota, Montana, and Washington join the Union — bringing the United States up to 42. Oklahoma, which won't be admitted for another 18 years, ushers in its territorial land rush with a near riot. More than 20,000 people line up to await the cavalry bugle signaling the opening of unstaked territory. The mob is controlled by a circle of marshals — most of whom have already secretly staked out the choicest claims.

To the east, heavy rains so swell the Conemaugh River that it ruptures the dam above Johnstown, Pennsylvania. Six valley towns are submerged beneath a wall of water that reaches 100 feet, as 2,200 people drown. Better news comes to the country with the founding of the Mayo Clinic . . . with Thomas Edison's development of the first movie film . . . and with the new Bessemer steel I beams, making possible steel-skeleton, rapid-construction skyscrapers.

The Eiffel Tower is officially opened, to the consternation of 100 leading French artists and authors. Their petition, penned by notables Guy de Maupassant and Alexandre Dumas, compares the "horrid nightmare" to "a huge, black factory smokestack." Elsewhere in Paris, World's Fair visitors gawk at the new liquid-fuel-burning, combustion engine automobile exhibited by Austrian Karl Benz. And in Japan, a new constitution provides for the basic rights of the people while bestowing nearly limitless powers on the emperor . . . its author.

In these early years, Dr. Abbott brings to his medical practice, to his drugstore, and now to his fledgling granule-manufacturing business a stock in trade that consists mainly of good health, relentless optimism, unstoppable energy, and a reasonable disregard for debt.

His remarkable vigor and quick wit are apparent to all. The alertness of his intellect, however, astounds even his closest associates. His ideas are definite and are expressed freely, frankly, and boldly.

Much of Dr. Abbott's strength of character was formed early in life. The son of Vermont farmer Luther Abbott and his wife, Wealtha Barrows, Wallace Calvin spent his early years much like any other hardworking farm boy. The hard school of farming helped give him the tremendous physical endurance that would carry him through many later struggles.

Because his father believed elementary schooling was sufficient, young Abbott was 20 years old before he was able to continue his education. Industrious years followed — including two at Vermont's St. Johnsbury Academy, where he completed the four-year college-preparatory course in half the usual time. The young scholar's energy and determination led one professor at the University of Michigan Medical School to remark, "Go anywhere, Abbott. You will succeed wherever you go."

Today, in his medical practice, Dr. Abbott is never satisfied with the old-fashioned ways of fighting disease, and is constantly on the lookout for a better method. It is this nagging curiosity, as much as anything else, that helps him more than double the business to $4,500 in its second year.

TOP: *Standing 5'4", Dr. Abbott is poised for success. Before setting up practice in Ravenswood, he serves briefly as a physician's assistant in his home state of Vermont.* BOTTOM: *Costing more than $1 million and standing 984 feet tall, the Eiffel Tower is completed for the 1889 Paris Exposition.*

17

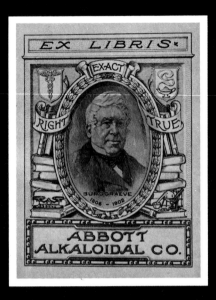

The Sherman Antitrust Act to curb monopolies in the United States is introduced this year by Senator John Sherman of Ohio. It will be passed with little opposition. William Jennings Bryan is elected to Congress, his first public office, on the Democratic ticket from a heavily Republican district in Nebraska. Idaho and Wyoming become the 43d and 44th states. Wyoming's entry is noteworthy because it gives women the right to vote, making it the first state to grant women's suffrage. Mississippi unbalances the liberal scales by becoming the first state to restrict the rights of blacks to vote.

All citizens can vote in Spain once they reach the age of 24 under the new universal suffrage grant, and further progress comes to Europe as England institutes free elementary education. Less harmony is found in Argentina, where a national uprising leads to bitter fighting, resignation of the cabinet, and establishment of a radical government that will last 40 years.

Two new phrases are on American lips this year. "Everybody talks about the weather, but nobody does anything about it" will be credited to Mark Twain — a surprise to Charles Warner, who wrote it first in the *Hartford Courant*. And *How the Other Half Lives* is the title of a new book on poverty and the slums written by Jacob Riis. In later years, his book will become an important factor in labor reforms, slum clearance, and improved building codes.

The U.S. population grows to 63 million this year. Economic estimates indicate that 1 percent of the people have more wealth than the other 99 percent.

TOP LEFT: *Showing his continued indebtedness to the concepts of Dr. Adolphe Burggraeve, Dr. Abbott uses a bust of Burggraeve on his company's book plate.* **TOP RIGHT:** *With the workload for granule production steadily increasing, Dr. Abbott hires his first nonfamily employee, Josephine "Jo" Fletcher.* **BOTTOM:** *Squalor, crime, and overcrowding in New York City's slums are revealed in the photographs of Jacob Riis, best known for his 1890 book* How the Other Half Lives, *a scathing indictment of the city's tenement system.*

The 32-year-old Dr. Abbott discovers a logical new rule for growth: Family ties breed low-cost productivity. He installs his parents and his sister Lucy in a two-story frame house two blocks north of the drugstore. Their parlor he uses to store spare cans of granules. Their kitchen becomes an extra laboratory, and their sink yet another production center. Each member of the family is now working for the company. Month by month the orders begin to pile up. Dr. Abbott breaks the familial bond and hires his first nonfamily worker. Jo Fletcher fills the pill bottles, sweeps the floor, and stamps the envelopes. Her salary of $6 per week is considered only slightly ostentatious for the times.

Dr. Abbott's production methods and quality control do not differ a great deal from his compounding days as a pharmacist. Instead of pouring elixirs from one flask to another, he uses molds of hard rubber and his spatula to form the moistened masses of material into tiny granules. His production guides are old copies of the *Dosimetric Medical Review*, Dr. Burggraeve's *New Handbook of Dosimetric Therapeutics*, plus his own lore of chemistry and the making of pills. The result? According to Dr. Abbott's own persuasive logic: "I now have granules which are accurate ... the solubility rapid and perfect ... and the keeping quality assured without gum or any other material that will harden with age and render the granule worthless."

It would appear that he must be doing something right. The demand for these accurate granules far exceeds the needs of his own practice. And the Abbott Alkaloidal Company, in only its third year, does a business of $8,000.

19

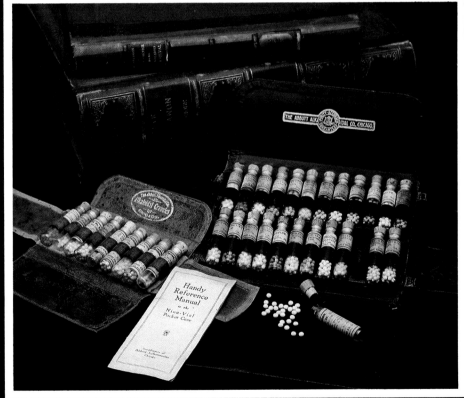

Charters are granted to three important American schools: the University of Chicago, Houston's Rice Institute, and Pasadena's Throop Polytechnic Institute, which will be known in later years as Cal Tech. The nation's first correspondence school also opens — with the unlikely idea of teaching by mail safer mining methods to workers in coal mines.

British, French, Belgian, and Swiss authors and publishers gain protection as Congress passes the International Copyright Act. Prior to this, American publishers could freely copy the works of foreign authors, depriving them of their royalties. In time, the copyright will be extended to include most other countries. Meanwhile, tremors of all kinds are felt around the world: a 30-second earthquake shakes three-fifths of Japan, killing or injuring 24,000 . . . the Great Famine of 1891-92 breeds unrest across Russia . . . civil war rocks Chile, a troubled land that will see 100 changes of government over the next 29 years . . . and 41 banks go under in Australia. At least in Hawaii the news is good. A new queen is proclaimed — Liliuokalani, composer of the song "Aloha Oe."

In the U.S., necessity continues to spawn invention. The first patent for a motion picture camera is filed by Thomas Edison. Lesser-known inventor Whitcomb Judson comes up with a novel idea for a fastener. It's called a zipper. And in Springfield, Massachusetts, a new game is invented at the YMCA Training College by a Dr. James Naismith. Because he strung up a couple of peach baskets at each end of a gymnasium, he'll call it "basketball."

Dr. Abbott adds writing to his repertoire with frequent contributions to the columns of the widely read professional publication, the *Medical World*. In one issue, readers are liable to hear of his experiences with victims of the U.S. influenza epidemic that came halfway around the world from St. Petersburg, Russia. "Out of several hundred cases, I lost only one," writes Dr. Abbott, "and that was a plethoric, rheumatic woman at the climacteric period with cerebritis." Fortunately, most of the Doctor's patients aren't afflicted with such a diversity of symptoms.

Unfortunately, not all the readers of the *Medical World* have yet become believers in dosimetry. Some call it quackery. Some insist that the granules are too expensive, unnecessary, and even too burdensome. And some believe that any physician who dispenses his own medicine is little more than a peddler.

Dr. Abbott bristles at this. "With dosimetry," he writes, "the practitioner has no fear of losing himself in a labyrinth of idiosyncrasies, temperaments, variety of pharmaceutical preparations, decoctions, tinctures, or infusions. The true dosimetric treatment is the easiest method on earth. It is simply helping nature.

"With two years' experience in dosimetry," continues Dr. Abbott, "my results leave me with no desire for the high-priced, much-extolled French granules. I consider a handy case of active remedies in a convenient form far superior to the time-honored methods of bottles full of nauseous mixtures and boxes of unsightly pills prescribed by the busy doctor and waited for by patients."

TOP: *In 1887, Thomas Edison sets out to do for sight what his gramophone had done for sound. By 1891, he has developed a simple "peep show," which quickly evolves into the forerunner of the modern motion picture camera.* **BOTTOM:** *As early as 1892, the Abbott Alkaloidal Company lists five different types of pocket medicine cases for sale in its product catalog. The smaller cases sell for $1.00, the larger for $1.50.*

21

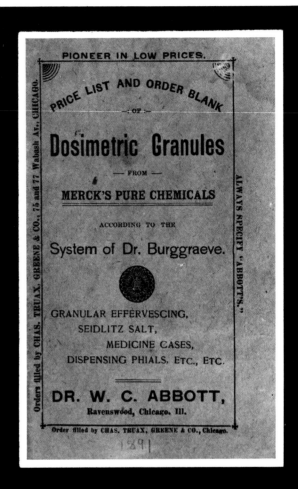

PIONEER IN LOW PRICES.

PRICE LIST AND ORDER BLANK

— OF —

Dosimetric Granules

— FROM —

MERCK'S PURE CHEMICALS

ACCORDING TO THE

System of Dr. Burggraeve.

GRANULAR EFFERVESCING,
SEIDLITZ SALT,
MEDICINE CASES,
DISPENSING PHIALS, ETC., ETC.

DR. W. C. ABBOTT,

Ravenswood, Chicago, Ill.

Order filled by CHAS. TRUAX, GREENE & CO., Chicago.

Orders filled by CHAS. TRUAX, GREENE & CO., 75 and 77 Wabash Av., CHICAGO.

ALWAYS SPECIFY "ABBOTT'S."

Grover Cleveland returns to the U.S. presidency as he and Adlai E. Stevenson defeat Benjamin Harrison. Ellis Island, in New York harbor, becomes the golden door for immigrants entering the U.S. Over the next 62 years, until its closing in 1954, it will process 20 million future American citizens.

The first American gasoline automobile is made by Charles and Frank Duryea, Chicopee, Massachusetts, bicycle makers. They test it indoors, to avoid derisive cries of "Get a horse." The World's Columbian Exposition is dedicated in Chicago and a man named George W. G. Ferris dedicates his own invention to the exposition. He calls it a Ferris Wheel. In France, chemist Henri Moissan invents the electric oven. And Dutch physicist Hendrick Antoon Lorentz, who will later share a Nobel prize for physics, discovers electrons. Born this year: Josip Broz Tito, future president of Yugoslavia and Communist leader, and Tafari Makonnen, who as emperor of Ethiopia will be better known by the name Haile Selassie.

The first heavyweight championship boxing match under the new Marquis of Queensberry rules is fought this year. The rules dictate gloves and three-minute rounds. "Gentleman Jim" Corbett becomes the new champion when he knocks out the great John L. Sullivan in the 21st round at New Orleans.

A Manual of Bacteriology, the first comprehensive work on bacteriology in the United States, is published by Lieutenant Colonel George M. Sternberg. The following year, he will be named U.S. surgeon general.

Dr. Abbott had discovered the power of advertising. In the June 1891 issue of the *Medical World,* he had placed this notice:

> Wanted: Every reader of the *MEDICAL WORLD* using or interested in DOSIMETRIC GRANULES to send me their address at once. Dr. Wallace C. Abbott, Ravenswood, Chicago, Ill.

This first ad cost 25¢. It would return $8 in orders — a 32-1 ratio. Other notices followed, word for word the same as the first. And the readers responded — some with questions about dosimetric granules, others with requests for a catalog, and a surprising number with orders for the new granules.

Dr. Abbott realizes that he must come up with a catalog. His first effort covers 14 pages and more than 150 products. The prices, as well as the compounds, may seem a little strange to us today: zinc valerianate for convulsions, and acetanilid as a painkiller, each at 10¢ per 100 granules — or 65¢ per 1,000 for the quantity user. Most prominently featured is Granular Effervescent Seidlitz Salt. Hardly an alkaloidal granule, this cure-all is described as "indispensable in the best application of the methods which should govern alkaloidal medication. Minor ailments often require nothing more than clearing the alimentary canal of indigestible, fermenting residues. It freshens and purifies the blood, the source of all health."

Thus state-of-the-art therapy, pre-turn of the century, concerns itself more with the expurgation of evil bodily spirits than it does with the disease-specific therapeutic approaches that will come years later.

TOP: *Dr. Abbott's first product catalog (actual size, 3⅝" × 6") lists a total of 163 different items in its 14 pages, including 157 types of granules and tablets, five granule cases, and Seidlitz Salt.* BOTTOM: *After processing at Ellis Island in Upper New York Bay, new arrivals to America receive a ferry ride to the mainland to begin a new life. At its peak during the first decade of the 20th century, Ellis Island will process as many as 15,000 immigrants a day.*

The Panic of 1893, one of the worst in American history, sets in as foreign investors withdraw capital from the U.S. economy. On Wall Street, stocks drop sharply and only a last-minute loan of $6 million by clearinghouse banks averts a money panic. One outstanding reason behind the crisis: the amount of paper money in circulation is nearly twice as great as the gold in the U.S. Treasury. The value of the silver in a U.S. silver dollar drops below 60¢.

The World's Columbian Exposition in Chicago attracts more than 21 million visitors — about one out of every three people in the U.S. The Cherokee Strip, six million acres between Kansas and Oklahoma purchased from the Cherokee Indians in 1891, opens up for land rush to more than 100,000 settlers. A revolution in Hawaii deposes Queen Liliuokalani and the Republic of Hawaii is established. At the same time, France makes Laos a protectorate. The illegal immigration of Chinese workers for cheap labor is stopped, and the first Chinese are deported from San Francisco under the Geary Chinese Exclusion Act. On a more liberal note, New Zealand grants women the right to vote.

Other news of social significance to Americans: Violators of the Antipolygamy Act of 1882 receive a presidential pardon — if they'll agree to practice monogamy. And the Anti-Saloon League is organized in Oberlin, Ohio, with the intention of invoking Prohibition. Mass exodus to the West is immediately considered by the town's topers.

TOP LEFT: *Dr. William Thomas Thackeray is instrumental in shaping the future of Dr. Abbott. In addition to introducing him to Dr. Burggraeve's concepts of dosimetry, Thackeray will give Dr. Abbott the* Alkaloidal Clinic. TOP RIGHT: *As keen a businessman as he is family physician, Dr. Abbott frequently uses "bounce-back" offers and testimonials to fortify his advertising (from the* Medical World*).* BOTTOM: *More than 21 million visitors file through the turnstiles of the World's Columbian Exposition, better known as the Chicago World's Fair of 1893. Many of them take the ride of their life on a device designed specifically for the Expo by George Ferris.*

By 1893, Wallace and Clara Abbott no longer live in the rear of the People's Drug Store. One block to the east, at the corner of Wilson and Hermitage avenues, the Doctor builds a rambling, three-story wooden house, with broad porches and an ornate cupola. The massive structure will still stand nearly a century later.

One of the most colorful characters to come into the life of Dr. Abbott at this or any other time is another physician — white-mustachioed William T. Thackeray. A hospital corpsman with the Union forces during the Civil War, Thackeray completed his training as a doctor after the war. Several years later, still an army medical officer, he took part in the Carlist Rebellion in Spain as director of a medical unit. He and an aide were captured, court-martialed, and sentenced to be shot. An hour before the scheduled execution, Dr. Thackeray was released and banished from the country.

Returning to the U.S., he served as an army doctor with troops fighting the Sioux Indians. After a stint in private practice, Dr. Thackeray became a medical technician and then a sales representative with Parke, Davis and Company. His job: to promote new products at medical conventions. At an American Medical Association meeting, he came across an idea he thought perfect for his company. In fact, he was so enamored that he bought, on the spot, the entire exhibit — featuring dosimetric granules and the crude machines that made them. When Parke, Davis had no interest in the idea, Dr. Thackeray left the company and organized his own Metric Granule Company in Chicago.

One of his new company's first customers is Dr. Wallace Calvin Abbott.

This is a year of severe economic depression in the U.S., with rising unemployment, falling prices, and labor unrest.

Jacob Coxey leads his "Coxey's Army" of the unemployed from Ohio to Washington, D.C., to petition Congress for money to create emergency work projects. He stands on the U.S. Capitol steps to make his plea. Capitol guards arrest him for trespassing.

In Ohio, 136,000 coal miners strike for higher wages. In New York, 12,000 tailors strike in protest against sweatshop conditions. And in Chicago, the Pullman Palace Car Company reduces wages, leading to a strike marred by violence and bloodshed.

In France, army officer Alfred Dreyfus is accused by his homeland of selling military secrets to Germany. Dreyfus will be convicted of treason by a court-martial, sentenced to life imprisonment, and sent to Devil's Island. Several years later, new discoveries pointing to his innocence will reopen the case and divide the nation, with lasting political and social repercussions.

William Jennings Bryan is defeated in his bid for a U.S. Senate seat and becomes editor of the *Omaha World-Herald,* a position that will give him an influential role in the political development of the West. And "The Sidewalks of New York" is composed by Charles Lawler; 30 years later, it will become even more popular when it's revived as Al Smith seeks his nomination for the presidency.

Despite the nation's worsening financial depression, Dr. Abbott's sales climb to $29,000. All is not so fortunate, however, for Dr. Thackeray. Both his business and his journal fail. One day, when the two men meet on the street, Dr. Abbott asks him what he intends to do with the *Alkaloidal Clinic.*

"I'm going to give it to you, Brother Wallace, if you'll have it, because I know you'll make it go," replies Dr. Thackeray.

Under Dr. Abbott's editorship, the magazine does grow — from 12 to 24 to 36 pages — all crammed with his wit and wisdom on a wide range of medical topics, along with letters, articles, and advertisements. Also notable are Dr. Abbott's crusading epithets against what he considers to be unwholesome habits. Tobacco and alcohol users are high on his list of pet peeves. Cigarette users, Dr. Abbott is convinced, are "uncertain and unstable to say the least, if not actually dishonest."

Fellow physicians are invited to contribute their own words of wisdom to the pages of the *Alkaloidal Clinic,* and occasionally, their answers to readers' questions are unabashedly blunt. "Madame," one troubled correspondent is advised, "the way to prevent conception is easy. Do not marry. What the dickens did you get married for? A home? What is a home without babies?"

Another is offered this sage advice: "Yes, I believe in old women marrying young boys. It is tough on the boys, but helps the old women to keep young and the boys to forego cigarettes."

TOP: *Under the direction of Dr. Abbott, the new version of the* Alkaloidal Clinic *flourishes, with an average circulation by 1896 of 17,362, as seen here on the* Clinic's *letterhead.* CENTER: *A specialty of the house, Buckley's Uterine Tonic is sold by the Abbott Alkaloidal Company for a variety of ailments, "from intermittent bilious fevers to painful menstruation."* BOTTOM: *Like the Wright brothers after them, America's Duryea brothers are a couple of bicycle mechanics with an inventive spirit. They built the nation's first auto in 1892, and, in 1894, they complete their third model, shown here driven by Charles Duryea.*

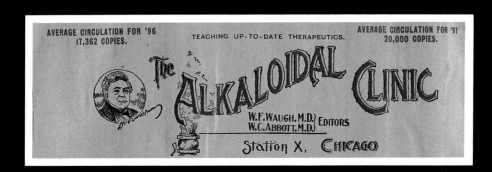

AVERAGE CIRCULATION FOR '96
17,362 COPIES.

TEACHING UP-TO-DATE THERAPEUTICS.

AVERAGE CIRCULATION FOR '97
20,000 COPIES.

The ALKALOIDAL CLINIC

W.F. WAUGH, M.D. } EDITORS
W.C. ABBOTT, M.D.

Station X, Chicago

A year of portentous events: Wireless telegraphy is invented by Italy's Guglielmo Marconi ... X rays are discovered by German scientist Wilhelm Roentgen ... and French chemist Louis Pasteur dies.

In the U.S., George Westinghouse makes a significant contribution to industry with his construction of huge power generators at Niagara Falls. The first patent for an automobile powered by a gasoline engine is issued to George B. Selden and is immediately challenged by Henry Ford. In Waukegan, Illinois, the first American contest between self-propelled vehicles is won by a Benz motor wagon — imported from Germany by Oscar Bernhard Mueller. It is one of only two cars to finish the race.

Back in the birthplace of the Benz, Germans mark the opening of the Kiel Canal, connecting the Baltic and North Seas and transforming the small northwestern town of Kiel into the country's chief naval base and, later, a principal shipping and industrial center. The nations of Europe continue to divide up Africa as Belgium acquires a colony called the Belgian Congo — which 65 years later will win independence and in 1971 will change its name to Zaire. Japan defeats China, to end the two-year war between those nations.

Culture is having its day in America with the publication of Stephen Crane's *The Red Badge of Courage* and Gelett Burgess' *The Purple Cow.* In later years, the first will become America's classic Civil War novel and the other one of the most widely known pieces of verse in the land. And Charles Dana Gibson makes his "Gibson Girl" the ideal of most Americans.

Now, with business booming, is the time to add a few more willing workers. Dr. Abbott has a unique system for screening potential female employees. All must work for a week or more at the new Abbott domicile — cleaning, dusting, making beds. This way, Dr. Abbott believes, he can determine which girls might be most helpful to him in his work.

Ida and Emily Richter are two who pass the domestic test. Emily becomes an office worker, and Ida the Doctor's private secretary. Ida's hours are in direct contrast to her salary of $8 per week. Although Dr. Abbott allows her to cease taking dictation and to go to her bed in an upstairs room by 10:00 P.M., he often awakens her at 3:00 A.M. to transcribe a particularly eloquent passage that has just occurred to him.

Relatives and friends are not neglected. Lucy Abbott, the Doctor's sister, and James Ranson, husband of Clara Abbott's sister Susie, are both conscripted to fill orders and answer inquiries. Henry Shattuck, a friend since boyhood days in Vermont, keeps the books. And Luther Abbott, the Doctor's father, continues to help out by filling bottles and pasting shipping labels.

TOP: *American illustrator Charles Gibson will be remembered for his pen-and-ink renderings of the ideal American girl — the "Gibson Girl."* BOTTOM: *In the words of Dr. Abbott, "I went about the thing in a very modest way, one helper at a time, and I remember how puffed up with pride I was when my force had grown to five or six good girls." Dr. Abbott's sister Lucy is seated to his left.*

This is an election year in the U.S., and William Jennings Bryan delivers his stirring speech "You shall not crucify mankind upon a cross of gold" at the Democratic convention. His oration, which advocates the free coinage of gold and silver, electrifies and unifies the party. He is nominated as presidential candidate the next day. Bryan will lose the election to the governor of Ohio, William McKinley, his Republican opponent.

Gold is discovered in Rabbit Creek, a tributary of the Klondike River in the Yukon territory of northwest Canada. When news of the strike reaches the U.S., thousands leave their homes to join the Klondike Stampede. Total production from this one strike will exceed $175 million.

Dorothy Dix (Mrs. Elizabeth Gilmer) begins her "advice to the lovelorn" column in the New Orleans *Picayune*. Billy Sunday begins his evangelical career and will become the greatest single influence for Prohibition. William Allen White gains a nationwide reputation overnight with his editorial in Kansas' *Emporia Daily and Weekly Gazette* on "What's the Matter with Kansas?"

Meanwhile, the European nations flex their muscles. Italy invades Ethiopia over a dispute in the interpretation of an 1889 treaty that established the African nation as an Italian protectorate. Although the Italian army withdraws in defeat, renewed threats will come 40 years later when Mussolini conquers Ethiopia on the road to World War II. France annexes the African island of Madagascar, a move met with fierce resistance. On a more pacific note, the Olympic Games resume after a 15-century hiatus. They are held this year in Athens, Greece. A small band of travel-weary Americans triumphs in 9 of the 12 events.

TOP: *Dr. Abbott (left) confers with James Ranson, husband of one of Clara Abbott's sisters and early employee of the Abbott Alkaloidal Company.* CENTER: *Coupons such as this were used frequently by Dr. Abbott.* BOTTOM: *William Jennings Bryan delivers the eloquent "Cross of Gold" speech that endears him to delegates at the 1896 U.S. Democratic convention. Bryan gets the nod but is defeated by William McKinley.*

With the *Alkaloidal Clinic,* Dr. Abbott now has diversified well beyond his drugstore, his medical practice, and his granule-manufacturing plant. He purchases the frame structure next door to his main building and establishes the Clinic Publishing Company — complete with presses, bindery, composing room, editorial offices, and library. With a corps of 15 typesetters and pressroom workers, he prints all his own magazines, pamphlets, booklets, order sheets, and prescription pads. He even takes job-printing orders from the neighborhood Beckley-Ralston Cycle Company.

Dr. Abbott believes in healthy habits. He exhorts all his employees to follow his lead by riding bicycles to and from work, and arranges to get substantial discounts from Beckley-Ralston and deducts $1 per week from purchasers' wages until the vehicles are paid for.

This is the era of the first generic drug controversy. Dr. Abbott, naturally, is right in the middle of it. When the American Pharmaceutical Association expresses displeasure with physicians who buy directly from Dr. Abbott and other granule-makers, Dr. Abbott defends his own brands. "It is a well-recognized fact," he states, "that these products *do* differ . . . even if they are made from set pharmaceutical formulae, and one must learn how to handle them before he can be assured of his result. The 'just as good' and 'so much cheaper' are accountable for much of professional failure and set up a bigger row of gravestones every year than many are aware."

William McKinley is inaugurated as the 25th U.S. president, succeeding Grover Cleveland. Two days before leaving office, Cleveland vetoes a proposed immigration bill that would require a literacy test. The basis of his disapproval: that the bill is "a radical departure from our national policy."

Congress votes $50,000 for relief of Americans trapped during the Cuban Rebellion. The struggle broke out in 1895 as a revolt against Spanish rule and is partly a result of the aftereffects of the Panic of 1893, which caused severe economic depression in the Cuban sugar industry. American sympathy for the Cubans — and against Spain's repressive measures — is aroused by the yellow journalism of William Randolph Hearst's *New York Morning Journal* and Joseph Pulitzer's *New York World.* Congress can well afford the $50,000 largess, as $750,000 in gold arrives in San Francisco and is followed three days later by another $800,000, the first shipments from the Klondike strike.

A series of revolts force Turkey to relinquish its hold on the Mediterranean island of Crete, paving the way for Crete to join Greece following the Balkan Wars of 1912-13. "On the Banks of the Wabash," one of the most popular songs ever written in America, is composed by Paul Dresser, who grew up on the banks of the Wabash River in Terre Haute, Indiana. His real name is Dreiser, and he is the brother of novelist Theodore Dreiser, who wrote the first draft of the song's lyric.

Dr. William F. Waugh, editor of the *Medical Times* in Philadelphia, joins actively in editing the *Alkaloidal Clinic.* Dr. Waugh collaborates with Dr. Abbott on so many medical articles that the two are soon calling themselves the "Alkaloidal Twins." Their jointly written *Text Book of Alkaloidal Therapeutics* quickly becomes the standard reference on the subject. Dr. Abbott advertises it in his own journal as "a storehouse of ideas that any progressive physician can convert into 'coin of the realm.'"

Dr. Waugh also brings to the burgeoning company his own ideas for new products. His area of specialty seems to be cathartics. The Waugh-Abbott Intestinal Antiseptic Tablet, for example, blends the sulphocarbolates of lime, soda, and zinc. This and Abbott's Saline Laxative — "It does the work and never gripes!" — are both popular and profitable.

Testimonials for both the publications and the products pour in. Most are dutifully reported in the pages of Dr. Abbott's journal. Dr. W. H. Blythe, of Pleasanton, Texas, writes: "My *Alkaloidal Clinic* for all of last year cost me one dollar. As a premium I received a nine-vial pocket case of granules. Dr. Waugh's *Manual* cost me one dollar so, all told, I was out two dollars. But I had on hand the *Manual,* a year's bound volume of the *Clinic,* and a nine-vial pocket case (not yet empty) out of which I've realized $6.50, leaving me already $4.50 ahead." And from Dr. S. D. Wetherby, of Middletown, Kentucky, "I would rather practice without my saddle pockets than to be without the *Clinic* and your little granules."

Thus, the prolific physician-publisher increases his business to $86,000.

TOP: *Shown here in the basement of the house on East Ravenswood, early granule production would have a difficult time meeting today's standards of pharmaceutical manufacturing.* **BOTTOM:** *On August 16, 1896, gold is discovered in Rabbit Creek, a small tributary of Canada's Klondike River. News of the discovery reaches the U.S. in January 1897, and the Klondike Stampede is on.*

The U.S. battleship *Maine* arrives in Havana harbor. One month later it mysteriously explodes, with 260 seamen lost. American sympathies, already strong for Cuba in its revolt against Spanish tyranny, make intervention inevitable.

In quick order, President McKinley recalls U.S. consuls from Cuba ... asks Congress for authorization to use armed force to compel the Spanish evacuation of Cuba ... and obtains a Congressional resolution demanding Cuban independence. Spain's refusal results in the American blockade of all Cuban ports and the president's call for 125,000 volunteer soldiers. The Spanish-American War runs from April to mid-August and is fought throughout the Caribbean and the Pacific.

Lieutenant Colonel "Teddy" Roosevelt organizes his "Rough Riders" cavalry for service in Cuba. In the Pacific, Admiral Dewey's fleet destroys the Spanish at Manila Bay and goes on to assist in the occupation of Manila. When the Americans fire on Guam, the Spanish commander there apologizes for not returning the "salute." He doesn't know about the war, and there isn't any ammunition on the island, anyway.

The war ends with the surrender of 24,000 Spanish troops at Santiago. America suffers 5,462 casualties. Fewer than 400 are killed in battle or die of wounds; more than 90 percent are felled by disease. A treaty is signed in Paris as the U.S. acquires Puerto Rico and Guam and pays Spain $20 million for the Philippines. Cuba gains its independence, thus ending almost 30 years of rebellion against Spanish rule.

Even though 1898 is a hard-times year, Dr. Abbott's business moves up to $100,000. Still he finds that he must spend most of each "Editorial Chat" in the *Alkaloidal Clinic* exhorting new readers to subscribe and old readers to renew. Subscriptions are a dollar a year — less if you can line up a friendly colleague. "If times are hard, Doctor, and you can't spare the dollar, hustle around and get us three new subscriptions and we'll advance you one year," implores Dr. Abbott.

Sometimes, he finds, subscribers are as hard to keep as they are to get. So he wraps all copies of expired issues in a pink wrapper as a gentle reminder. After six months, the pink wrapper is replaced with a bright red one. Most of the time it works. Circulation is now more than 20,000 copies a month — making the *Clinic* the fourth most widely read medical and surgical journal in the country. Advertising rates reflect the advance: they are now $3 per column inch and $30 for a full-page ad.

The editorial pages, meanwhile, contemplate such vexing medical questions as suitable remedies for catarrh, the indigestion of constipation, carbuncles, la grippe, diphtheria, and scurvy. One poser which receives much attention is "When should syphilitics marry?" The consensus seems to be that it is safe only at the end of the sixth year. The more venturesome in the profession, however, feel that the disease loses its contagiousness so rapidly that maybe two years is enough. All this, of course, in an era when the therapeutic treatment consists mainly of waiting. And praying.

TOP: *Dr. Abbott confers with his private secretary, Ida Richter. Though very demanding about neatness and order in the plant, he apparently doesn't apply the same standards to his desk.* **CENTER:** *The staff of the original Clinic Publishing Company is called out for a midday photo.* **BOTTOM:** *Teddy Roosevelt and the "Rough Riders" storm San Juan Hill during the Spanish-American War, as immortalized by this 1898 lithograph by George H. Harris & Sons, after the painting by W. G. Read.*

PHÉNOL SODIQUE
STOPS BLEEDING   HEALS ALL WOUNDS

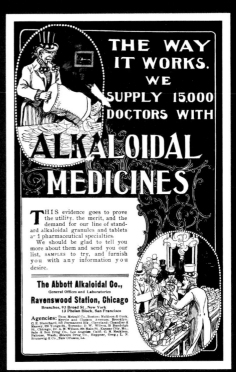

THE WAY IT WORKS. WE SUPPLY 15,000 DOCTORS WITH ALKALOIDAL MEDICINES

THIS evidence goes to prove the utility, the merit, and the demand for our line of standard alkaloidal granules and tablets and pharmaceutical specialties.

We should be glad to tell you more about them and send you our list, SAMPLES to try, and furnish you with any information you desire.

The Abbott Alkaloidal Co.,
General Offices and Laboratories
Ravenswood Station, Chicago
Branches, 93 Broad St., New York
13 Phelan Block, San Francisco

One of the new U.S. acquisitions, the Philippines, shows its recalcitrant side as Filipino insurrectionists and American forces clash. General Arthur MacArthur, father of General Douglas MacArthur of World War II fame, commands the U.S. troops. Rebellion against American rule will last over two years.

Congress creates a commission to study plans for building an interocean canal in Central America. The need is clear — a year earlier, a U.S. battleship took 67 days to sail from San Francisco to Key West. The first U.S. mail collection by motor is made in Cleveland. The vehicle makes 126 stops along 22 miles of streets in two hours, 27 minutes — less than half the six hours required by horse-drawn wagon. The Post Office learns from this experience and sets up a motor vehicle division — in 1914.

Horatio Alger's death underscores his prolific series of over 135 books with combined sales of more than $16 million. Among the more successful titles: *Ragged Dick, Luck and Pluck,* and *Tattered Tom.* (Tom, incidentally, was a girl.)

In the rest of the world, peace has its moment but war rules the day: Czar Nicholas II of Russia invites 26 nations to attend the first international discussion of disarmament at The Hague, Netherlands. Meanwhile, the discovery of diamonds and gold in the Dutch-ruled South African republic of Transvaal sets off the three-year Boer War between the British and the Boers, Dutch farmers whose ancestors settled in the region in the 17th century. Lord Kitchener commands the victorious British troops.

Dr. Abbott gains a remarkable addition to his editorial staff this year, in the person of Dr. Ephraim M. Epstein.

A native of Bobrusk, Russia, Dr. Epstein studied theology and languages at an Andover, Massachusetts, seminary for three years before switching to medicine. Returning to Europe, he practiced medicine in Constantinople and Vienna, and served as a surgeon in the Austrian navy. Back in the U.S., the peripatetic Dr. Epstein set up practice in Cincinnati, next was named the first president of South Dakota University, then pulled up stakes again to teach at Bethany College in West Virginia. Along the way he learned to speak and read Greek, Hebrew, Latin, Arabic, Russian, German, French, Italian, Spanish, and a smattering of Slavic languages. He also became an ardent advocate of alkaloidal therapy.

All these qualifications serve him well as a regular contributor and critic for the *Alkaloidal Clinic.* Dr. Epstein dissects, much as a drama critic reviewing the latest Broadway play, each clinical case. Occasionally, he'll even note one of his own esoteric remedies: "A first-born child came into the world small, feeble, and exceedingly jaundiced. A dough of finely sifted rye flour was wrapt from head to foot. This was removed twice in 24 hours. It was also bathed daily in a strong decoction of bean, to which a liberal amount of beer was added. In about two weeks, the child regained strength and grew up well."

TOP LEFT: *Drawing upon topical elements of the day, this product ad depicts American sailors aboard a warship in Manila Bay protecting America's new holdings in the Philippines.* **TOP RIGHT:** *A typical ad from the* Alkaloidal Clinic *of the times might go so far as to enlist the help of Uncle Sam in unloading mail bags full of orders for Abbott remedies or handing out product samples to interested customers.* **BOTTOM:** *At the turn of the century, all bottling and storage of granules takes place in this room of the East Ravenswood building.*

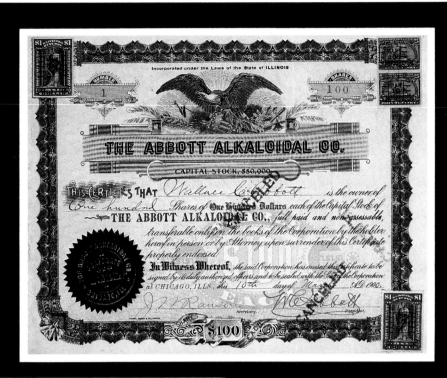

The U.S. reaches a total population of over 75 million as incumbent President McKinley and Theodore Roosevelt win the election from William Jennings Bryan and Adlai Stevenson. Over 73 percent of eligible voters turn out. Roosevelt is unhappy with his vice-presidential nomination, since he campaigned through 24 states and across 21,000 miles while McKinley sat at home on his front porch.

Illiteracy in the U.S. reaches a new low of 10.7 percent — about half of what it was in 1870. The fledgling automobile industry reaches new highs with 8,000 autos in the land — but only 10 miles of concrete pavement. There are 1.3 million telephones in use, and more than 12,000 pairs of silk stockings will be sold — only enough for 1 pair for each 3,100 women. Meanwhile, four billion cigarettes are produced — but they're still considered, by some, to make the smoker look effete.

The Boxer Rebellion erupts in Peking, China, as the effort of a secret society of Chinese to expel foreigners from the land. The quantum theory is proposed by the German physicist Max Planck, and the cause of the dreaded yellow fever is discovered by Walter Reed, a U.S. army surgeon. The Hawaiian Islands are constituted as U.S. territory and Sanford Dole becomes the first governor of Hawaii.

Mrs. Carry Nation continues her bottle-busting, bar-breaking antiliquor rampage through Kansas. And Casey Jones dies at the throttle trying to slow down his locomotive to save his passengers' lives.

The business is officially incorporated as the Abbott Alkaloidal Company — and will retain that name for the next 15 years.

With the press of business ventures, plus his own vastly increased writing and editing demands, Dr. Abbott is forced to cut back on his extensive medical practice. He still makes himself available, however, to employees and friends, pedaling briskly on his bicycle to their homes whenever summoned. But day by day the Doctor finds himself more desk-bound. His routine is unswerving: He's into the office at seven each morning, long before his first employee arrives. His giant desk is heaped with a prodigious pile of drafts of articles for the *Alkaloidal Clinic,* correspondence, and semicomposed dunning letters. The discards cascade in a mound covering his stockinged feet.

Each letter gets close clinical attention; there is no such thing as a form reply. To a physician who hasn't ordered for a long time, Dr. Abbott writes: "In looking over our records I find that we have not had an order from you for some months. Now, we don't like to lose a customer any better than you like to lose a patient. We are still hustling at our end, and I suppose you are at yours. Why not bring together your need and our ability to supply through the medium of a nice order?"

To a red-wrapped subscriber, Dr. Abbott pens: "It has just come to my attention that you are behind with the *Clinic.* I know of course that it is not intentional. If you owed us a thousand dollars instead of this mere pittance, I shouldn't even have to ask you for it. But we need the money. Hence this letter and the enclosed bill. Right now will suit us tip top!"

TOP: *The new century is ushered in by the incorporation of the Abbott Alkaloidal Company. This is the company's first stock certificate.* **BOTTOM LEFT:** *John Talbot oversees the smooth operation of early tablet-making and coating equipment.* **BOTTOM RIGHT:** *In an era of great national prosperity, U.S. President William McKinley is enthusiastically nominated for a second term, as shown in this colorful campaign poster of 1900. McKinley wins the election but is assassinated six months later.*

Queen Victoria, who has been Queen of England for 64 years, dies. She is succeeded by her son Edward VII. President McKinley is shot to death while attending the Pan American Exposition in Buffalo, and Vice President Theodore Roosevelt is sworn in as America's 26th president.

Armed revolt against U.S. occupation in the Philippines finally ends. It has been the most unpopular war ever fought by the U.S., with many Americans believing the Filipinos should be given their independence. The Supreme Court rules that territories acquired as a result of the Spanish-American War are neither foreign countries nor part of the U.S. This becomes an important point in establishing tariff policy toward the possessions.

America's Yellow Fever Commission reports that experiments definitely prove the disease is transmitted by mosquito. Dr. Carlos Finlay, of Havana, has been trying to convince the medical profession of this same theory for 20 years and has been consistently ridiculed. Two doctors in the four-man U.S. team sent to Cuba to conduct experiments contract yellow fever and die. Meanwhile, the first British submarine is launched and, a little farther east, in Germany, so is the first Mercedes automobile.

The first great U.S. oil strike, the Spindletop claim near Beaumont, Texas, signals both the beginning of fabulous growth for the Southwest and years of continuous savage financial struggles over oil rights. Andrew Carnegie sells his interest in Carnegie Steel and will spend the next 18 years distributing $350 million to a variety of worthy causes.

With sales up to $133,000, it's time for a major expansion. The frame cottage next to the main building is demolished, and in its place is erected a fine new four-story brick building, 58 x 160 feet. It will be used to house all publishing projects, as well as the business, editorial, and advertising offices of the Clinic Publishing Company.

The manufacturing facilities, meanwhile, remain unchanged. Dr. Abbott's original kitchen laboratory was moved in the winter of 1892-93 to his parents' old frame house. That house, finally replaced in 1908, will be outgrown time after time, built upon and added to and gerrymandered about as space is repeatedly found inadequate. The basement laboratory has a very low ceiling and a very high density of unpleasant smells and noises. In the center of the room, a large gas engine powers the shafts and pulleys that lead to the coating pans and tablet machines. The air is hazy and heavy with particles of whatever drug is being produced. Nose masks are unknown at the time; it's not unusual for workers to be overcome by heat or fumes.

The finished pills and granules are hauled by a rope elevator in an air shaft to the bottling and shipping room on the floor above. On the third floor are huge barrels of saline solution, ready to be tapped to fill the orders for Abbott's Saline Laxative. All finished stock is kept in a two-story shed connected to the rear of the building by an enclosed runway.

All of which makes for less-than-ideal surroundings — but for a few more years, at least, the uncomfortable set-up will have to do.

TOP: *In 1901, the frame cottage housing the Clinic Publishing Company is demolished and in its stead is erected this four-story brick building.* BOTTOM LEFT: *One of the Clinic's first undertakings in its new quarters is the publication of* Helpful Hints for the Busy Doctor. BOTTOM RIGHT: *The longest reign in British history, 64 years, ends in 1901 with the death of Queen Victoria, four years after this photo was taken of her breakfasting with Princesses Beatrice and Victoria.*

This is a year for famous births ... and deaths. Aviator Charles Augustus Lindbergh, singer Marian Anderson, and poet Ogden Nash come into the world, while explorer Cecil Rhodes and novelists Bret Harte and Émile Zola pass on to the next.

Internationally, America's treaty with Denmark for purchase of the Virgin Islands is approved by the U.S. Senate but rejected by the Danish Rigsdag — it will take $25 million and 15 more years before St. Croix, St. Thomas, and St. John become U.S. property. In Panama, the Isthmian Canal Act authorizes the building of a canal — but only after a $40 million concession from the Panama Canal Company of France and a revolt by Panama against Colombia. In a move that solidifies the division of Europe into two opposing camps — a rivalry that will eventually erupt into World War I — Germany, Austria, and Italy renew their Triple Alliance agreement for six more years.

Back home, the country is raving about Hughie Cannon's new hit "Bill Bailey, Won't You Please Come Home?" And the most popular show in New York, *Florodora,* closes after 547 performances. Audiences will long remember the six comely girls in the Florodora Sextette who sing "Tell Me, Pretty Maiden."

In sports, the first postseason college football game is called "The Tournament of Roses." Michigan wallops Stanford, 49-0. More serious news comes with the strike of 140,000 anthracite coal miners in Pennsylvania. The workers want an increase in wages and an eight-hour day. After five months President Roosevelt establishes a commission to arbitrate. Meanwhile, the average wage of shopgirls in Boston remains at about $5 a week.

The *Alkaloidal Clinic* has grown in stature, in size, and in cost. The November issue reaches one-fourth of the American medical profession. It sets a record when it carries almost 200 pages — 111 editorial and 80 advertising. A full-page ad now costs $55 — up from the $30 of only four years ago. Subscription prices, however, are still a bargain at only $1 for 12 monthly issues.

From Syrup of Figs ("the family laxative") to Buffalo Lithia Water ("for Bright's Disease, Stone in Bladder, Renal Calculi, Gout, Rheumatism, Uric Acid Diathesis, etc."), the pages of Dr. Abbott's journal are replete with remedies for almost every esoteric ailment of the day. Nerve tonics, digestive stimulants, and constipation cures seem to be the most popular. But a wide variety of physical paraphernalia also comes in for prominent mention. Abdominal supporters, body braces, pessaries, elastic stockings, and an adult-sized Empire Umbilical Truss ("an abdominal supporter with button inserted at the navel") make it evident that the frailties of the human body of 1902 need every bit as much help as the profession can muster.

Two nonmedical signs of the times vie for the busy physician's attention. He can get a "handsome, roomy business buggy with full leather top plus wings and side lamps" for only $33.50. The more venturesome and affluent, however, can make his house calls in a brand-new Oldsmobile for $650. The advertisement promises that "each working part is made from materials of the highest grade, finished and fitted with mathematical accuracy."

TOP: *Dr. Abbott takes time to pose with office staff.* BOTTOM LEFT: *Alkaloidal literature, products, and fob using Abbott's first logo — "Purity-Accuracy Guaranteed."* BOTTOM RIGHT: *Sextette and swains sing "Tell Me, Pretty Maiden" in* Florodora, *America's smash musical hit of the early 1900s.*

43

Chicagoans mourn the death of 589 people in the December 30 fire at the city's Iroquois Theatre during a performance by Eddie Foy. The hue and cry that results leads to improved safety codes, better fire walls, and more theatre exits.

Wisconsin becomes the first state to adopt a mandatory primary election system. New Hampshire, meanwhile, takes a progressive step when it replaces 48 years of complete Prohibition with a system of liquor licenses.

President Teddy Roosevelt has an active year: He creates a ninth Cabinet office — the Department of Commerce and Labor. In another 10 years, it will be split into two separate offices. He sanctions a payment of $10 million in gold, plus an annual fee of $250,000, for full control of the 10-mile canal zone in Panama. He exercises that full control by ordering the warship USS *Nashville* to Panama to insure "free and uninterrupted transit" across the isthmus. And he brings a Japanese instructor into the White House to teach the first presidential jiujitsu.

Significant happenings in the world of transportation: A Packard automobile goes across America from San Francisco to New York in 52 days — the first time a gasoline-driven automobile has made the trip under its own power. While its driver is concerned simply with *getting* there, in Great Britain he'd also have to watch his speedometer — the country has just set a 20-mile-per-hour speed limit for autos, including the first motor taxis, introduced this year. Down in Kitty Hawk, North Carolina, Wilbur and Orville Wright's heavier-than-air machine makes its first flight, at a speed of 35 miles per hour. The flight lasts 12 seconds.

Dr. Abbott writes that he has no salesmen at all, and it isn't his way to "camp at a physician's door with long-winded talk and a bag of samples." He depends, instead, on his own powers of written persuasion to convert doubtful and skeptical prospects into the believers who will later become the backbone of the Abbott business.

He is a natural at putting the personal touch into his correspondence. The Doctor is not addicted to form letters; each is a personally written lesson in human interest. Nor does he believe that the story of alkaloidal therapy can be told convincingly in a few simple paragraphs. So he works 14 to 16 hours a day — much of that time spent writing the letters, editorials, and advertising copy that are beginning to win a host of followers.

The prerogatives of success (and sole ownership) are such that Dr. Abbott can increase both his staff and his own salary. From a base 10 years earlier of $37.50 per week plus another $12.50 a week for his work on the *Clinic,* the Doctor's weekly income now reaches a lofty $275.00 plus another $25.00 for his counsel on the *Clinic.* Dr. Waugh's $65.00 per week is second highest, followed by James W. Ranson, $50.00; Henry B. Shattuck, $30.00; and Frederick K. Hunsche, $27.50.

Exclusive of Dr. Abbott, the other 62 employees earn a total weekly wage of $646.73 — an average of $10.43.

TOP: *Fred Hunsche (right), chief pharmacist, oversees two workers in the company's formulation room.* BOTTOM: *The Wright brothers' first flight lasts a mere 12 seconds, just long enough for them to make history with the world's first successful heavier-than-air flying machine.*

44

U.S. President Theodore Roosevelt and his running mate, Charles W. Fairbanks of Indiana, sweep the Republican party to its most overwhelming victory since Ulysses S. Grant steamrollered Horace Greeley in 1872. Some consider the Prohibition party "wry drys" when they nominate a Dr. Silas Swallow.

Elsewhere in the nation, a number of firsts are recorded. At the St. Louis Exposition, German inventor Dr. Rudolf Diesel gives the first demonstration of a new kind of engine. The first speed law is passed by New York State: 10 miles per hour in closely built-up districts, 15 in villages, 20 in open country. New York City marks both the first use of motorcycle policemen and the first arrest of a woman for smoking a cigarette while riding in an open automobile on Fifth Avenue.

Around the world, the year sees the outbreak of the Russo-Japanese War over Russian expansion in Manchuria, the eradication of yellow fever in the Panama Canal Zone, and the founding of the Rolls-Royce Company in Great Britain. Russian playwright Anton Chekhov dies; Spanish painter Salvador Dalí and Russian choreographer George Balanchine are born.

In sports, the first Olympic Games held in America open in St. Louis. The U.S. wins 21 events and the unofficial championship. And Cy Young, of the Boston Americans, pitches the first perfect major league baseball game when he doesn't allow a single Philadelphia player to reach first base.

The addition of two new employees makes 1904 a remarkable year. Both are writers, but there the similarity ends. They are as disparate as two persons could be. They will, however, share one notable distinction. Both will become outstanding presidents of Abbott Laboratories.

Dr. Alfred Stephen Burdick is tall, scholarly, distinguished, contemplative. Son of an Eastern Seaboard clergyman, he spent two years as a schoolteacher after graduating from Alfred College. Coming to Chicago to study medicine at Rush Medical College, young Burdick later turned to teaching medicine at Illinois Medical College. A prolific writer, he soon became editor of the *Medical Standard*. It is here that Dr. Abbott discovers his talents. He hires Dr. Burdick as associate editor of the *Alkaloidal Clinic*. A handshake plus $40 a week seal the deal.

Simeon DeWitt Clough, aggressively red-haired and standing hardly a hand taller than Toulouse-Lautrec, is a product of Chicago's bustling West Side. His boyhood was a lesson in growing up the hard way. From hawking newspapers on the street to night classes in stenography and accounting to correspondence courses in advertising, young Clough schooled himself as an enthusiastic, though florid, writer. By 1903, his inspirational messages and advertising copy are written for *Tengwall Talk*, house organ of a loose-leaf binder company acquired by Dr. Abbott. It isn't long before the Doctor converts Clough to writing and selling ads for the *Alkaloidal Clinic*. His salary, another contrast to Dr. Burdick, is $12.50 a week.

TOP: *The Abbott family portrait: the Doctor's wife, Clara; the Abbotts' only child, Eleanor; and Dr. Abbott.* BOTTOM: *Denton True Young, the great "Cy" Young, shows the form for which baseball will proclaim him one of its best pitchers of all time.*

Norway and Sweden part company, while the provinces of Alberta and Saskatchewan unite with the Dominion of Canada. With more human attachments in mind, Sigmund Freud publishes his book *Three Contributions to the Theory of Sex.*

U.S. President Roosevelt urges Russia and Japan to end hostilities by joining him in a peace conference. They accept his offer and after two months of negotiation sign their peace treaty at Portsmouth, New Hampshire. Roosevelt will be honored for his role of mediator with the Nobel Peace Prize.

Grover Cleveland tries for equal statesmanship, but fails miserably, when his opposition to women's suffrage is voiced in, of all places, the *Ladies Home Journal.* "Sensible and responsible women do not want to vote," he writes. "The relative positions to be assumed by man and woman in the working out of our civilization were assigned long ago by a higher intelligence than ours."

The *Ladies Home Journal* is also in the news for its exposé of patent medicines. The most startling charge is that Mrs. Winslow's Soothing Syrup, for teething babies, soothes them with a hefty dose of morphine and has been labeled "poison" in Great Britain.

Progress of a sort is made when the number of automobiles registered in the U.S. rises to 77,988. This represents an increase of 7,688 in the last decade. Even so, most people still regard the noisy contraptions as useless toys. Meanwhile, the Pennsylvania Railroad and the New York Central inaugurate 18-hour runs between New York and Chicago. One week later, both trains suffer accidents.

Disaster strikes on the morning of November 9, 1905. While Dr. Abbott and DeWitt Clough are in New York City, they learn that their brick building housing the power plant, printing presses, and editorial and advertising offices has caught fire. As the neighborhood newspaper describes it: "It was one of the fiercest fires ever seen in this part of the city. The entire structure, four stories high with a floor space of over 50,000 square feet, going down in but little over an hour."

Dr. Abbott catches the next train home and arrives in time to see the still-smoking ruins. Even in adversity, his comments stress the positive. "Fortunately," he says, "the wind was in a lucky direction. Otherwise, we'd have lost our laboratories. Though our machinery plant is gone, our subscription records were saved and, with the presses and the willing hands of the great city, we shall go on. Watch us grow!"

The growth resumes immediately. To the building contractor who estimates six months are needed to reconstruct, Dr. Abbott gives only three — but promises a hefty bonus if he can do it. (He does meet the 90-day deadline, but only after conscripting a crew of workers from the many saloons up and down Lincoln Avenue.) Dr. Abbott, meanwhile, contracts with local printers to publish a special insert for the *Alkaloidal Clinic.* All four pages cover the holocaust, including a plea for patronage.

Final irony comes when the year's sales figures reach a new high of $200,000 — the exact loss from the fire.

TOP: *Catalogs and pamphlets such as these are routinely mailed to physicians.* CENTER: *The disastrous fire of 1905 leaves the four-story brick building of the Clinic Publishing Company in ruins.* BOTTOM: *U.S. President Theodore Roosevelt poses for the press with Japanese and Russian envoys aboard the* Mayflower.

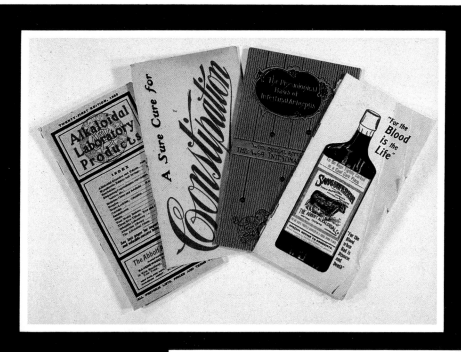

The San Francisco earthquake, most damaging ever in U.S. history, finally ends after two days of unceasing tremors. The fires resulting from it rage on for three more days. With 452 dead, 225,000 left homeless, and over $350 million in property loss, the damage from the quake itself is less than that caused by the fires and looting.

The U.S. Pure Food and Drug Act is signed into law after James R. Mann dramatically recites in Congress a list of adulterants found in coffee, including "roasted peas, beans, wheat, rye, oats, chicory, brown bread, charcoal, red slate, bark, and date stones." This so inspires Dr. Harvey Wiley, the Act's leading proponent, that he asks President Roosevelt to ban saccharin. The president, who routinely uses the substance, turns him down.

João Franco becomes prime minister of Portugal, Giovanni Giolitti of Italy, and Peter Stolypin of Russia. Franco will leave the country two years later when King Carlos is assassinated, Giolitti will have a longer and more fruitful career as the father of major social and agrarian reforms, and Stolypin will make his mark by executing hundreds of revolutionaries and carrying out massive repression through his secret police agency.

Meanwhile, Upton Sinclair's lurid novel *The Jungle* turns the stomach of Americans as it exposes the industry practice of putting tainted meats on the market and starts a scandal that leads to passage of the Meat Inspection Act. Zane Grey's *The Spirit of the Border* starts him on a career of writing colorful Westerns that will span 54 novels selling over 15 million copies.

With presses repaired, new equipment purchased, and a gleaming new five-story brick building in place, Dr. Abbott's enterprise is back in business by March 1906. But not on the same basis.

Changes are taking place. Despite Dr. Abbott's original aversion to salesmen, Clough and Dr. Burdick convince him that a sales force must be added if the company is to grow. Dr. Thackeray is named sales manager, and soon "Abbott Missionaries" make their rounds in a variety of intriguing ways: by oxcart in Arkansas, by horseback with stuffed saddlebags in Missouri, by buggy in Kentucky, and by horseless carriage in Michigan. The Doctor, however, stays with his bicycle.

At home, the *Alkaloidal Clinic* undergoes a subtle restyling by Dr. Burdick. The name is changed to the *American Journal of Clinical Medicine*. More important, the articles no longer deal only with alkaloidal therapy but encompass a broad range of medical subjects. Clough, meanwhile, adds yet another title to his repertoire, becoming business manager. The little man quickly reverses the journal's trend of mounting losses. He raises subscription rates from $1.00 to $1.50, raises advertising rates to $400 for a full page, streamlines accounting methods, and slashes office expenses. Further revenue-producing measures that he proposes (and has accepted) include the idea to spin off the company for which he formerly wrote ad copy, Tengwall File and Ledger, at a profit close to $15,000. And bonds at $20 each in the Abbott Alkaloidal Company are advertised to physicians all over the country.

TOP: *At 5:13 A.M. on April 18, 1906, the ground beneath San Francisco begins to tremble, as the worst quake in U.S. history hits the West Coast.* CENTER: *The Abbott Alkaloidal Company calling card lists the company's four branch offices and a sampling of product specialties.* BOTTOM: *Dr. Abbott goes for a spin in the* Alkaloid, *owned and driven by Abbott salesman H. S. Jones.*

The Abbott Alkaloidal Co.

Manufacturing Chemists

RAVENSWOOD STATION, CHICAGO

Branches: New York City, N. Y.; Oakland, Calif.;
Seattle, Wash.; London, England

SPECIALTIES:
Abbott's Ready-in-Dispense;
Alkaloidal Granules and Tablets;
Saline Laxative; Solitbis; Nuclein;
W-A Antiseptics—Intestinal, Vaginal
and Dermal; Neuro-Lecithin; Calcidin;
Calcalith; Bilein; Sanguiferrin; Hyos-
cine, Morphine and Cactin Comp.; and
Other Success-Making Specialties

51

Tragedy lays a heavy and frequent hand on the news when U.S. coal mine disasters claim the lives of 361 people in Monongah, West Virginia, and another 239 in Jacobs Creek, Pennsylvania. About the same time, the steamer *Larchmont* founders in Long Island Sound, causing 131 deaths, and a train wreck on the Père Marquette Railroad near Salem, Michigan, costs 30 lives.

In a lighter vein, Boston begins to make its mark on the cultural world when it suppresses Elinor Glyn's novel *Three Weeks*. The romantic tale is spiced with a few episodes of illicit sex. The novel is formally banned in 1908, but not before selling 50,000 copies in its first three weeks. The first American appearance of Richard Strauss' opera *Salomé* is several veils too few for proper Bostonians, so Mary Garden is forced to sing it elsewhere.

Great Britain launches two of the largest steamships in the world, the *Lusitania* and the *Mauretania*. Each weighs 31,000 tons. The *Lusitania* breaks the transatlantic speed record by making the journey from Queenstown, Ireland, to New York Harbor in five days, 45 minutes.

The General Appropriations Act is approved by the U.S. Congress, increasing the salaries of cabinet members, the speaker of the house, and the vice president to $12,000. Senators and representatives are raised to $7,500. Those increases come in the nick of time as a currency panic begins with a run on New York's Knickerbocker Trust. Within a day and a half, the bank's entire reserves are depleted. Quickly, other banks throughout the country are forced to close as the bad news spreads.

The 1907 depression, coming only two years after the disastrous fire, finds the company in tenuous financial condition. Orders continue to come in, but payments fall far behind. Company revenues can't keep up with sharply rising costs. Often, there's not enough cash on hand to meet day-to-day expenses.

Dr. Abbott tries every cure he knows to solve the dilemma. He plunges into a virtual round-the-clock existence at the office — managing the plant by day and directing the executive, sales, and advertising policies at night. What little sleep he gets is on the cot in his office. Some employees, he realizes, must be laid off. Others show their loyalty by volunteering for a 50 percent pay cut, with the balance on promise. Several key employees sign away any pay increases with the promise of stock reimbursement later. Some who accept this offer — and hold their stock through the years — will become North Shore millionaires. The Doctor even allows a few of his employees to invest in his gold mines, chief of which is the "Little Mattie," on Chicago Creek in Colorado. They all prove unproductive; the yield of low-grade ore is too poor to process. Even so, all employees who invested are paid in full when the mines are finally discontinued.

When sales of the $20 cooperative bonds lag, Dr. Abbott tries to improve his cash position with a new investment offer — $200,000 worth of seven percent preferred stock. There are few takers. It is at this precise time that the Ravenswood Exchange Bank (in which Dr. Abbott has a "considerable" interest) fails, with an indebtedness of $400,000.

TOP: *This artist's rendering, circa 1907, presents Dr. Abbott's vision of the Chicago "home office" of the Abbott Alkaloidal Company. It includes a center administration building that will never be built.* BOTTOM: *Set off by failures of the Knickerbocker Trust Company and the Westinghouse Electric and Manufacturing Co., a currency panic sweeps the U.S., creating mad "runs" on banks, such as this one in New York City.*

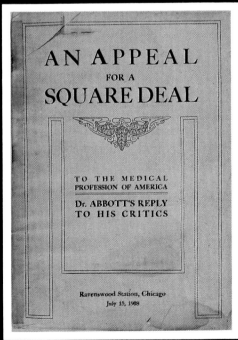

AN APPEAL
FOR A
SQUARE DEAL

TO THE MEDICAL
PROFESSION OF AMERICA

Dr. ABBOTT'S REPLY
TO HIS CRITICS

Ravenswood Station, Chicago
July 15, 1908

54

Republicans William Howard Taft and James S. Sherman defeat William Jennings Bryan and John W. Kern in the U.S. presidential election. The campaign's only real stir comes when the Socialist Labor Party nominates a Martin Preston as its candidate. He has at least two strikes against him: he's under the constitutional age and he's serving a jail term in Nevada for murder.

Elsewhere, progress comes in a variety of ways. Henry Ford introduces his famous Model T at a price of $850. Sixteen years later, the price will drop to $290 because of Ford's manufacturing efficiencies. The new 47-story Singer Building in New York sets a record as the world's tallest building, but it will hold that title for less than a year. The building is barely topped off when New Yorkers are treated to their first sky advertising. A plane towing a box kite rigged with a dummy on a trapeze flies over the new skyscraper, advertising a new Broadway show. In Berlin, the first steel and glass building goes up. The A.E.G. Turbine factory demonstrates the simple, utilitarian, modern style that is making designer Peter Behrens famous.

At Fort Myer, in Arlington Heights, Virginia, Orville Wright's airplane crashes, causing the first air fatality when his passenger, Thomas Selfridge of the U.S. Army, dies. And in Sicily and Calabria, a massive earthquake kills 150,000 people.

The great around-the-world automobile race, from New York to Paris by way of Alaska and Siberia, is won by an American after a leading German team is penalized for shipping its car to Seattle by rail. The only other car to finish, an Italian entry, crosses the line two weeks later.

A strange vendetta between the American Medical Association and Abbott is inspired by Dr. George H. Simmons, secretary of the AMA and editor-in-chief of its influential *Journal of the American Medical Association.*

What started out in 1905 as Simmons' personal crusade against the patent-medicine industry and their worthless nostrums reaches several of Dr. Abbott's products. Specifically, Dr. Simmons questions the efficacy of *Bilein*, an Abbott bile salt product, and the attributes of the *H.M.C.* Tablet as an anesthetic. The attacks soon spread into a series of venomous articles, each more ruthless than its predecessor.

Dr. Abbott becomes convinced the crusade has turned into a conspiracy when he is denied advertising space in the *Journal,* and when the editorial barrage spreads to many AMA-controlled state and county medical societies. His letters of refutation are seldom printed, and then only after severe editing. His counterattack comes in July 1908 in the form of a carefully prepared 48-page rebuttal, titled *An Appeal for a Square Deal,* which he sends directly to doctors throughout the U.S. Headlines in Chicago papers read, "Doctors' War Grows Bitter." Finally, DeWitt Clough, through his acquaintances at the AMA, negotiates an understanding that ends the feud, permitting Abbott to once again advertise in the *Journal.*

TOP: *Dr. Abbott's home in the Ravenswood section of Chicago was built in 1891.* BOTTOM LEFT: *To counter a sharp attack from the American Medical Association, Dr. Abbott prepares this 48-page defense of his company's practices.* BOTTOM RIGHT: *These entrants in the great around-the-world auto race from New York to Paris will likely look a little less fresh at the finish.*

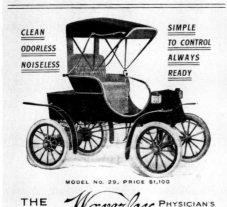

In Your Daily Rounds, Doctor

You can save from two to three hours, an item of great importance in your practice, by the use of a POPE WAVERLEY ELECTRIC.

CLEAN
ODORLESS
NOISELESS

SIMPLE
TO CONTROL
ALWAYS
READY

MODEL No. 29, PRICE $1,100

THE POPE *Waverley* PHYSICIAN'S ROAD WAGON

The above model is designed especially to meet the requirements of the physician. It is made roomy, with a broad and high back seat, fully upholstered, for comfort; the top is large and extends well forward for protection from the weather. An ideal runabout throughout.

POPE MOTOR CAR CO., Waverley Dept., **INDIANAPOLIS, IND., U. S. A.**

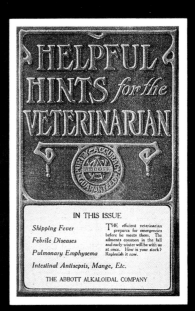

HELPFUL HINTS for the VETERINARIAN

PURITY ACCURACY GUARANTEED
ABBOTT

IN THIS ISSUE

Shipping Fever

Febrile Diseases

Pulmonary Emphysema

Intestinal Antisepsis, Mange, Etc.

THE efficient veterinarian prepares for emergencies before he meets them. The ailments common in the fall and early winter will be with us at once. How is your stock? Replenish it now.

THE ABBOTT ALKALOIDAL COMPANY

The big news comes when six people discover the North Pole — and one more claims to have beat them to it. American Commander Robert E. Peary, with his black servant Matt Henson and four Eskimos, makes a mad dash from their advance camp, reaching 90 degrees north for the first time in recorded history. Later in the year, Dr. Frederick Cook, of Brooklyn, will claim to have reached the Pole a year earlier. His claim is not believed.

U.S. President Taft opens up 700,000 acres to settlers in Washington, Montana, and Idaho. The 100th anniversary of Abraham Lincoln's birth is celebrated by issuance of the Lincoln penny, which replaces the Indian head penny in circulation the past 50 years. W. C. Handy, a band leader in Memphis, writes the campaign song for E. H. Crump in the Memphis municipal election. Originally called "Mister Crump," the song is later renamed "Memphis Blues" and as such becomes the first blues rhythm to be published.

Elsewhere in the world, French aviator Louis Blériot becomes the first person in history to reach Britain who does not come by water. He pilots his plane across the English Channel to land at Dover. The Wright brothers win the first U.S. Army contract to construct a plane. Halley's Comet is first sighted at Heidelberg. It's a rare person who will see it twice: the next appearance will be 77 years later, in 1986. And the first wireless message is sent, from New York City to Chicago.

The momentum begins to build as the company reaches annual sales of $445,000. DeWitt Clough is more than a little expansive when he suggests it's time for Dr. Abbott to switch from his bicycle to one of the new electrically driven autos. One of the most popular of these is the Waverley, manufactured in Indianapolis. Clough suggests that he might even be able to get a deal on one. The Doctor immediately accepts.

After considerable correspondence, Clough is able to secure a full year's advertising contract in *Clinical Medicine* in exchange for a new Waverley plus two or three hundred in cash. Thirty days later, a Chicago railroad terminal advises him that the new auto has arrived and should be sent for at once. Clough is so exuberant he calls for the car himself, not stopping to consider that he's never before driven an auto — or even been in one. The freight handlers help him get the car down to street level and even show him how to push the steering lever to the right to turn left and vice versa. As Clough describes it, "It was only by a miracle, plus driving the thing at three miles an hour up Michigan Avenue, that I finally arrived in front of Dr. Abbott's home."

Dr. Abbott is as pleased with the car as a boy with a new toy. He, too, however, has never driven anything without handlebars. Backing out of the garage one morning, he forgets to change gears. The car bolts backward through a sturdy garden fence and into a tree, spraining the Doctor's arm. The Doctor does not report the accident, but when he comes to the office with his arm in a sling, the secret is out. It's enough to send him back to his bicycle.

TOP: *French aviator Louis Blériot poses with his wife and plane after becoming the first to fly across the English Channel.* BOTTOM LEFT: *One of the ads run by DeWitt Clough in the* Alkaloidal Clinic *in exchange for the Doctor's new Waverley automobile.* BOTTOM RIGHT: *Upon creation of the company's first veterinary department in 1909, Dr. Abbott begins publication of this monthly journal, similar to* Helpful Hints for the Busy Doctor.

1 9 1 0

The first plane takeoff from the deck of a ship is made near Hampton Roads, Virginia. And the first night flight is taken by Frenchman Émile Auburn.

The Boy Scouts of America are formally chartered by W. D. Boyce, a Chicago publisher. The Camp Fire Girls are organized one month later. Eight states have now adopted Prohibition. Meanwhile, the Christian Endeavor Society of Missouri tries to ban all motion pictures that depict kissing between people who are not relatives. This may be where the term "kissin' cousins" first comes into prominence. A British comedian named Charlie Chaplin is the leading performer in a vaudeville act called "The Wow-Wows." It is hardly a strong stepping-stone.

For the first time since 1894, a Democratic Congress is elected, by a country dissatisfied with President Taft's vacillating tariff policies. In the same election, a young man from Dutchess County, New York, wins his first seat in the New York State Senate. His name: Franklin Delano Roosevelt. President Taft appoints the governor of New York, Charles Evans Hughes, to the Supreme Court. Despite the fact that full grade-school education has been completed by less than half the population over 25, illiteracy in America reaches a low of 7.7 percent — a decline of 3 percent since 1900.

Elsewhere in the world, the Union of South Africa is formed, Korea is formally annexed by Japan, China abolishes slavery, the Mexican Revolution breaks out, and both King Edward VII and Count Leo Tolstoy die.

Now there are more than 700 products in the Abbott catalog. Sales cross the magic half-million threshold to reach $546,000, and the customer list totals 50,000 of the country's 130,000 physicians, plus 1,000 in Europe and 500 in Latin America. Expansion has been the key word with branches now in New York, San Francisco, Seattle, and Toronto, a European agency in London, and new operations in India.

To the fast-growing company, three new employees will each contribute decades of productivity. Edward Hawks Ravenscroft, educated as a civil engineer, has two prior ties to Dr. Abbott. Not only did he supervise the 1908 construction of the company's new five-story fireproof building, but in 1896 he had married Dr. Abbott's sister Lucy. Serving as chairman of the board from 1933 to 1946, Ravenscroft will apply his skill and knowledge in finance to help guide the company through good times and bad.

Joseph Favil Biehn, M.D., previously director of the Chicago Health Department laboratories, supervises the biological laboratories at Abbott. He will set up a veterinary department and begin arrangements for the company to move into the dental field. As head of the medical department, Dr. Biehn will be a prime factor in molding Abbott's reputation in pharmaceuticals.

Ferdinand H. "Fred" Young, assistant manager of a Peoria drug-making company although only 20 years old, is hired at 40¢ an hour in alkaloidal production. Later, as head of all manufacturing, he will become the dominant force in helping Abbott achieve breakthroughs in the production of penicillin and I.V. solutions.

In 1910, three new faces appear at Abbott: TOP LEFT, *E. H. Ravenscroft.* TOP RIGHT, *Dr. J. F. Biehn.* BOTTOM LEFT, *F. H. "Fred" Young.* BOTTOM RIGHT: *"Life's Happy Hours — Best I Guess is the Old Recess." The caption to this photographic idyll to American childhood was penned by James Whitcomb Riley, enormously popular during this period for his idealized poems about small towns and simple people.*

59

Abbott's Booster

TO OUR MEN AND BRANCHES

PRIVATE

| Second Year | May-June, 1912 | No. Two |

I WANT MORE SMOKE

You men who are out on the road these days getting the orders, or trying to get them, are exactly the fellows who are supposed to keep the smoke coming out of the towering chimney of this plant. It is upon you that we depend.

The volume of smoke emitted by the chimney the last thirty days has been by no means inconsiderable; it has been sufficient to darken the landscape around here all right. But still I am not satisfied. Not quite!

I want more smoke.

Now, beginning next week. I am going to make it a point to watch my chimney every day at high tide, to see if I am getting it. So get busy, every one of you, and shoot in the orders— the fuel that makes the smoke that comes out of the towering chimney over the engine house.

I want smoke and plenty of it—the densest, the blackest smoke that ever wended its way skyward. And when the warm breezes commence to blow in I don't want to see the smoke line getting any smaller around or thinner or less black than it is right now—or will be in a week from now.

I want more smoke and I want it all spring and summer, without lull or intermission. If I do not get it I shall be very disappointed, I can tell you.

So please knuckle down—all—and keep the stream of orders coming in uninterruptedly. Let's all do our very best to make this year a record-breaking one. We can; we've got a good start; and the outlook is fine.

Keep pushing Calcidin hard—and harder yet. In these spring months, with their changeable weather, there is no end to the indications for it. Statistics show that there are more cases of pneumonia in the late spring than in mid-winter. And the crop of "colds" and catarrh is a bumper one.

All together now, for more smoke and a big year! You know me—"I want what I want when I want it."

This is the year for antitrust suits in the U.S. The Supreme Court breaks up John D. Rockefeller's Standard Oil Company. The trust is reorganized into six separate corporations. Two weeks later, the same thing happens to James B. Duke's American Tobacco Company. The corporations that emerge include American Tobacco, P. Lorillard, Liggett & Myers, R. J. Reynolds, and the British-American Tobacco Company.

A National Health Insurance Bill is introduced to Britain's Parliament by Lloyd George. Italy declares war on Turkey, and the event marks the first offensive use of aircraft when the Tripoli coast is bombed. A revolution overthrows the Manchu dynasty in China, and the Chinese Republic is proclaimed. The calendar is reformed, pigtails abolished, and Sun Yat-sen established as the new republic's leader.

America's first annual Indianapolis 500 auto race is won by Ray Harroun, who averages 75 miles per hour in his Marmon Wasp. A record transcontinental airplane flight is made, with the journey from Sheepshead Bay, New York, to Pasadena, California, completed in 3½ days' flying time. In reality, the trip takes 49 days, since the pilot crashes no fewer than 19 times. "Alexander's Ragtime Band" by Irving Berlin popularizes, outside the Mississippi Delta, the ragtime music that Scott Joplin pioneered.

Meanwhile, a young Polish chemist, Casimir Funk, coins a new word. He feels that if enzymes are to work, they will require coenzymes. He calls these "vitamines" in the belief that they are essential to life.

Some of the flavor of Dr. Abbott's brand of leadership is captured in his communications to fellow employees. Short, pungent phrases are his rule. Notes to those in low positions as well as high are routine. Many of these come from his "memory rester" — a small black notebook he carries with him at all times. He can be seen penciling in reminders and observations almost any time of the day, anywhere in the plant.

Dr. Abbott is in the habit of personally checking the flow of work, popping up in the lab one day, the shipping room the next. A forceful man, even concerning tiny details, he hates to waste a moment. If an employee tosses a wad of paper at the wastebasket — and misses — he'd better not take the time to pick it up. That's the janitor's job, insists the Doctor.

When he feels a push is needed, he's never afraid of speaking up. "Do it now!" is one favorite note. The next level comes when he tells employees, "I want more smoke!" They know exactly what he means. And when operations run into an occasional snag, "Back up and try again!" becomes his maxim. Old-timers recall one occasion when *everything* seemed to go wrong. This called for a company-wide clarion: "Everybody get busy — the Doctor."

Inspirational messages are not limited to employees. For medical readers, he has two concise points of advice. "Clean out, clean up, and keep clean!" is a small dose of sage thinking that could pertain to an entire spectrum of medical conditions. But his favorite reminder to physician customers is "Equalize the circulation, eliminate wastes, stop autotoxemia, maintain systematic aesepsis, stimulate innervation, and feed the tissues."

TOP: *The Doctor probably used this mailing department of the Clinic Publishing Company for his direct mail campaigns.* BOTTOM LEFT: *Dr. Abbott continually pumps advice and product information into his sales force by means of this monthly publication created by DeWitt Clough in 1911.* BOTTOM RIGHT: *Ray Harroun wins the first Indianapolis 500 auto race in his Marmon Wasp.*

The world is shocked when the "unsinkable" British luxury liner the SS *Titanic,* on her maiden voyage, scrapes an iceberg in the North Atlantic and sinks within 2½ hours. Only 711 of the 2,224 aboard are saved.

Back in the U.S., former President Teddy Roosevelt bolts the Republican party to run as the "Bull Moose" candidate on the Progressive party ticket. He beats the incumbent, President Taft, but Governor Woodrow Wilson of New Jersey walks away with the election, giving the Democrats control of the White House for the first time in 15 years.

A Dutch airplane designer named Anthony Fokker opens an aircraft factory in Johannesthal, Germany. By coincidence, English aeronaut Thomas Sopwith establishes Sopwith Aviation in Kingston-on-Thames. The products of these two will duel for air supremacy of Europe over the next six years.

The first full-length foreign movie ever shown in America, a 40-minute French film called *Queen Elizabeth* and starring Sarah Bernhardt, opens at New York's Lyceum Theatre.

Jim Thorpe, an American Indian from Pennsylvania's Carlisle Indian School, wins both the decathlon and the pentathlon at the 1912 Olympic Games in Stockholm. He is proclaimed the "world's greatest athlete." Later, gold medals and all honors will be stripped from him when it is learned that he played one semester of semi-pro baseball as part of a summer job in college. It is an injustice that will not be corrected during his lifetime.

After 20 years as Dr. Abbott's secretary, Ida Richter becomes the first person to retire from the company — and probably one of the most important.

As Dr. Burdick sees her: "Never could I slight a piece of work that she would not overtake me in the fault; never did I leave anything undone, unwittingly or not, that she did not bring it to my attention; never did I half-finish a job that she wouldn't come to me and explain that 'the Doctor wants things to come to him finished.'

"When we left school," Burdick continued, "we dreamed of the great things we would do. We despised the little ones, thinking they were suited only for fellows who didn't know quite as much as we did. And yet, I give it as my opinion that nine-tenths of the failures in life are due to despising or overlooking detail. If you can watch a person early enough, and if his or her head is not too badly swollen, something of this truth may be got into it. But, woe to the one who doesn't think it necessary to his or her career to know, and knowing do, the little things.

"This is where Miss Richter got in her work among us. Dr. Abbott told me that, without her help, he might have failed; that it was the unceasing devotion of Ida and her sister Emily that contributed more perhaps than the work of any two other persons to establish the Abbott Alkaloidal Company and the *Clinic* on a sound business basis."

TOP: *After 20 years of devoted service as Dr. Abbott's private secretary, Ida Richter retires. Her parting words at the banquet given in her honor: "I can truly say . . . that I felt I was having a small part in something that was for the uplift of mankind."* BOTTOM: *Family and friends await survivors of the sinking of the British liner SS* Titanic.

Henry Ford establishes a high wage of $5 a day for his workers, and will watch the price of his Model T drop from its highest point of $950 to $290 because of his efficient new assembly-line production. Meanwhile, the average English worker still earns less than 1 pound per week ($5 in U.S. currency).

Low wages may be a contributing factor as suffragettes demonstrate in London. Their like-minded neighbors to the north celebrate as Norway gives the vote to women. Meanwhile, the Balkan Wars — fought by Bulgaria, Turkey, Serbia, Russia, Albania, and Greece for possession of the European territories of the declining Ottoman Empire — come to an end with the defeat of Bulgaria. The nationalism heightened by the wars will be one cause of World War I.

This is the year Camel cigarettes are introduced by R. J. Reynolds Company. Made mainly of a flue-cured bright tobacco, they are combined with a sweetened burley from Kentucky and Turkish tobaccos to become the first modern blended cigarette. Liggett & Myers, well known for its Fatima, Picayune, and Piedmont brands, tries to match Camel with a new blend called Chesterfield. Perhaps it's a coincidence that this is also the year in which the American Cancer Society is founded.

In sports, a little-known college football team from northern Indiana, Notre Dame, startles the sports world and the powerful Army team with its strategic use of a new weapon called the forward pass. Notre Dame wins 35-13 as Charles "Gus" Dorais completes 17 of 21 passes to Knute Kenneth Rockne.

In 1912 sales declined from $600,000 to $538,000. While sales recover to $587,000 in 1913, the downturn, the first in the company's history, is both sobering and ominous. Dr. Abbott finds that his 25-year-old alkaloidal business is beginning to have the same obsolescence as the fledgling automobile industry. Discarded models, in drugs as in cars, are becoming routine.

The Doctor bombards his 35 salesmen with incessant exhortations in the pages of the new monthly publication *Abbott's Booster* to consider each sales point as "daily food. Digest it well, and everybody hustle!" is his order. He constantly emphasizes that alkaloidal granules are to be pushed hard. "Regardless of all else, put these to the front on every possible occasion. Don't forget to suggest them in bulk and *never* write down an order for less than 1,000 unless the customer insists that you do so!"

Some customers do insist. A typical order of the day reads:

1 doz. Saline Laxative (small)	$ 2.25
1,000 Strychnine Arsen. 1/128 gr.	.65
500 Colchicine 1/128 gr.	.75
1,000 Trip Arsen. w/Nuc #1	1.65
6 tubes *H.M.C.* #1	2.50
	7.80
15% discount	− 1.17
	6.63
Wells Fargo express	.21
	$ 6.84

P.S. — Our chicken cholera remedy is effective and profitable.

Perhaps there's hope in the chicken cholera remedy — at least more than in the fading alkaloidal business.

TOP: *The 1913 team of Abbott managers and key personnel. (Standing, left to right) DeWitt Clough; E. H. Ravenscroft; Franklin Summers; and Dr. Abbott. (Seated, left to right) W. R. Laughlin; C. O. Brown; and Alfred Burdick.* BOTTOM: *University of Notre Dame's left end, Knute Rockne, will go on to become the school's head football coach from 1918 to 1931, keeping his team constantly in the limelight with a record of 105 wins, 12 defeats, and 5 ties.*

Austria declares war on Serbia in late July — one month after a 19-year-old Serbian terrorist guns down Archduke Francis Ferdinand and his wife. Within four days, Germany declares war on Russia, and two days later, on France. The next day, Belgium is invaded by German troops and Britain declares war on Germany. The lamps begin to go out all over Europe when Japan gets into the act by declaring war on both Germany and Austria.

The Panama Canal opens to traffic with a 51-mile system of locks connecting the waters of the Atlantic and Pacific. Cost of completion totals some $367 million and 30,000 lives. Mohandas Gandhi returns to India after practicing law for 21 years in South Africa. He attracts wide attention when he inaugurates the first of 14 political fasts.

In the U.S., the Federal Trade Commission is established, with a mandate of checking the growth of monopolies and safeguarding business competition. The first stoplight in America controls traffic at Euclid Avenue and East 105th Street in Cleveland. Novelist Edgar Rice Burroughs publishes his classic *Tarzan of the Apes.*

Walter Hagen wins the U.S. Open golf championship at age 21. In later years, he will add another U.S. Open, five PGA championships, four British Opens, and a French Open. Of longer-lasting significance is the invention by Mary Phelps Jacob. She patents the idea of combining two pocket handkerchiefs, a strip of pink ribbon, and thread to form what she calls a "backless brassiere."

The heart of the Abbott business has always pulsed with four or five laxatives and cold remedies, a number of antacids, and an occasional heart drug. Constipation, catarrh, and gut miseries are common maladies of the times. With the world standing on the threshold of rapid progress in chemistry, medicine, and technology, Dr. Burdick realizes that the vogue for alkaloids has already peaked. He argues long and hard before he gets the Doctor's blessing to switch the research emphasis away from more alkaloidal remedies and into the exciting new field of synthetic medicinals.

The idea is still more of a wish than a practice. Though the United States has almost illimitable sources to draw on for raw materials through its coal mines, coke ovens, and gas plants, the manufacture of synthetic chemicals up to now has been limited to saccharin and aspirin. And these are made in the U.S. entirely by German-owned corporations. American chemists so far are inadequately trained to undertake the tremendous problem of manufacturing medicinal chemicals, as compared with those German scientists whose work already rests on the secure foundation of many years of great achievement.

TOP: The Abbott Alkaloidal Company periodically represents itself with handsome exhibits at trade shows and conventions. Here Sarah Drake demonstrates granule manufacturing at a meeting of the American Medical Association. CENTER: *Abbott's Saline Laxative and W-A Intestinal Antiseptic are wide-selling specialties of the day.* BOTTOM: *On August 15, the Panama Canal is opened for traffic.*

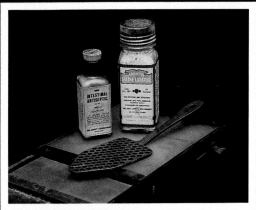

The Great War grows more intense on both the Eastern and Western Fronts, and the Germans begin a submarine blockade of Britain. In May, the British steamship *Lusitania*, queen of the Cunard line, is torpedoed without warning by a German U-boat off the coast of Ireland. It sinks within 18 minutes, killing 1,198, including 128 Americans. Indignation over the sinking makes U.S. entry into the war inevitable.

In April, the Germans use chlorine gas in the Belgian city of Ypres to rout French colonial troops, the first use of poison gas. Britain reciprocates in September. By then, Russia has lost all of Poland and Lithuania to the Germans. British and French troops attack Turkey's Gallipoli Peninsula in an attempt to seize the Dardanelles and open up supply lines for Russia. Four British warships are sunk by mines, and the land forces eventually abandon the campaign. Blame for the costly failure falls on Britain's 41-year-old first lord of the admiralty, a man named Winston Churchill.

In the U.S., racial tensions are heightened by the first showing of D. W. Griffith's full-length movie *The Birth of a Nation*. The situation isn't helped when a new Ku Klux Klan, dedicated to white supremacy, is started in Stone Mountain, Georgia. Meanwhile, black prizefighter Jack Johnson loses his heavyweight championship to Jess Willard, the "great white hope," in a 23-round bout in Havana.

The company name is changed to Abbott Laboratories. The switch marks two important trends: first, the growing influence of Dr. Burdick, and second, a totally new direction for the company.

Dr. Abbott sees an opportunity to finance the transition, and the need for infinitely more research, in his own way. After all, he reasons, might not the same idea he used before to assuage his nonpaid employees — the issuance of stock certificates — work now to attract new investors? And what better market to pursue than his own physician customers?

Stock in Abbott Laboratories is issued at 10 shares for $100. Ten shares is the least an investor can buy. There is no upper limit. The stock is listed as a seven percent preferred and is offered to a preferred list of physicians. Dr. Abbott's letter reads with considerable gusto.

My dear Doctor:

Here's the story — *plain English in cold type!* I could not tell you more if I talked a week. This A. A. Co. preferred is a ripping good thing ("good" for both of us) and I want you in: even if for no more than ten shares ($100.00) as a "starter." Please give me a chance to show you what, with your help cooperatively, we can do. If you are "in" by May 1st, you shall have the full quarter's dividend, April, May, and June, paid July 1st. Kindly use the enclosed order blank and personal return envelope. I'll see you through. Don't get left.

Fraternally,

W. C. Abbott

It is an offer that "can't be refused," though some do. Most of those who take the offer will hold the stock only a few years.

TOP: *Seen here with his trainer, Jack Johnson was the first black American boxer to win the heavyweight crown. In 1915, he loses to Jess Willard in the 23d round of his final title defense.* **CENTER:** *While Dr. Abbott claims to be giving the story "in cold type" in this business appeal for the purchase of Abbott preferred stock, he actually has the letter reproduced and distributed in his own hand, presumably for dramatic effect.* **BOTTOM:** *The staff of the newly named Abbott Laboratories takes time out to celebrate with a costume party in the Clinic building loft. Dr. Abbott, perhaps master of ceremonies, appears with megaphone.*

My dear Doctor:-

Here's the story — plain English in cold type! I could not tell you more if I talked a week.

This A.A.C. preferred is a ripping good thing ("good" for both [us]) and I want you in; even if for no more than ten shares ($100 ea) as a "starter."

Please give me a chance to show you what, with your help, cooperatively, we can do. If you are "in" by May 1st you shall have the full quarterly dividend, April, May and June, paid July 1st.

Kindly use the enclosed order blank and personal return envelope & I'll see you through. Fraternally,

The war in Europe continues to take a heavy toll: the Battle of Verdun on the Western Front rages from February to July, with 350,000 French lives lost and almost as many German. Next, the Battle of the Somme is fought along a 15-mile front and becomes the bloodiest in British history, claiming 600,000 Allied casualties and 500,000 Germans. At the battle's conclusion, the Allies drive the Germans back about seven miles, most of which Germany will regain in 1918.

A U.S. military expedition, under the command of Brigadier General John J. Pershing, goes in pursuit of the Mexican revolutionary General Francisco "Pancho" Villa. Pershing will spend nearly a year fruitlessly searching the Mexican mountains for Pancho Villa. He'll finally withdraw his forces after arbitration settles differences between the U.S. and the Mexican government.

President Wilson narrowly wins reelection on a platform that includes the slogan "He kept us out of war." His Republican opponent, Charles Evans Hughes, goes to bed believing he has won the presidency. But late returns come in from California to give Wilson a slim majority of 23 electoral votes.

At the University of Berlin, a general theory of relativity is announced by Albert Einstein. Explained by a single set of equations, it revolutionizes the world of physics. Closer to home, an important advance in the prevention of internal blood clotting comes with the discovery of heparin by a Johns Hopkins medical student. This will lead to the discovery of Dicumarol, isolated from spoiled sweet clover, as a longer-lasting method of anticoagulation, with less frequent injections required.

Dr. Burdick becomes responsible for the acquisition of one of the first of the new synthetics Abbott will produce. An avid reader, he constantly pores over medical journals from around the world. Early in 1916, he is intrigued to read about a new, nontoxic, and extremely potent antiseptic developed on European battlefields.

The antiseptic is the discovery of Dr. Henry D. Dakin, a young English chemist attached to a French army unit. Dr. Dakin sees thousands of men wounded in battle brought to his field hospital for surgery, but with wounds so infected that many die before they can be placed on operating tables. What is critically needed is a germicide that will kill parasitic life without affecting living tissues or irritating the raw surfaces of the wound.

Customary antiseptics often hinder rather than help recovery; some, in fact, are so lethal that many physicians revert to soap, water, and alcohol instead. After experimenting with more than 200 different mixtures and sterilizing solutions, Dr. Dakin finds the answer: a white, crystalline, chlorine-containing substance, soluble in water and with intense antiseptic action. It accomplishes in five minutes the same degree of sterilization that bichloride of mercury takes seven hours to produce; it is at least 50 times as effective against certain bacilli as carbolic acid. The battlefield outcome is impressive: with recovery rate increased remarkably, cases that formerly required three or four months of treatment now require only a quarter of the time.

Within six months of Dr. Burdick's introduction to Dr. Dakin's discovery, Abbott has arranged to market *Chlorazene*, the "precious fluid" many physicians regard as the greatest surgical find since Joseph Lister introduced antiseptic surgery in 1867.

TOP: *The elusive Pancho Villa, Mexican bandit and revolutionary.* CENTER: *This early American Gothic pose was captured in the filling room of the manufacturing plant on East Ravenswood, built in 1908.* BOTTOM: *In this family portrait, Dr. Abbott displays the Beckley-Ralston bicycle that has become his trademark.*

Russian troops mutiny, and collapse of the Russians on the Eastern Front follows. This combines with the growing strength of the Hindenburg line in the West to give Germany confidence to resume unrestricted U-boat attacks on all shipping, including that of neutral United States. In early April, President Wilson proclaims that "the world must be made safe for democracy," as Congress votes 373-50 to declare a state of war against Germany. One member of the House to vote against entry into the war is Representative Jeannette Rankin, who has been in office just one month as the first female member of Congress.

On the Western Front, French troops lose heart after suffering heavy losses. They, too, mutiny. The brunt of the Allied war effort now falls on the British Tommies. Three months later, American troops land in France, but their first shots in trench warfare aren't fired until early November.

Revolution sweeps through Russia as Czar Nicholas II abdicates in favor of his brother, Michael. When Michael declines to succeed him, the Romanov dynasty founded in 1613 comes to an abrupt end. Over the next few months, the Bolsheviks will overthrow two provisional regimes before Nikolai Lenin seizes power and establishes the Communist party. He names Lev Bronstein, recently returned from exile in the U.S. and England, as commissar for foreign affairs. Bronstein now goes by the name Leon Trotsky. A 39-year-old native of Soviet Georgia who calls himself Joseph Stalin becomes commissar for national minorities.

As the war surges on in Europe, the shortage of essential drugs and chemical supplies from Germany becomes more acute. So serious is the situation that the British actually permit one German ship to pass through their blockade on humanitarian grounds — because it is carrying several hundred thousand ampules of Salvarsan, Dr. Paul Ehrlich's "magic bullet" compound for syphilis. There are said to be 10 million cases of syphilis in the United States, so demand for the drug is enormous. Humanitarian cooperation soon ceases, however, when the dwindling supplies command prices as high as $35 per tube.

The German patent monopoly and the experience and capability of German manufacturers of synthetic chemical and medicinal products seem invincible. Those few American firms that try to break the hold by making similar products soon find that the price of the German counterparts quickly drops below actual manufacturing cost. Germany's world market at this time is so vast that it can afford to sell at a loss in the United States to squelch competition.

For major U.S. companies, this is a prime reason to intensify efforts. One immediate problem is that of German patents. Such important medicinals as Salvarsan, Veronal, Luminal, Atophan, and Novocaine are all enemy property. The U.S. government is eager for these compounds to be produced in America. And when the United States actively enters the war, that difficulty is overcome with the passage of the Trading With The Enemy Act, authorizing the Federal Trade Commission to license U.S. firms to manufacture German products.

TOP: *Posters like this hang in recruitment centers across America, as the nation enters the war.* BOTTOM: *The immediate and overwhelming success of the potent antiseptic Chlorazene continues through the years with several adaptations, among them Halazone, a water purification tablet used by the millions during World War II.*

72

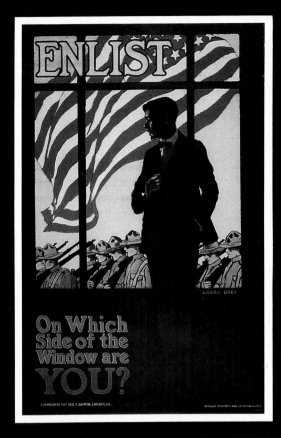

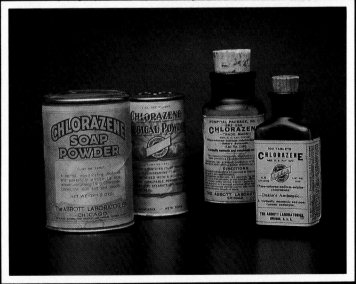

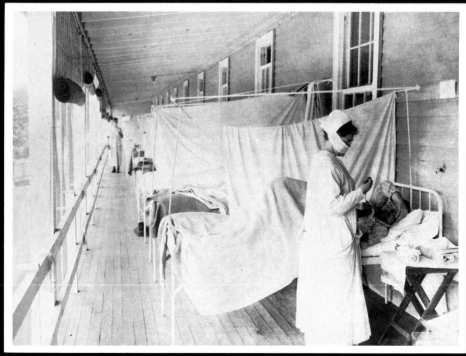

74

The German spring offensive on the Western Front gains momentum and valuable ground over depleted and dead-tired British and French reserves. Finally, in June, over 250,000 fresh American troops come into action at the Battle of the Marne. It marks the turning point. Throughout the summer, the build-up continues as more U.S. soldiers arrive. At long last, victories begin to come. First, U.S. Marines capture Belleau Wood after weeks of bitter fighting. Then, General Pershing mounts a major offensive at Saint-Mihiel as the Germans fall back to the defense line they left behind in 1914.

In the air, Germany's famed "Red Baron" — Manfred von Richtofen — is credited with 80 Allied kills before he is shot down. France's René Fonck, on the other hand, gets less acclaim although he shoots down 75 enemy planes. America's best-known ace, Captain Eddie Rickenbacker, wins the Congressional Medal of Honor for combined balloon and aircraft kills of 26.

By October, 1.2 million American troops are fighting the battle of the Meuse-Argonne. Their objective: to snap the German railroad supply line at Sedan. It works, and the Armistice of November 11 finally signals an end to war. A tragic incongruity: In four years of war, 8.5 million soldiers on both sides have been killed. Yet in only 10 months of 1918, the worst pandemic ever to afflict mankind — Spanish influenza — sweeps through Europe, America, and the Orient. The toll: 21.6 million dead.

TOP LEFT: *Dr. Roger Adams begins his 40-year association with Abbott by synthesizing key products to replace German products no longer available as a result of the war. Due to Adams' work, Abbott is able to move ahead rapidly in the synthetic drug business.* TOP RIGHT: *An assortment of Abbott synthetic drugs, shown with patriotic literature of the day.* BOTTOM: *Makeshift arrangements in the flu ward of Walter Reed Hospital in Washington, D.C., show the desperate conditions caused by the worst flu epidemic in modern history. Worldwide, 21.6 million lives are lost.*

Events stimulated by the war, in particular the opening up of enemy patents to U.S. firms, have impressive significance for Abbott. A series of investigations are already well under way at the company to develop synthetic products superior to the German originals. Even so, the risks of developing processes for commercial production under licenses made possible by the Trading With The Enemy Act are great. Large amounts of money must be devoted to research, the profitability is doubtful, and postwar conditions might bring their future value to naught. Finally, each firm must deposit a five percent royalty on sales to protect the German patent holders. But the company sees it as a patriotic duty.

And in synthesizing German products, Abbott is well ahead of the competition. Soon, the German sedative Veronal becomes the Abbott Barbital. The anesthetic Novocaine is reproduced as Procaine. And Atophan, the German remedy for gout, lumbago, neuralgia, and rheumatism, becomes Cinchophen. Benefits to the American public are immediate. Procaine sells within the year at a lower price than the German Novocaine, and Barbital's price is one-third to one-fourth Veronal's.

The man behind these breakthroughs is a brilliant young chemist, Dr. Roger Adams, hired as a consultant by Abbott in 1917. After studying in Berlin at the Kaiser Wilhelm Institute, Adams served at both Harvard and the University of Illinois. He seems to have a knack for gathering about him top graduate students. One of the best of these is a promising Ph.D. chemist from the University of Illinois. His name: Dr. Ernest Henry Volwiler. Like Dr. Abbott, he was reared on a farm and taught in rural schools. In later years, also like Dr. Abbott, he will head Abbott research and will go on to become Abbott president and chairman.

SUMARIO.

A new republic is formed at Weimar as the Treaty of Versailles forces the Germans to pay huge reparations in land, money, iron ore reserves, and coal deposits. Alsace-Lorraine is returned to France, Belgium and Poland get other territories, and all German colonies are divided up by the Allies. The U.S. Bayer Company, whose German parent makes aspirin, is seized as a war spoil by the U.S. alien property custodian.

Chaos confronts not only Germany but the winners as well. Russia is embroiled in a civil war between the Bolshevik Red Army and a White Russian Army. Inflation rips through France. And in America, New York City's cost of living zooms 79 percent higher than in 1914. The war has cost the United States $22 billion in only two years, plus over $10 billion in war loans to Allied powers.

The U.S. Senate rejects the Treaty of Versailles and membership in the League of Nations. Labor unrest and race riots in 26 cities rock the nation. In Boston, police strike and an orgy of looting and robbing follows. Steelworkers in Gary, Indiana, walk out, and John L. Lewis orders bituminous coal miners to strike.

U.S. racing gets its first Triple Crown winner as Sir Barton sweeps the Kentucky Derby, the Preakness, and the Belmont Stakes. The country gets its first sports scandal as the Chicago White Sox throw the World Series to the Cincinnati Reds.

TOP: *The ready availability of cheap immigrant labor, coupled with intolerable working conditions throughout the industry, cause America's steelworkers to go on strike.* BOTTOM LEFT: *A sign of the company's early expansion into international markets, this Spanish-language edition of the* American Journal of Clinical Medicine, *formerly the* Alkaloidal Clinic, *is circulated in Mexico and other Central American countries.* BOTTOM RIGHT: *Dr. Abbott, with wife Clara, joins in the company picnic. His health at this point is failing rapidly.*

The transition from alkaloids to medicinal chemicals is fast becoming fact. So widely accepted are the new Dakin antiseptics plus the new synthetics freed up from German patents that sales leap — from 1916's $664,000 to $904,000 in 1917 and over the million-dollar barrier to $1,259,000 in 1918.

Beyond this is the undeniable reality that the company has taken its biggest step toward becoming a full-fledged, research-driven pharmaceutical firm. As inevitably accompanies such developments, more men of keen potential and ability have been drawn to the company. One of these has good reason to remember his introduction to Abbott. James F. Stiles, Jr., who came into the company in 1913 as a shipping room packer, claims a lifelong tie to Dr. Abbott. It is a valid claim. The good Doctor, it seems, spanked the first breath of life into the infant Stiles as attending physician at his birth in 1892. Stiles will later serve as company treasurer and, still later, as chairman of the board. His most lasting contribution, however, will come at midcareer when he initiates a broad range of employee fringe benefits, including a stock purchase plan that will allow generations of Abbott employees a comfortable retirement.

Others, too, grow on the job. Elmer B. Vliet first visited the company in 1917 when he was a chemistry student. He remembers the occasion vividly because at a company-sponsored dinner that evening, Dr. Burdick announced America's entry into the war. Two years later, after serving with the Chemical Warfare Service's research section in Washington, young Vliet joins the company as a research chemist. Over the next 40 years, his path will wind through most areas of research, until in 1959, his career, too, culminates in the chairmanship of Abbott.

77

U.S. population reaches 106 million as city dwellers for the first time outnumber rural residents. One in every 3 Americans still lives on a farm, a ratio that will drop to 1 in 30 over the next 60 years. Illiteracy reaches a new low of six percent of the population and life expectancy reaches a new high of 54.1 years. Prohibition goes into effect early in the year, but some diehards continue to buy their booze illegally or else make their own bathtub gin.

Women's suffrage is proclaimed in effect just in time for the national elections, and female voters do their bit to help Ohio's handsome, genial, and colorless Warren G. Harding defeat a fellow Ohioan, Democratic Governor James M. Cox, for the presidency. America's first broadcasting station, KDKA in Pittsburgh, gives the results of the Harding-Cox campaign.

The League of Nations meets for the first time in its new headquarters in Geneva, but its membership includes neither the U.S.S.R. nor the United States. The Hague is selected as the seat of the League's World Court, which later will become the International Court of Justice, judicial arm of the U.N. The court's first decision settles a dispute between Albania and the British-held island of Corfu by determining that Albania was responsible for the mines in the Corfu channel that sank several British vessels.

With rapid sales growth — revenues more than doubled in four years — comes an urgent need for expanded production facilities. A new single-story building is erected adjacent to an apartment building on Ravenswood Avenue. It creates more problems than it solves, however. Nearby residents are quick to complain as objectionable chemical fumes fill the neighborhood. The Chicago Fire Department joins the dissidents as frequent small fires plague the new facility. These repeated incidents soon lead to a heightened search for a new, less populous area for expansion.

Nothing could be less populous than the location proposed — a barren 26-acre tract of industrial ground in the city of North Chicago, 30 miles north of the company's present site. Curious to see the area, Drs. Abbott and Burdick motor out from Ravenswood in Jim Stiles' car. Less than halfway there, the trip is almost aborted due to a tire puncture. No spare, no tire pump, not even a service station nearby. Finally, a passing motorist helps them out, and they continue their journey to what will become the new plant site.

Plans for the new buildings are quickly drawn, with priority given to those designed for chemical production. But Dr. Abbott has a better idea. "Why not," he proposes, "just ask Merck and Company for the blueprints of their plant at Rahway, New Jersey?" Understandably, Merck refuses to release their drawings. Ravenscroft and Vliet go to Rahway anyway, spend 20 minutes scanning the plant from a nearby railroad platform, and report back the results of their trip. On the humid morning of June 9, 1920, Dr. Abbott turns the first furrow of ground at North Chicago, then invites all those around to join him for a picnic lunch on the grounds. The new plant, as it turns out, looks nothing at all like Merck's.

TOP: Posing behind a single-row, horsedrawn plow during ground-breaking ceremonies for the North Chicago plant undoubtedly takes Dr. Abbott back to his boyhood days on a Vermont farm. CENTER: After the ceremonies, several Abbott employees, including Dr. Burdick (standing, far right) and Dr. Abbott (seated, far right), join in a picnic on the North Chicago grounds. BOTTOM: Passage of the 19th Amendment marks the end of a long battle by America's suffragettes.

Just to work, and to get, as I give, "the square deal" Fraternally yours

Univ. of Mich. '85

The superiority of air power over sea power is convincingly demonstrated by U.S. Brigadier General Billy Mitchell when he sinks the former German battleship *Ostfriesland* and the condemned battleship the USS *Alabama* with concentrated air bombing off Hampton Roads, Virginia. They are the first warships ever sunk by bombs from U.S. planes.

Southern Ireland gains dominion status in a treaty signed with England, but the six counties in Protestant Northern Ireland remain part of the United Kingdom, and conflict will go on between the two for well over half a century. In the U.S.S.R., sailors mutiny as the nation's economy collapses. Industrial and agricultural production fall off and food and fuel shortages immediately become acute. With winter comes famine and three million Russians starve to death.

The United States has its problems, too. U.S. workers strike as employers cut back wages by 10 to 25 percent. Business failures plague the country as nearly 20,000 companies fold and 3.5 million Americans are out of work. A wave of lawlessness sweeps the South, with whippings, brandings, tarrings, and destruction of property by the now-rampaging Ku Klux Klan.

In the face of the hard times, it's ironic that the first million-dollar prize fight is held in Jersey City. Jack Dempsey wins the heavyweight championship with a fourth-round knockout of Georges Carpentier.

All chemical manufacturing has been transferred to North Chicago. Although new construction is progressing rapidly, Dr. Abbott is not to see his vision become a reality. Several years earlier, he suffered attacks of typhoid fever and inflammatory rheumatism. While his recovery at the time seemed complete, the illnesses left behind the beginnings of a chronic disease of the kidneys.

Over the past three years, even when his health seriously began to give way, Dr. Abbott has kept on. There have been periods, at first short, when he would have to yield and rest. For a while, he could come back quickly, but from year to year the periods of ill health have become more prolonged and his recuperation slower. His once boundless energy is now the exception.

If he had been a man who spared himself, he might have lived to a ripe old age. But the tremendous business burdens, plus his routine of working night and day, take their toll. Finally, on July 1, 1921, the 63-year-old Dr. Abbott walks slowly home from the Ravenswood plant for the last time and takes to his bed. Three days later he is dead.

In 33 years, Dr. Wallace Calvin Abbott built a $1,453,000 organization based on his conviction that he could improve the practice of medicine with better forms of medication. During this time, there were two drastic depressions, two wars, bank failures, fires, and other emergencies. Not many men of his time will leave such a rare legacy of accomplishment and tradition in the face of such difficulties.

The choice of successor is immediate. Gentle-spoken, scholarly Dr. Alfred S. Burdick is elected by company directors to the post he has actually been filling for several years.

The man fondly known simply as "the Doctor" dies on Independence Day, 1921. This was his favorite portrait.

81

This is a year for discovery. First, King Tut's tomb, crammed with Egyptian treasures dating to 1567 B.C., is unearthed at Luxor. Of the 27 tombs near Thebes, Tut's has been the only one spared from looting. Another discovery, of the Sumerian Royal Cemetery at Ur on the Euphrates River in Iraq, provides the first historical evidence of the legend of the 3000 B.C. Mesopotamian civilization of Sumer.

Key medical discoveries mark the year when Dr. Alexis Carrel of the Rockefeller Institute announces his discovery of leukocytes, or white corpuscles, as the agents in the blood that prevent the spread of infection. Work progresses that will lead to the discovery of vitamin D, later known as the "sunshine vitamin," following the recent revelation that sunlight can be successful in the treatment of rickets. Finally, two Canadian researchers find that the hormone insulin, which they've isolated from animal pancreatic tissue, gives diabetics their first available medical treatment and a new lease on life.

A discovery of slightly lesser significance comes when a 97-pound weakling named Angelo Siciliano, who will change his name to Charles Atlas, announces that "dynamic tension" exercises have turned him into the "World's Strongest Man." The last revelation comes when King Victor Emmanuel III discovers something about human nature when he summons a 39-year-old journalist to form a ministry so he can restore order and bring about reforms. His act marks the beginning of Benito Mussolini's fascist dictatorship in Italy.

TOP LEFT: *By 1922, activity in the Clinic building has been consumed almost entirely by pharmaceutical manufacturing.* TOP RIGHT: *The company's directors named Dr. Alfred Burdick as successor to Dr. Abbott. Piloting the company through a period of rapid expansion, Burdick will serve as president until his death in 1933.* BOTTOM: *Dr. Alexis Carrel of the Rockefeller Institute is not a new name to medical science. Ten years prior to his 1922 discovery of white blood cells, he was awarded the Nobel prize for his work in organ transplantation and blood vessel suturing.*

With the solid establishment of its synthetic drugs, Abbott has become well placed on the medical map. Even so, President Burdick recognizes that one vital ingredient is missing: a stronger, more diversified research organization. Hearing rumors that Philadelphia's Dermatological Research Laboratories might be acquired, Dr. Burdick and DeWitt Clough begin meetings with the company. The competition among bidders is fierce; DRL is renowned as a leader in antisyphilitic research in the U.S. But Abbott has two advantages: DRL doesn't want to affiliate with a German company and its president, Dr. Jay Frank Schamberg, confides, "I like what I hear about Abbott Laboratories and the way it operates." Both Burdick and Clough amaze themselves when they acquire DRL's plant and patents for $150,000 and the entire inventory for only $31,000 more.

The acquisition involves far more than physical facilities. A number of men whose futures will be linked with Abbott for many productive years come along with the deal. Chief among these is Dr. George W. Raiziss, a Russian-born chemist who studied widely in Europe. He will lead Abbott research efforts into germicides and antisyphilitics for many years. Another key new employee is DRL's aggressive sales manager, Raymond E. Horn. In later years, he will revolutionize Abbott sales techniques and become the fifth Abbott president.

"The purchase of the Dermatological Research Laboratories was an exceedingly fortunate venture," Dr. Burdick writes to Mrs. Abbott. "I think it is perfectly safe to say that we will make during the first year of operation enough to pay for the entire plant." Dr. Burdick's prediction is valid. Well before the next year ends, the full purchase price will have been paid and expectations for future productivity, both medically and commercially, will remain high.

German inflation soars out of control as the mark falls from 1921 levels of four to the dollar, to four billion to the dollar by November. Prices rise so fast that workers are paid daily, then several times a day. Peasants swap eggs, milk, butter, and potatoes for Persian rugs and Rembrandt oils. Adolf Hitler, 34, tries to capitalize on the social unrest by staging his "Beer Hall Putsch" in Munich. His Nazis try to seize the city government, but the party is ousted and Hitler sentenced to five years in prison. He'll serve nine months and spend them writing *Mein Kampf* (My Battle).

On the other side of the world, Tokyo and Yokohama suffer an earthquake that sees over 140,000 killed, 752,000 injured, and 83,000 homes completely destroyed. Tokyo's Imperial Hotel, which was designed by Frank Lloyd Wright, is left intact.

In the U.S., President Harding dies of apoplexy in a San Francisco hotel room, and Calvin Coolidge is sworn in by his father, a notary public, the next morning. Both Montana and Nevada enact the country's first old-age pensions as they allot a monthly $25 to qualified septuagenarians. Across the country, the Dempsey-Firpo fight at New York's Polo Grounds sets a new standard for viciousness. In less than four minutes, 12 knockdowns are recorded, most famous of which comes in the first round when the "Wild Bull of the Pampas" knocks Dempsey completely out of the ring and into the laps of sportswriters. He comes back, however, to kayo Firpo in the next round and retain his championship.

TOP: *Introduced in 1923, Butyn will number among the most successful synthetic drugs to come out of Abbott's postwar research program.* CENTER: *Having joined Abbott Laboratories in 1918, Dr. Ernest Volwiler quickly distinguishes himself as one of the company's outstanding scientific minds. Here he is shown in the lab built in 1920 expressly for his work.* BOTTOM: *In this lithograph of America's 1923 Dempsey-Firpo fight, George Bellows captures one of the most famous knockdowns in the history of the fight game.*

Although Abbott is already licensed to produce Cinchophen, Barbital, and Procaine, the wartime-acquired versions of Germany's Atophan, Veronal, and Novocaine, Dr. Burdick realizes all too well that the marketing lives of these products may be short. With the patents on each due to expire this year, he sends Drs. Volwiler and Adams back to their labs to find suitable substitutes.

The task is improbable and painstaking. Novocaine, the immensely popular local anesthetic created in 1906, has had a long-standing advantage over cocaine. It has lower toxicity and presents no peril of strong addiction. On the other hand, the drug does not work as fast as cocaine. So, how to uncover a chemical relative which combines the positives of both and the negatives of neither? The research is grindingly slow. Strangely enough, the war has provided a solution. It is butyl alcohol, known to the laboratory chemist but procurable only at a prohibitive price in the quantities needed for manufacture. The substance is a by-product of the synthetic production of acetone, which is required as a solvent in the making of explosives. Butyl alcohol soon becomes the keystone of the Abbott scientific search.

Forty different compounds are produced in the lab, then carefully tested on animals. Only one has decided advantages over the products already available. It is named *Butyn,* and its advantages are numerous: faster-acting and more powerful than either cocaine or Procaine, it costs less to produce, is not habit-forming, and can be applied on the surface of the skin or by injection. Thus, diligent molecular manipulation opens the way to better anesthesia in operations on the mucous membranes of the eyes, nose, and throat.

Nikolai Lenin dies at 53 of a stroke in the Soviet Union and the city of Petrograd is immediately renamed Leningrad in his honor. A power struggle will now begin between Leon Trotsky and Joseph Stalin. In Washington, D.C., Woodrow Wilson dies at his home after four years of suffering from paralysis and failing memory, and President Coolidge wins reelection on a platform of "Coolidge Prosperity." In Britain, the first Labour government takes office under Ramsay MacDonald. Newly independent Albania comes under the rule of Ahmed Zogu, who will proclaim himself King Zog.

After a series of decreases, the price of the Ford Model T hits its lowest point: $290 without a self-starter. Back in 1908, the original price of a Model T was $850. Now, more than half the cars in the world are Fords. After a sensational trial — with defense attorney Clarence Darrow introducing novel forms of evidence — two university students, Nathan Leopold, 18, and Richard Loeb, 17, are sentenced to life imprisonment for the thrill slaying of 14-year-old Bobby Franks. Darrow's novel defense is based on psychiatric examination and it saves them from the gallows, although Loeb will later be killed in prison.

University of Illinois halfback Harold "Red" Grange receives the opening kickoff from undefeated Michigan State and races 95 yards to a touchdown. He scores three more touchdowns in the next 12 minutes and a fifth later in the game — all of which inspires sportswriter Grantland Rice to dub him the "Galloping Ghost" of the gridiron.

TOP: *Manager's conference, 1924. (Standing, left to right) DeWitt Clough; James Ranson; Fred Young; Alfred Bays; and Robert Plummer. (Seated, left to right) Henry Shattuck; R. C. Sohoni; Alfred Burdick; E. H. Ravenscroft; and C. O. Brown.* BOTTOM LEFT: *The year 1924 ushers in construction on Building M-1 at the North Chicago site. The foundation for Building A-1 appears in the foreground.* BOTTOM RIGHT: *Having seen his grand objective for world peace eroded, U.S. President Woodrow Wilson retired to semiseclusion after finishing his second term in 1920. He dies four years later on February 3, 1924.*

The death this year of Clara Ingraham Abbott brings to light an unusual trust she has set up in her will. It stipulates that 15 years after her death, half the estate she inherited from Dr. Abbott is to be distributed to "benefit the cause of medical, chemical, or surgical science." When Mrs. Abbott dies, her estate is estimated at $800,000 in company stock. Fifteen years later, when the first distribution from the Clara Abbott Trust is made, the value of this stock will be more than $9 million.

The largest single grant — $1.5 million — will go to Northwestern University, where the money will be used to finish a 20-story dormitory for professional students on the Chicago campus. During World War II, Abbott Hall will serve as a U.S. Navy midshipman's training school, turning out more than 20,000 officers. A second early bequest of $1 million will go to the University of Chicago and will be called by Chancellor Robert Maynard Hutchins "not only one of the greatest but one of the most useful in recent years." With the Abbott money in hand, he will secure an additional $1.5 million grant from the Rockefeller Foundation and create the Abbott Memorial Fund for the Endowment of Research in the Biological Sciences.

In 1940, the Clara Abbott Foundation will be established with a transfer of 12,000 shares of stock left by Mrs. Abbott. In accordance with the terms of her will, this gift will be used to help needy Abbott employees with funds for home loans, medical expenses, and assistance with other financial difficulties. Still later, the Foundation will inaugurate a program of college grants and loans for sons and daughters of Abbott employees. Over the next 50 years, more than 11,000 educational grants will be made.

The Scopes "monkey trial" attracts more attention than any other legal proceeding in U.S. history. John T. Scopes, a 25-year-old Tennessee schoolteacher, is accused of teaching evolution when he acquaints his class with the 1859 writings of Charles Darwin. His defense lawyers include Clarence Darrow, and one of the prosecuting attorneys is former Secretary of State William Jennings Bryan. The high point of the trial comes when Bryan takes the witness stand to defend his Fundamentalist doctrine. He is completely humiliated by Darrow. Scopes is convicted on a technicality and fined $100, but Bryan will die within the week of apoplexy.

Cancer kills Chinese republican leader Sun Yat-sen and he is succeeded by General Chiang Kai-shek, 38, who immediately makes a Russian general his unofficial chief of staff. Hitler publishes Volume I of *Mein Kampf* and reorganizes the Nazi party, with 27,000 members. It is only 7 years since the close of the last World War and 14 before the next will begin.

Alphonse Capone, a 26-year-old Italian-American from Illinois, takes over as boss of Chicago racketeering and soon controls all bootlegging, gambling, and prostitution in the city. In this era of Prohibition, he grows rich by smuggling vast quantities of whiskey and rum into the U.S. from Canada and the Caribbean. Elsewhere in the U.S., the Charleston becomes the rage in dance steps and King Vidor's *Big Parade*, starring John Gilbert and Renée Adorée, is the film hit of the year.

With sales now at $2.2 million and research expenditures at $100,000, Dr. Burdick decides to spin off the original property in Ravenswood and consolidate all facilities at North Chicago. An eager buyer is a small Chicago pharmaceutical firm looking to expand — G. D. Searle & Co.

In this same year, a portent or two of things to come: first, Abbott gets into the milk business. One early preparation is Lactigen, a milk sterilized by a steam process and then packaged, with the fat removed, in sterile ampules. An adjunct comes when Dr. Burdick believes the company has a chance for "volume sellers" in baby foods. Within the year, the company realizes that consumer marketing of baby foods is better left to those more experienced. It will be another 39 years before Abbott gets solidly into pediatric nutrition when it merges with M & R Dietetic Laboratories of Columbus, Ohio, the producers of *Similac*, which coincidentally is also introduced this year.

Similac, developed by Alfred Bosworth, is closer to mother's milk and more appropriate nutritionally than the cow's milk from which it is made. Stanley Ross, who with his brother-in-law Harry Moores had started Moores and Ross Milk Company in 1903, recognizes the significance of Bosworth's work and agrees to produce and market his product. It is initially called *Franklin* Infant Food, after the Franklin Brewery, a building purchased to meet the needs of the expanding business. The label features a baby picture of Ross' son Dick. This marks Dick Ross' debut in the family business which he will one day head.

TOP: *The old Franklin Brewery building becomes the main plant site for M & R Dietetic Laboratories of Columbus, Ohio, now Abbott's Ross Laboratories division.* BOTTOM LEFT: *Richard M. Ross very early on finds himself in pictures. For two years, before receiving the name* Similac, *every can of* Franklin *Infant Food will bear Mr. Ross' baby photo.* BOTTOM RIGHT: *Clarence Darrow leans back on the table for the defense during America's Scopes "monkey trial."*

89

The power struggle between Joseph Stalin and Leon Trotsky is resolved when Trotsky is expelled from the party by the Politburo and Stalin establishes himself as virtual dictator of the Soviet Union. Another long-term reign begins in Japan when Emperor Yoshihito dies at age 47 and is succeeded by his 25-year-old son, Hirohito.

Matinee idol Rudolph Valentino dies of a ruptured ulcer during the New York City opening of *Son of the Sheik*. Distraught crowds line up for 11 blocks to view the body. New Yorker Gertrude Ederle, 19, becomes the first woman to swim the English Channel. After 14 hours, 31 minutes, of slogging through heavy seas, she beats the world record by almost two hours. The feat costs her a permanent hearing loss. Harry Houdini suffers an even worse loss when he locks himself underwater in an airtight coffin containing only enough oxygen to sustain a man for 5 or 6 minutes. The escape artist stays down for 91 minutes, damaging his appendix, an injury which kills him three months later.

U.S. auto production reaches 3.7 million — up nearly seven times from 1914 — and a new invention called power steering is installed in a Pierce-Arrow. It will be another 25 years before the inventor can convince Detroit automakers to start commercial production of it. Two important vitamin findings occur when researchers show that rats can be cured of the vitamin deficiency causing human pellagra on a diet from which the heat-labile part of vitamin B has been removed. Elsewhere, a German biochemist and an American pediatrician move closer to demonstrating that irradiation converts the substance ergosterol into vitamin D.

A near-miss of a merger occurs when Frederick Stearns and Company, of Michigan, indicates interest in joining forces with Abbott. The company, 12 years older than Abbott, originated the idea of ethical drug specialties. It sounds like an attractive venture to both parties. Negotiations break down, however, when agreement can't be reached on a new name for the combined operation. The compromise suggested is "Allied Laboratories." Dr. Burdick, after spending a sleepless night pondering the proposal, declines, saying, "We might lose our identity, and we should not do that. I hope we will be known as Abbott Laboratories long after we're all gone."

What will eventually become the beginning of a breakthrough for a short-acting hypnotic comes unannounced to Abbott this year when a young organic chemist leaves Ann Arbor for North Chicago. He is Dr. Donalee L. Tabern, a gifted scientist who has paused along the academic trail long enough to acquire three degrees from the University of Michigan. In later years, he will spark the development of those "hot" pharmaceuticals known as radioactive drugs. Now, however, he joins a scientific partnership with Dr. Volwiler that will launch the two of them on careers that will prove to be extremely advantageous to both medicine and Abbott.

Tabern's work involves barbituric acid derivatives — a direct outgrowth of the work done three years earlier by Dr. Volwiler in the development of the sedative *Neonal*. The advantage of observing Dr. Volwiler's studies on barbitals soon leads Dr. Tabern into the laboratory production of barbiturates containing branched chains in their structure. It is a study that will consume more than 10 years and will result in a product that half a century later will still be the world's most widely used induction anesthetic.

TOP: *Passing the test of time, many turn-of-the-century Abbott products are still present in the 1926 price list.* **BOTTOM LEFT:** *A long and bright career with Abbott begins for Dr. Donalee L. Tabern.* **BOTTOM RIGHT:** *Hollywood revels in glamour and romance, as Rudolph Valentino (shown opposite Vilma Banky in* Son of the Sheik*) dominates the silver screen during the 1920s.*

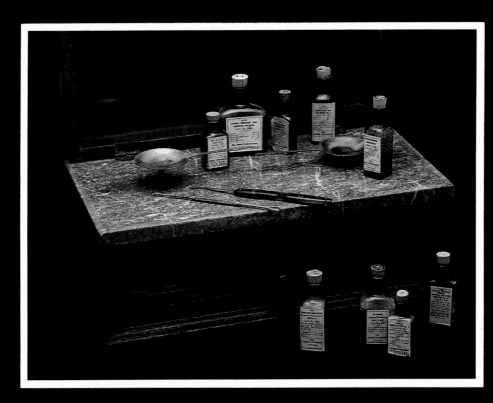

Charles Augustus Lindbergh, a 25-year-old airmail pilot, startles the world when he makes the first nonstop solo flight across the Atlantic in his single-engine *Spirit of St. Louis.* He has to use a periscope to see what lies ahead, since his forward vision is blocked by the gasoline tank and engine. Lindbergh covers the 3,600 miles from New York to Paris in 33 hours, 29 minutes, and the "Lone Eagle" becomes an instant world hero.

Al Capone lists his earnings as $105 million for the year. It is an all-time record for the highest gross income by a private U.S. citizen, and beats Henry Ford's best year by $35 million. Crime, according to Capone, pays. So do telephone calls. Transatlantic telephone service between New York and London begins this year. Three minutes of conversation cost $75, or 15 pounds. The first movie Oscars are presented this year, and *Wings,* starring Buddy Rogers, Clara Bow, Richard Arlen, and Gary Cooper, wins the award for best picture.

Prospectors strike oil in northern Iraq. It takes 10 days to cap the 80,000-barrel-a-day gusher and prevent it from reaching the Eternal Fire, a natural gas leak a mile and a half away that has been burning for thousands of years. A Peruvian pilot flying over the desolate plains of southern Peru spots enormous drawings of birds, reptiles, and animals. The mysterious drawings were made by an ancient pre-Inca civilization and are visible only from the air.

The intrigue of a supposedly secret formula leads to an exciting occurrence on a Saturday night in June.

Eight masked men, all dressed in dark suits and armed with revolvers and machine guns, overpower the two Abbott night watchmen at the gate and take over the North Chicago plant for seven hours. The would-be thieves ransack the plant from top to bottom, purposely ignoring thousands of dollars' worth of office equipment and lab instruments and untold quantities of valuable chemicals and narcotics.

They seem to know exactly what they're looking for, and they're in no hurry to execute the robbery. While one group empties desks and files, another goes through every locker. They move from building to building at their own pace, strewing the floors with mounds of papers. They methodically blast open two safes with charges of nitroglycerin. The only clue they leave behind is a trail of cigarette butts.

The bound and gagged Abbott security men finally free themselves the next morning, unharmed except for minor rope burns. Over the following weeks, the newspapers conjecture that the bandits were after an Abbott secret formula for a synthetic, nonhabit-forming narcotic with painkilling potency. The description is a dead ringer for *Butyn,* the Abbott local anesthetic.

"They took no money," says an Abbott official, "because there was none. Quite a few stamps are missing, but I'm afraid they were all precanceled. If they found any formulae in our files, they weren't very secret. This product has been on the market for four years, is patented, and its formula has appeared in medical journals many times. They really could have saved themselves a whole lot of time just by reading a library copy of the AMA *Journal.*"

TOP: *It will take America's Charles Lindbergh two days — May 20 and 21, 1927 — to write his name in the history books as the first to complete a nonstop solo flight across the Atlantic.* BOTTOM: *Various processes for large-scale manufacturing of synthetic drugs are developed in this lab in Building B-1 of the North Chicago plant.*

California's Herbert Hoover wins the U.S. presidential election by a landslide over New York's Catholic governor, Alfred E. Smith. "The slogan of progress," says Republican Hoover, "is changing from a full dinner pail to a full garage." His opponent misquotes Hoover as saying, "a chicken in every pot and two cars in every garage." The phrase sticks and haunts Hoover through the Great Depression years.

The antibiotic revolution begins when Scottish bacteriologist Alexander Fleming accidentally discovers penicillin. Surprisingly, bacteria are destroyed by the mysterious mold.

Amelia Earhart becomes the first woman passenger on a transatlantic flight when she and two male pilots cross from Newfoundland to Wales. From the opposite direction comes the first commercial flight of the German dirigible *Graf Zeppelin.*

In the U.S., CBS is founded this year by the 27-year-old ad manager of La Palina cigars, William S. Paley, when he sees his cigar sales soar after radio advertising. And musical history of a sort is made when two future legends — Lawrence Welk and Rudy Vallee — form their first small bands.

The second big acquisition, and another indication that Dr. Burdick intends to turn Abbott into a growth company, is the purchase of John T. Milliken and Company for $125,000. Interest is first sparked by a representative of A. G. Becker, an investment firm, who tells Dr. Burdick that the St. Louis company is having a rough time financially and might be bought for a bargain price. There seems to be a sound reason for the low price. The Milliken product line is composed of age-old galenicals with only a few specialties, mostly copied rather than developed by research.

On the surface, the acquisition sounds like a giant step backwards. Milliken has a history of marketing failures. Almost everything it touches turns into a dud. Originally started because of the personal antipathy of founder John Milliken toward some of the officials of Lambert Pharmacal of St. Louis, the company hired chemists to try to duplicate Lambert's Listerine formula. Milliken called his antiseptic *Pasteurine.* Its market life was mercifully short. Other company products have been equally anonymous. Although company revenues have ventured as high as $700,000 in the nine years since John Milliken's death, the business has languished.

There are, however, some positives. The Milliken plant and laboratories are well equipped with modern machinery and manufacturing facilities for making their liquid extracts. The company has expert technical people plus a traveling force of 40 salesmen. But the hidden plum, and the real reason for the acquisition, comes from the more than 20,000 retail druggists on its customer rolls. Thus, the beginning of the Abbott direct retail distribution plan. It will make the $125,000 well spent even after the products are discarded.

TOP: *The library in Building A-1 of the North Chicago plant supplies Abbott scientists and researchers with professional literature important to their work. On the right is Elmer B. Vliet, an Abbott chemist who will eventually become chairman of the board.* CENTER: *The North Chicago plant is an impressive complex by 1928.* BOTTOM: *Tied to its mooring mast in Los Angeles, the German dirigible* Graf Zeppelin *dwarfs the Goodyear blimp, anchored next to it.*

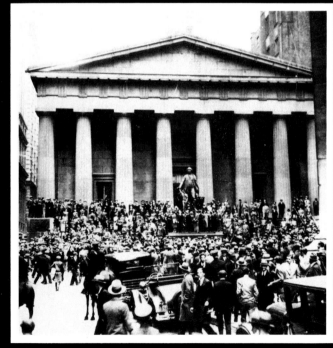

The index of common stock prices reaches an all-time high in September as prosperity surges throughout America. Stocks have been on a steady rise since 1926. In early October, a small downward trend begins, the result of a drop in U.S. iron and steel production plus a rise in British interest rates that pulls European capital out of the American money market. On Tuesday, October 29, the stock market crashes as speculators who have bought on margin are forced to sell. Within three weeks, more than $26 billion in paper value is lost — a sum greater than the entire cost to the U.S. of World War I.

Canada and the U.S. sign an agreement to preserve the beauty of Niagara Falls. The two countries will also agree to begin work on allowing greater use of the water for the production of electricity. Elsewhere, the Serbo-Croat-Slovene Kingdom becomes Yugoslavia, and the Lateran Treaty establishes an independent Vatican City.

The United States now has 20 million telephones — twice as many as the rest of the world combined. Most are crude wooden boxes hung on the wall and cranked furiously to call Central. Other noteworthy events: Seven-Up is introduced under the unlikely name of "Lithiated Lemon," Popeye is introduced in a cartoon strip, and Amos 'n' Andy are fast becoming a radio legend.

In Chicago, gang warfare reaches an all-time high in brutality on Valentine's Day when seven members of the "Bugs" Moran gang are machine-gunned to death in a North Clark Street garage by hoodlums dressed in police uniforms. Police suspect the rival Capone gang, but are never able to prove it. Three months later, Al "Scarface" Capone is sentenced to a year in prison for carrying a concealed weapon. It is faint reprisal.

TOP: *Abbott goes public in 1929. Originally offered at $32.00, Abbott common stock rises to $40.50 in its first day of public trading.* BOTTOM: *Panic-stricken investors gather on Wall Street, as the stock market plunges a record 38.33 points, marking the beginning of America's Great Depression.*

This, the year of the Wall Street stock market crash, is the very time Abbott picks to offer its shares to the public. Prior to March, the company's stock had been closely held with only a couple of exceptions. In the years of the Panic of 1907-8, when Dr. Abbott had trouble meeting his payroll, he offered shares to employees in lieu of salary. Most employees considered their certificates as little more than sentimental souvenirs of a troubled time. As the owners of a stock with no market value, they had no choice but to hold onto their shares, whether they wanted to or not.

The stock is listed on the Chicago Stock Exchange and closes 1929 at $37.25 per share. Those who have held their original shares can reap a small fortune by selling off. Those who choose to hold the stock longer, however, will eventually realize a large fortune.

A holder of 100 shares of this first public issue will receive one share for every three held in 1935; a three-for-one stock split in 1936; one share for every twenty held in 1939; a two-for-one split in 1946 and again in 1949; a three-for-one split in 1964; and two-for-one in 1975, 1978, 1981, and 1986. In other words, 100 shares of stock in 1929 will have become 80,256 shares by 1986. All in all, it's not too bad a track record for a company that started as a dispensary in an apartment kitchen.

97

98

U.S. stock prices regain almost half their 1929 losses in early spring, then break again in June and begin a long decline that signals the reality of a business depression. Other signs are equally ominous: more than 1,300 banks close, unemployment passes the four million mark, and the GNP falls from $90 billion this year to less than $56 billion in 1933. To make matters worse, an unprecedented drought parches the South and Midwest as major crops produce barely $8 per acre.

Right-wing coalitions and revolution rock the world. Heinrich Brüning forms a rightist government in Germany, and Joseph Pilsudski follows suit in Poland. Revolution in Argentina brings José Uriburn to power, and in Brazil, Getúlio Vargas rides the waves of upheaval to head a new dictatorship.

In the U.S., this is the year Lowell Thomas begins his nightly radio network news program. He will stay on the air for the next 46 years. The nation is talking about Grant Wood's painting *American Gothic*. He uses his sister and dentist as models in what starts out as a satiric portrayal of rural Iowa farmfolk but changes to a labor of love as the painting progresses.

It is a year for firsts: the automatic toaster, the Toastmaster, by McGraw-Electric; the first true supermarket in Jamaica, Long Island; sliced bread by Wonder Bread; the first stewardess for United Airlines (she is both a registered nurse and a student pilot); and the first year of the 44-year reign of Ethiopia's new emperor. He is 39-year-old Tafari Makonnen, who promptly changes his name to Haile Selassie. He will be hailed as the new "king of kings."

The earlier work on barbituric acid derivatives by Drs. Volwiler and Tabern shows exciting possibilities. Some of the new compounds tested are characterized by a more rapid onset, an appreciably shorter period of action, and a greater safety margin than existing sedative-hypnotics. One in particular stands out. For clinical tests, the compound is labeled "Abbott 844." It is referred to the eminent Dr. John S. Lundy, head of the anesthesia department of the Mayo Clinic. The drug's first recipients are Dr. Lundy's wife; Dr. Charles Mayo, cofounder of the institution; and former heavyweight boxing champion Jack Dempsey. Before the year is out, more than 2,000 successful clinical tests will have been done.

Dr. Lundy takes the initial letters of the promising compound's chemical name, ethyl l-methylbutyl, and adds the "al" which is a common suffix for barbiturates — thus, *Embutal*. But Drs. Volwiler and Tabern prefer the sodium salt form of the drug, because it is easier to produce and more quickly absorbed. So the first letter of the chemical symbol for sodium (Na) is added and the name becomes *Nembutal*.

Dr. Lundy's clinical trials show that a dose of only one and one-half grains can put a patient to sleep in less than 20 minutes. An even more valuable finding: small doses of *Nembutal* given at bedtime the night before and again on the morning of surgery provide excellent sedation before a longer-lasting anesthetic is administered. Patients recover faster and without the hangover and nausea that so often follow surgery. Soon, there is growing recognition of the drug's versatility as an oral sedative-hypnotic to ease childbirth, control convulsions, relieve insomnia, and alleviate disorders ranging from seasickness to delirium tremens. *Nembutal* will become one of Abbott's best-known and longest-lived products.

TOP LEFT: *The stark portrait of a midwestern farmer and his wife brings immediate acclaim for Iowa artist Grant Wood. Entitled* American Gothic, *the painting will remain Wood's best-known work.* TOP RIGHT: *The development of* Embutal, *later marketed as* Nembutal, *is a milestone in the company's search for a better sedative.* BOTTOM: *Ampule production of the day is all done by hand.*

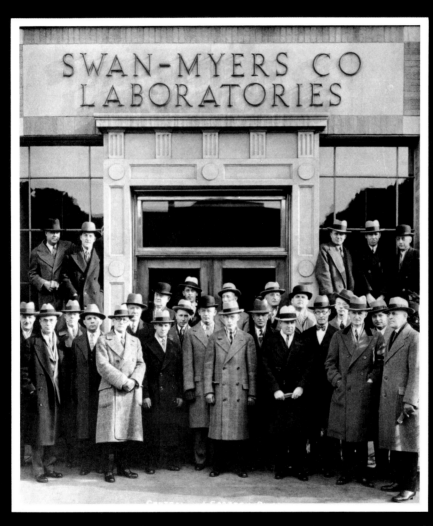

SWAN-MYERS CO
LABORATORIES

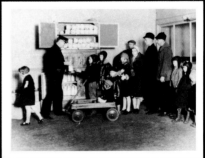

The Great Depression deepens as financial panic engulfs most of the world. Britain abandons the gold standard and watches the pound sterling drop from $4.86 to $3.49 almost overnight. Japan will drop the gold standard later in the year and Germany, France, and Austria all will need loans to keep them from bankruptcy. In the U.S., three banks a day are failing as the total climbs to 2,300. Unemployment now reaches eight million as automobile sales collapse and two of every three workers in major industrial cities are laid off.

Penicillin is used effectively at England's Royal Infirmary to treat three patients with pneumococcal and gonococcal infections. Strangely, no further efforts will be made to pursue penicillin's therapeutic powers until the end of the decade. Columbia University physical chemist Dr. Harold C. Urey pioneers the production of atomic energy when his discovery of heavy water leads to the separation of other isotopes.

London's small ballet company, the Vic-Wells troupe, receives enthusiastic audiences at every performance and will grow to become Britain's Royal Ballet company. The U.S. Congress votes to designate "The Star-Spangled Banner" as the national anthem, and Kate Smith makes her radio debut singing "When the Moon Comes Over the Mountain." The sports world is saddened when Knute Rockne dies in an airplane crash in Kansas. Chicago mob boss Al Capone is sentenced by a federal court to 11 years and a $50,000 fine for evading $231,000 in income taxes. He will serve 8 years and be released from prison a syphilitic vegetable.

Abbott acquires, for 25,000 shares of stock worth about $1 million, the Swan-Myers Company of Indianapolis. It is the third major merger for Abbott in nine years. The company's specialties include ampules as well as cold, catarrh, and hay fever remedies, none of which will survive the next decade. The people from Swan-Myers will be vastly more important to the future of Abbott.

Swan-Myers has been led since 1913 by Rolly M. Cain, who has built the business from $35,000 to over $1 million a year. He will join Abbott as vice president of sales and bring with him more key people than have come with any previous merger: Edgar B. Carter, Swan-Myers' scientific and production chief; such able scientists as Dr. Hobart W. Cromwell, the chemist team of Dr. E. E. Moore and his wife, Marjorie, and Oren C. Durham, the botanist who is developing into the nation's foremost authority on ragweed pollen; and an agile-minded young copywriter named Charles S. Downs.

The idea for the merger comes about during a pharmaceutical convention in Hot Springs, Virginia. Following the day's program, DeWitt Clough and Rolly Cain are recalling the early history of each company. Toward the close of the conversation, Clough casually asks: "Would Swan-Myers be interested in joining forces with Abbott? I think it might be a good idea for both companies." It is a brand-new idea, so new that Clough hasn't even cleared it with Dr. Burdick. Startled, Cain replies: "You've caught me somewhat by surprise. Let me sleep on it." A few weeks later, Cain tours the Abbott plant. After several more visits, the deal is sealed. Out of it will come, among other things, the only father-son presidency in Abbott history.

TOP: *Subjects of note in this early 1930s photo are Rolly Cain (front row, second from right) and his son, George (second row, second from right). Both will eventually become Abbott presidents.* BOTTOM LEFT: *These Abbott employees are busy bottling and finishing Viosterol in the newly constructed Building M-2 at the North Chicago plant.* BOTTOM RIGHT: *Food lineups such as this one at a milk station in Grand Rapids, Michigan, are common sights during America's Great Depression.*

101

It is another trying year for the U.S. as President Hoover tries desperately to stem the flood tide of depression. He grants generous credits to industry, orders a check on government spending, and even cuts his own salary by 20 percent. None of his efforts seem to work as unemployment reaches 13 million. Nationally, wages are 60 percent less than in 1929, as breadlines form in many cities. Nearly 20,000 businesses go bankrupt and there are 21,000 suicides. Voters recognize the need for a change, and Franklin D. Roosevelt — with his promise of a "New Deal" — is elected in a Democratic landslide.

An army made up of 20,000 poverty-stricken World War veterans and their families marches on America's capital to demand cash payment for veterans' certificates — a measure that has been passed by the House but narrowly defeated in the Senate. They camp in the city's parks, dumps, warehouses, and empty stores until federal troops finally drive them out.

Elsewhere in the news: The U.S. mourns the kidnapping-death of 20-month-old Charles A. Lindbergh, Jr. When the baby's body is found, outraged public opinion forces adoption of the death penalty in federal kidnapping cases. The government of the U.S.S.R. begins its second Five-Year Plan to gain full control of industry and agriculture. The result is widespread famine. Mahatma Gandhi begins a "fast unto death" protest against British treatment of India's lowest-caste "untouchables." After six days of fasting, Gandhi obtains a favorable pact for better treatment of his people.

The middle of the depression years find Abbott moving rapidly into the field of nutritionals. The start is no more than a belief that there must be a better source of vitamins A and D than cod liver oil, which Dr. Burdick calls "a disagreeable substance given to disagreeable children."

While other drug manufacturers promote the nutritional virtues of the cod, Abbott tries a different tack. Carl Nielsen, head of pharmaceutical research, leads the search for more potent vitamin sources. He already knows that Norwegian scientists have tested salmon, mackerel, red perch, shark, whale, and halibut. Of these, they found the oil from halibut livers to be amazingly rich in vitamin A. The question is: how to get enough livers to test?

Nielsen sends his assistant, Charles Lanwermeyer, off to the "meadows of the sea" in the North Pacific where halibut are plentiful. Although the annual catch runs at least 50 million pounds, Lanwermeyer discovers that fishing crews routinely dump thousands of pounds of the soft, spongy livers into the sea as they clean the fish. "Ain't no good to anyone" is the standard explanation. Lanwermeyer solves the dilemma by offering repeated rounds at a local pub to all who will load up 10-pound lard cans with halibut livers. He has more than enough takers. For four months, he ranges up and down the coast, hiring crews to haul in livers. The company now has a steady supply assured.

News from the laboratory is even better: oil from halibut livers contains from 75 to 125 times more vitamin A and 20 times more vitamin D than cod liver oil. Led by the new capsules of *Haliver* Oil, vitamins will account — within the next three years — for almost 25 percent of Abbott sales. It is a commercial as well as a nutritional breakthrough.

TOP: *One can only imagine what went through the mind of Charles Lanwermeyer when his boss, Carl Nielsen, approached him with a new assignment: "Charlie, you're going fishing." Here Lanwermeyer stands at the controls of halibut liver oil processing equipment in Prince Rupert, British Columbia.* BOTTOM: *WWI veterans dig in once again, this time within range of the U.S. Capitol. They are in Washington demonstrating for their soldier's bonus.*

103

Two significant 12-year terms start this year as Adolf Hitler and Franklin Roosevelt come to power. Ninety-two percent of Germans vote for the Nazis, as labor unions are suppressed, a boycott of Jewish businesses begins, and the first concentration camps are erected. Hitler's first 30 days are marked by a mysterious fire that damages the building housing the Reichstag, Germany's legislative body. Nazi leader Hermann Goering is believed to be behind it. Roosevelt's first 30 days are marked by a series of fireside chats. He tells the nation, "We have nothing to fear but fear itself," but America's 15 million unemployed are not completely convinced. Even for those with jobs, the economic outlook isn't bright — wage earner incomes are 40 percent below 1929 levels.

This is the year that causes panic among U.S. savers when a nationwide bank holiday is declared; ferrets out hoarders when an embargo is placed on gold holdings; and appeases the nation's drinkers when Prohibition is finally repealed. Chicago is involved in the national news even more than usual. Early in the year, Mayor Anton Cermak is fatally wounded in Miami by an assassin who claims he was aiming at president-elect Roosevelt. A fan dancer named Sally Rand attracts thousands to the opening of the Chicago World's Fair's "Century of Progress International Exposition" when she pirouettes seductively around the stage wearing nothing but a few ostrich plumes. And baseball's first All-Star game is played at Comiskey Park as the American League defeats the National, 4-2.

A two-year dip in depression sales bottoms out as revenues climb back over the $4 million mark, but the company is shaken early in the year when Dr. Burdick is stricken with pneumonia. After only a week's illness, he dies at Highland Park Hospital. His eulogy is simple and well earned.

"From the beginning of his association with Dr. Abbott in 1904," recounts a newspaper tribute, "Dr. Burdick realized, more than anyone else, the critical importance of research. He brought the first ideas of research into the company, and was instrumental in devoting much of the company's resources to research in chemistry, pharmacy, and medicine. During his presidency, the company absorbed two other large pharmaceutical houses: John T. Milliken and Company of St. Louis and the Swan-Myers organization of Indianapolis. In addition, he brought Dermatological Research Labs of Philadelphia into association with Abbott. During his 12-year tenure as president, Dr. Burdick's influence and contributions helped Abbott grow in importance in medical research and in the manufacture of synthetic chemicals."

But now the mood and the mode of the company change radically. The new president is S. DeWitt Clough, the former advertising copywriter. He believes devoutly in the power of words and ideas, and favors lush and colorful expression. His will become an era of exhortation, inspirational exuberance, and effusive persuasion. He is the "music man of the thirties." He is also exactly the right man at the right time for Abbott.

TOP: *"For his rare combination of head and heart," Dr. Burdick receives a portrait and a letter signed by each of Abbott's 750 employees. Mrs. Burdick stands to his left.* BOTTOM LEFT: *In large part due to the sales success of* Haliver *Oil in its various forms, Abbott is able to maintain a program of growth and expansion, while the rest of the country struggles under the Great Depression.* BOTTOM RIGHT: *The "Bavarian corporal" makes another rhetorical assault during the formative years of the Nazi party. In 1934, with the death of President Hindenburgh, Hitler will take the title* führer *(leader) and become chancellor of Germany.*

104

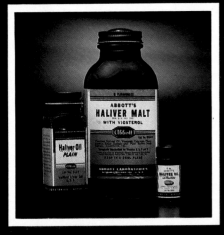

Plagued by searing midsummer heat, America's farmers watch their fields wither away in the most destructive drought the Midwest has ever seen. Dust storms across Kansas, Texas, Colorado, and Oklahoma blow hundreds of thousands of tons of topsoil all the way to the Atlantic Ocean. Drought and dust reduce the U.S. corn crop by nearly a billion bushels and send 350,000 "Okies" and "Arkies" on a western trek to California to find a new life.

The U.S.S.R. is admitted to the League of Nations — and five years later, when it attacks Finland, it will become the only nation ever to be expelled. Germany signs a mutual non-aggression treaty with Poland, traditionally an ally of France.

The infamous Bonnie and Clyde, Bonnie Parker and Clyde Barrow, are cut down in a hail of police bullets in Louisiana after a two-year crime spree in which they casually kill 13 people in four states. In Chicago, America's most wanted criminal, John Dillinger, is shot down in an FBI trap as he leaves the Biograph Theatre. New York police arrest a German-American carpenter named Bruno Richard Hauptmann for possession of ransom money paid in the Lindbergh kidnapping. Two years later, he will die in the electric chair.

For sports fans, the two most imposing figures in the country are Dizzy and Daffy Dean, brothers who roll up 49 victories between them as they pitch the St. Louis Cardinals to the world championship. Meanwhile, a black pitcher who isn't allowed to play in the big leagues, Leroy "Satchel" Paige, wins 29 games in 29 days for his Bismarck, North Dakota, semipro team. Fourteen years later, Paige will finally be admitted to the major leagues.

From the start of his term, President Clough sweeps into action with a fervor seldom seen. "Depression or no depression," he cries out, "we are going to build up this company!" He starts by changing the board so that only active Abbott executives are permitted to sit as directors. Although this limits outside thinking, Clough reasons that he can now get boardroom discussions every working day over the company's luncheon table — for free. The system will continue more than 25 years.

Emphasis now switches to educating doctors to prescribe, rather than dispense, Abbott drugs. To do this, Clough brings in Raymond E. Horn, the former Dermatological Research Labs sales expert, as his general sales manager. The two men are cut from the same mold: both approach the selling of Abbott with an aggressive evangelism that, happily, is infectious to both employees and customers. Together, they improve training methods for salesmen and insist on regular retraining for the more experienced men. New bonuses and special awards are given those who exceed their quotas. Those who don't, find that their wives are not invited to the semiannual sales conference.

The Study Club starts at the request of employees who want to continue their education. After-hour classes are held right at the plant; fellow employees are the instructors. Employees who attend courses at local schools have half their tuition refunded if they do well. Many employees get their diplomas this way, and Abbott has more promotable people. Everybody wins.

TOP: *Presumably too pressed by business to pause for the group picture, Abbott President DeWitt Clough appears as the man on the phone in this 1934 sales convention photo.* BOTTOM: *Wind and erosion reduce the south-central region of the U.S. to a wasteland — the Dust Bowl (near Dalhart, Texas). Photo by Dorothea Lange.*

A few breaks in America's depression clouds appear as unemployment and business failures drop, agricultural prices rise, and people begin to take new hope. Controlling many phases of life are a sudden rash of new federal agencies, from WPA, REA, and FHA to NYA and SEC. In this one year, 33 new agencies are created and the government payroll swells by 3.5 million people, all contributing to an increase in the national debt of nearly 20 percent.

"The federal government must and shall quit this business of relief," President Roosevelt tells Congress. It obeys and passes the Emergency Relief Act authorizing nearly $5 billion for work relief. The Works Progress Administration is organized to employ thousands of the jobless in construction projects, joining the two-year-old Civilian Conservation Corps, which already has 500,000 federal employees. But the New Deal suffers a stunning setback when the Supreme Court declares its cornerstone, the National Industrial Recovery Act, unconstitutional.

Across the sea, recovery of a different nature is under way as the first rumblings of a discontented nation are heard. Adolf Hitler vigorously denounces the Versailles Treaty which provides for German disarmament. With one hand, Hitler signs an agreement with Britain promising to limit expansion of the German navy, while with the other he organizes the Luftwaffe to give Germany vastly increased air capability. Meanwhile, his SS leader, Heinrich Himmler, starts a breeding program to encourage young women of "pure blood" to volunteer their services as mates of SS officers to produce a Nazi "super race."

In an era of advertising that borders on the flamboyant, one element of Abbott promotion is more benign than baroque. Under the direction of Charles S. Downs, the former Swan-Myers copywriter, the company issues a new publication, called *What's New,* for physicians. From the beginning, typography, art, and layout are unusually striking. The editorial content blends medical news from the nation's leading professional journals with original staff-written articles. One such article, dealing with the problems of Indian medical care, finds staff members traveling 20,000 miles to visit Indian reservations from Mexico to Alaska.

Each year at Christmas, *What's New* becomes less a medical journal and more a contemporary art and literature magazine. Some of the nation's most distinguished writers, including Carl Sandburg, William Saroyan, Edna St. Vincent Millay, Conrad Aiken, James Hilton, Ogden Nash, Clifton Fadiman, Leo Rosten, and Robert Frost, contribute noteworthy short stories, essays, and poetry to the publication.

But it is another of Downs' policies that draws the most acclaim. He directly commissions fine artists to design original work for the covers, inside illustrations, and even the advertisements in *What's New.* Thus, Abbott becomes the trendsetter of American corporations in sponsoring such artists as Ben Shahn, Thomas Hart Benton, Joseph Hirsch, Lawrence Beall Smith, Hans Erni, Peter Hurd, Adolf Dehn, Doris Lee, and Raoul Dufy. The idea and the execution draw such raves — from the art and advertising worlds as well as the medical community — that over the next 30 years, the Abbott traveling art collection will visit thousands of museums and universities throughout the world.

TOP: *Uncle Sam receives another battery of remedies for "depression" from "Dr." F. D. R. in this depression-era cartoon by Clifford Berryman.* BOTTOM: *Promoted to director of sales in 1934, Raymond E. Horn here doffs his hat before boarding a United Air Lines flight. Horn will become president of Abbott in 1947 and will serve until 1950.*

Although 80 percent of the press opposes him, President Roosevelt leads a Democratic landslide over Governor Alfred M. Landon of Kansas, carrying every state except Maine and Vermont. The election is so lopsided that the Democrats hold a three-to-one majority in both houses of Congress. The result establishes the credibility of the new Gallup Poll, which forecast it accurately, and destroys *The Literary Digest*, which predicted a Landon victory.

Overseas, Britain's King George V dies after a 26-year reign and is succeeded by his 41-year-old son, Edward VIII. The new king reigns less than a year as he abdicates to marry the 39-year-old American divorcée Wallis Warfield Simpson. Civil war breaks out in Spanish Morocco as army officers led by General Francisco Franco start a revolt against the weak government in Madrid. The insurgents are joined by German and Italian "volunteers," while the U.S.S.R. supplies the Loyalist government with equipment and advisers. The war spreads rapidly through Spain and soon develops into a practice run for the Nazis' Stuka dive-bombers and Panzer tanks. Britain, France, and the U.S. do not take sides, but 2,800 Americans volunteer for the Lincoln Battalion to fight for the Loyalists.

In Berlin, the martial presence is everywhere as the Olympic Games are held, but the "master race" Aryan athletes are embarrassed when a black American named Jesse Owens wins four gold medals.

With the success of *Nembutal* well established, Drs. Volwiler and Tabern now begin a persistent search to find an analogue of the hypnotic drug that might be useful as an intravenous anesthetic. There is certainly room for improvement in the field. Most general anesthetics have obvious drawbacks. Some have effects that last far too long; others can't maintain enough depth to carry the patient safely through surgery. Some interfere with the body cells' ability to utilize oxygen; others are too toxic for most patients to tolerate.

Volwiler and Tabern produce 200 different substances in the laboratory. Curiously, the very first compound they test — a sulphur analogue of *Nembutal* — turns out to have the most striking potential. Animals fall asleep before the injection into the vein can be completed. Better yet, each awakens after several minutes, alert and normal. Before the year is out, the new drug will have been given to 700 men and women with equally good results. In humans, the induction is smooth and pleasant, with no delirium or sense of suffocation. The drug starts to work — depressing the central nervous system — before the patient can count to 20. Recovery is swift, with little or no postoperative nausea.

The two researchers name the new drug *Pentothal*. Little do they realize the lifesaving services it will render in World War II. Neither can they possibly imagine that 50 years later it will still rank as the most widely used induction anesthetic in the world; nor that in 1986, they will be honored for their invention of *Pentothal* by induction into the National Inventors Hall of Fame, where they will join Thomas Edison, Alexander Graham Bell, the Wright brothers, and Henry Ford.

In another area of the company, a new business begins: that of supplying hospitals with bulk intravenous solutions.

TOP: *In 1936, civil war breaks out in Spain. By 1939, largely due to military assistance from Fascist Italy and Nazi Germany, General Francisco Franco will have achieved complete victory over the Loyalist cause.* CENTER: *Abbott enters the intravenous solution business.* BOTTOM: *Developed and marketed in 1936,* Pentothal *revolutionizes the field of anesthesia, allowing Abbott to boast, "To know intravenous anesthesia is to know* Pentothal.*"*

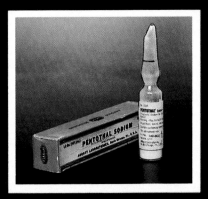

111

The year is one of uncertainty and uneasy waiting as the menace of a possible war becomes more evident. In Spain, the Italians and Germans pour in troops. German Junker and Heinkel bombers destroy the Basque villages as German warships devastate the coastal towns. German Jews are evicted from all trade and industry while Romanian Jews are forbidden to own land and are barred from all professions. The persecution deepens as Jews are barred from all parks, places of entertainment, health resorts, and public institutions. Not too much attention is paid when the first concentration camp opens at a place called Buchenwald. It will become infamous in later years when within its walls more than 56,000 Jews are killed by starvation, execution, and torture.

On the other side of the world, Japanese troops invade China in an undeclared war that will last until 1945. Despite fierce resistance, the Japanese sweep across China, and world opinion is roused by Japanese bombing of Chinese cities. Tension deepens when the U.S. gunboat *Panay* is sunk in Chinese waters by Japanese warplanes. Prime Minister Stanley Baldwin of Great Britain retires, to be replaced by Chancellor of the Exchequer Neville Chamberlain.

In the United States, President Roosevelt signs the Neutrality Act prohibiting the export of arms to belligerent nations and, after four years of recovery, the first signs of a business recession become apparent as a selling wave on the stock market drops the Dow-Jones average from its post-1929 high of 194.4.

Abbott stock is listed on the New York Stock Exchange on March 1, 1937, closing at $54.25 a share. The selling price reflects strong 1936 sales of nearly $7.8 million, and rapid expansion of company operations both at home and abroad.

Rolly Cain, now executive vice president, and President Clough have decided that the time has come for Abbott to expand its sales beyond U.S. borders. Actually, the company has long had a dribble of business coming in from foreign agencies that stock and sell Abbott products, but subsidiaries have only begun to be established in the last few years, under Cain's leadership.

Cain has traveled extensively, mainly in Europe, and has a more cosmopolitan outlook than many of his colleagues. He starts out by setting up a Canadian division in Montreal to handle the distribution of products everywhere in the British Empire except India. Next comes Abbott Laboratories de Mexico, S.A., to replace the agent the company has had there. Cain brings in an aggressive Abbott salesman, Manuel Doblado. The new man promises that, given the chance, he can turn the business around immediately. His plan is to stock every jobber in Mexico, advertise heavily, and set up a strong detailing system. It works. Within the year, Abbott business in Mexico jumps from what had been a static $5,000 to more than $100,000.

In quick succession, Abbott establishes subsidiaries in Argentina, Brazil, Cuba, and England, and sets up a new manufacturing plant near London. By the end of the decade, total sales of the export business will have grown from 1933's $62,000 to $1,624,000. Thus, Abbott will find itself a multinational long before the term becomes commonly known.

TOP: *The distinctive color of company labels becomes affectionately known as "Abbott blue." Various products of the period also show the octagonal logo that serves Abbott from 1932 to 1959.* BOTTOM: *A timely cartoon from the* Chicago Daily News *sends the American people a grim message of Hitler's lust for power and insatiable desire for German expansionism.*

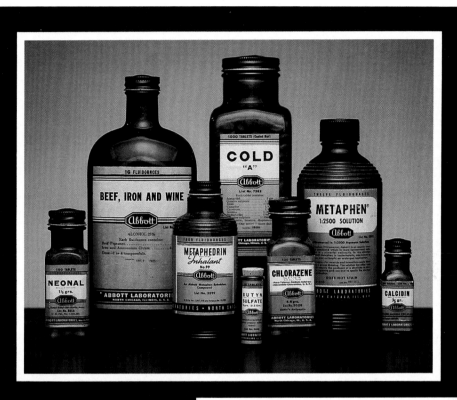

TAKE ME TO CZECHOSLOVAKIA, DRIVER

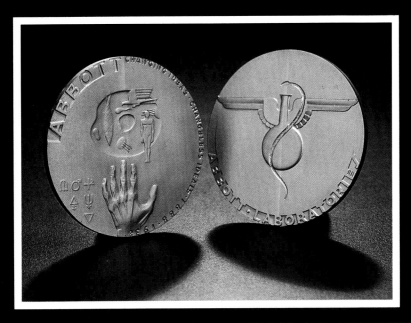

The center of U.S. government activity swings slowly in the direction of foreign affairs as isolationism vs. limited intervention becomes an active national issue. Although there is widespread nervousness about the possibility of war, few believe it can happen.

In March, Hitler annexes Austria to "protect" the six million Germans who live outside the Reich. In September, the Munich Pact is signed by Hitler, Mussolini, Chamberlain, and Daladier. It yields 16,000 square miles of the Sudetenland and all important Czech military strongholds to Germany as yet another appeasement to avoid a European war. Prime Minister Chamberlain tells the British people, "I believe it is peace for our time . . . peace with honor." The president of the Reichsbank tells Hitler that Germany's trade balance shows a deficit of 432 million marks and the country has been bankrupt since 1931.

Douglas "Wrong Way" Corrigan becomes a U.S. hero when, denied a permit to land in Europe, he flies to Dublin after claiming he was headed for California. President Roosevelt signs the Fair Labor Standards Act setting the minimum wage for all workers at 25¢ an hour. This immediately wipes out the 40,000-worker needlework industry in Puerto Rico where the hourly rate for *skilled* workers has been 25¢. The "War of the Worlds" radio broadcast by Orson Welles is so realistic that near-panics result as Americans think that Martians are landing in New Jersey.

The company's 50th anniversary is marked by the dedication of a three-story, $500,000 research center at North Chicago. The interior, created by well-known industrial designer Raymond Loewy, is commodious and striking. Visitors are greeted by Weimer Pursell's heroic mural, a floor and a half high, depicting the Abbott "Tree of Research" — a towering figure of a man/tree stretching skyward, its feet deep-rooted in the symbols of science and the men of research.

The building is a scientific workers' paradise. Here the tools of the trade are things called colorimeters and vitameters and fluorophotometers. There is a polariscope that uses a rotating beam of sodium vapor light shot through a prism to determine the identity, purity, and potency of substances in solution. There is a large machine called a spectrophotometer that, in a matter of moments, can detect traces of vitamin A, for example, that might take weeks to unearth through deficiency tests on animals. There is a microanalytical laboratory so small the entire lab can fit in the palm of a man's hand. The beakers, casseroles, combustion boats, and weighing tubes must be minute because the investigator is working with fractions of a drop and with compounds that may weigh as little as one fifteen-thousandth of an ounce. There is a distilling apparatus that can determine the nitrogen content of a speck of substance and do it in 20 minutes, as compared with the six hours required for the conventional search. And one balance is so sensitive that it is mounted in an air-conditioned room where the light is never turned off lest the temperature change upset the balance.

There is little doubt: Dr. Abbott, in his kitchen-sink detective work with active-principle alkaloids, never had it like this.

TOP: *Its mettle tested and found durable for half a century, Abbott celebrates its 50th anniversary with this commemorative medal. The theme of the anniversary: "Changing Ideas — Changeless Ideals."* **BOTTOM:** *The company also celebrates by opening its $500,000 research center at North Chicago, which houses the control laboratory shown here.*

115

the Abbott Tree

A spectacular upsurge in the U.S. economy comes as war orders flood the nation's factories. Most Americans agree that war is unthinkable but inevitable.

In Europe, one conflict ends almost as another begins. The three-year-old Spanish Civil War finally is over when Madrid falls to General Franco. A few weeks earlier, Germany invaded Czechoslovakia. In late August, Germany and Russia sign a mutual nonaggression pact. One week later, German troops and aircraft attack Poland. Britain and France immediately declare war on the Nazis. Three weeks later, Russia invades Poland from the east, causing Warsaw to surrender and Poland to be partitioned between Germany and the U.S.S.R. Winston Churchill, England's first lord of the admiralty, calls Russia's actions "a riddle wrapped in a mystery inside an enigma."

Back in the U.S., opening ceremonies at the New York World's Fair are telecast to the nearly 200 experimental receivers in the New York metropolitan area. Newspaper ads proclaim, "Sooner than you realize it, television will play a vital part in the life of the average American." It is one of the understatements of all time. On the opposite coast, the San Francisco World's Fair opens, but without television.

Despite the loss of the European markets, Hollywood produces one of the most expensive and successful pictures of all time, *Gone With the Wind*. Pictures of primitive Americana gain overnight fame for 79-year-old Grandma Moses when her paintings are shown at New York's Museum of Modern Art. One story that receives scant attention in the newspapers is the announcement that scientists have succeeded in splitting uranium by means of bombardment with neutrons.

TOP: *On the lobby wall of Abbott's new research building, Weimer Pursell paints a floor-and-a-half tall mural entitled* Tree of Research. BOTTOM LEFT: *Abbott's sales force receives a warm welcome during the company's annual sales convention.* BOTTOM RIGHT: *Scarlett O'Hara (Vivien Leigh) storms across the lawn of her beloved plantation, Tara, in* Gone with the Wind.

With its broadened business base, the company is called upon to produce an increasingly diverse catalog of health-care products. Into the receiving sheds at North Chicago come items from a shopping list that covers most parts and ports of the world. Great burlap bales of ma huang leaves arrive from China, with a thousand pounds of leaves needed to produce five pounds of ephedrine, a nasal decongestant. Huge boxes of quick-frozen thyroids, pituitaries, ovaries, and spleens come from the packing houses of the Midwest; rolls of gold foil from the Yukon; cans of deadly curare from the reaches of the Upper Amazon; demijohns of perfume oils from France; selenium from the copper mines of Chile; olive oils from Spain and Morocco; and tons upon tons of basic chemicals.

The new research building has a fully equipped auditorium. Talented employees see its potential and develop a show for fellow employees. The first effort, called *The Show is On,* gets rave reviews. The Spring Show becomes an annual event with names like *Ghost-Capades* in 1944 and *Bells A-Hoppin* in 1951. A star attraction is the Abbott Medicine Men, a group of four harmonizers that also steals the show at Abbott sales conventions. Another attraction: the Spring Show serves as an early singles club, and a number of new Abbott families result each year. Dr. Abbott, who took a personal interest in all his employees and their accomplishments, would have loved it.

117

The lightning-like speed of the German Blitzkrieg is evidenced in April as Nazi troops seize Denmark and Norway. Within 30 days, German panzer divisions sweep through the Netherlands, Luxembourg, and Belgium and race across northern France, stranding 380,000 British, Belgian, and French troops at Dunkirk. The evacuation of these men is finally completed after eight days of fierce fighting, but 40,000 Frenchmen are left behind. One week later, Mussolini declares, war on Britain and France. German troops enter Paris four days later and France signs an armistice. Hitler's Luftwaffe begins day and night bombings of Britain that will go on for months. At the height of the blitz, 180 German planes are shot down in a single day as Spitfire pilots frustrate the Luftwaffe. "Never in the course of human conflict was so much owed by so many to so few" says Winston Churchill, Britain's new prime minister, in praising the RAF.

In the U.S., President Roosevelt decides to take the unprecedented step of running for a third term, realizing that America is at a major crisis point. He defeats political newcomer Wendell Willkie because people feel it is better not to "change horses in midstream." Meanwhile, the first Social Security payments are made. The first check, for $22.54, goes to a Vermont widow. The annual total will be $75,844. U.S. unemployment remains at eight million with 16.4 percent out of work. The new 40-hour work week doesn't affect them.

An interesting insight into one of the quirks of the drug business comes after Abbott invests six years in pharmacological and clinical testing of a sulfa compound that, as it turns out, doesn't work well enough against the infections for which it is intended but is highly effective against an entirely different disease.

Two years after the German scientist Gerhard Domagk demonstrated how the sulfa compound he called Prontosil could fight bacterial infections, Abbott synthesizes a sulfa it names *Diasone*. When tested in the laboratory on mice, rabbits, and guinea pigs, *Diasone* shows promise in treating tuberculosis. But that is only the first step. Drug metabolism must be measured, possible toxicity gauged, and dosage levels determined. The investigation continues month after month and over a battery of tests. There are no shortcuts. After nearly $100,000 are spent, field trials on actual patients finally begin. Four months of intensive clinical studies are set up in TB sanitariums. Over one million doses are administered as the drug is given across the board to patients from the minimally afflicted to those with the most advanced cases. Almost all show some improvement, but the decision is obvious: *Diasone* is not effective enough to market. By an odd coincidence, however, some of the clinical doses have been given to leprosy patients who have tubercular symptoms. *Diasone* dramatically reduces their nodular lesions and skin ulcers, performing far better than the injections they've been enduring.

Although the market for leprosy drugs is limited, Abbott continues to produce *Diasone* at virtually no profit. That decision is particularly appreciated in those areas of the world where leprosy continues to be a disease both feared and difficult to treat.

TOP: *The German war machine, or* Wehrmacht, *pays a visit to Paris.* BOTTOM: *Whether it's 1940, 1960, or 1980, sales conventions most likely change only in the style of dress. In the front row of this 1940 Planned Progress Convention held at the Edgewater Beach Hotel in Chicago appear Abbott's officers: (left to right) Ferdinand H. "Fred" Young, Raymond E. Horn, Charles S. Downs, Rolly M. Cain, and James F. Stiles, Jr.*

The war in Europe explodes into a world-wide conflict as German troops invade the U.S.S.R. in June and Japanese planes attack Pearl Harbor in December. British intelligence predicts a Soviet collapse within 10 days and an American admiral comments, "We will clean up on the Japs by next Tuesday."

The attack on Pearl Harbor, which comes without a declaration of war, is an immense success for the Japanese. They lose only 29 of their 360 planes plus five midget submarines as they cripple the U.S. Pacific fleet. The attackers badly damage or sink the battleships *Arizona, Oklahoma, California, Nevada, West Virginia,* and *Utah;* damage nine other capital ships; destroy 188 U.S. planes; and kill 2,400 Americans. Calling December 7 "a date that will live in infamy," President Roosevelt calls for a declaration of war.

In the U.S.S.R., the German siege of Leningrad comes as the most severe winter in 30 years strikes the country. German bombing has knocked out communications, utilities, and food stocks in the city. There is no heat, no electricity, and virtually no food. Before the siege is lifted in 1944, one-third of Leningrad's three million people will have died of starvation. Britain is saved similar pangs when one million tons of foodstuffs arrive from the first U.S. Lend-Lease just in time to avert a drastic food shortage. Germany, meanwhile, has no such problems. It remains the best-fed nation of all European combatants, with a lenient rationing plan that gives Germans at least 95 percent of their regular prewar caloric intake.

Abbott becomes one of five pioneers in the U.S. to start commercial production of penicillin — 13 years after the drug was discovered. Back in 1928, Alexander Fleming accidentally found the first of the useful antibiotics. As he had often done before, Fleming had grown staphylococcal colonies in flat culture plates in his cramped laboratory in St. Mary's Hospital in London. When he uncovered the plates for viewing under a microscope, airborne mold spores floated in to settle on one of the culture plates. Later, when examining the plates again, Fleming noted that in the area around the blue-green mold, the staphylococcal colonies were being destroyed. Never before had he seen this around a contaminating colony. Further studies convinced him that the substance must have clinical value, if only it could be produced on a large scale.

Strangely, over the next 10 years, few scientists made the effort. Most investigators refused to believe that a mold whose spores were found in soil or air and were of the same family as the mold on stale bread could have medical value.

By 1941, with Great Britain deep into World War II, neither finances nor manpower can be spared for further investigation. So the British bring their penicillin-producing mold to America. Their objective: to search for firms that might volunteer facilities to start large-scale production.

Abbott is quick to accept the challenge. Within three months, the company adds a new facility, begins fermentation production in a series of flasks, and tests over 100 types of culture broths to find the best yield. The breakthrough comes when a new mold strain is discovered on an overripe cantaloupe in a Peoria, Illinois, fruit stand. From such an unlikely source, the possibilities of a miracle drug are nurtured.

TOP: *During the 1940s, the loading dock of Building M-1 at North Chicago serves the shipping needs of the entire company.* BOTTOM LEFT: *Abbott's newly expanded cafeteria in Building A-1 gives employees a chance to socialize over lunch.* BOTTOM RIGHT: *The threat of continental invasion has the West Coast on edgy alert, as news of the Japanese attack on Pearl Harbor makes headlines across America. The date — December 7, 1941.*

121

The year seesaws through a series of hard-fought, well-remembered actions. In January, the Japanese take Manila and invade the Dutch East Indies but suffer a naval setback when U.S. and Dutch forces attack a Japanese convoy. Singapore falls the next month as the fixed gun emplacements of the British naval base all point out to sea while the Japanese approach from the Malayan interior. In early April, U.S. troops on the Bataan peninsula surrender, although Corregidor will hold out for another month. Some consolation comes to America when Tokyo and Yokohama are raided by 16 B-25 bombers under the command of Lieutenant Colonel Jimmy Doolittle. The Japanese suffer consecutive heavy losses in May at the Battle of Coral Sea and in June at the Battle of Midway.

On the other side of the world, Cologne is raided by the RAF but bad news comes when Tobruk in Libya is taken by Field Marshal Erwin Rommel as his Axis forces go on to El Alamein, only 60 miles from Alexandria. In late summer, the Battle of Stalingrad begins. Lasting five months, it becomes one of the most savage conflicts in history. The vaunted German army of 20 divisions will have shrunk to 90,000 ill-fed, poorly equipped stragglers by the time it surrenders the following February. In November, a combined U.S.-British force of 400,000 men under the command of General Dwight Eisenhower lands at Casablanca, Oran, and Algiers to begin the African campaign and the long road back.

TOP: *Part of the "blood, toil, tears, and sweat" promised by British Prime Minister Winston Churchill involves endless work on correspondence, often as he travels war-torn England by train to "see things for [himself]."* CENTER: *Abbott takes advantage of its location directly adjacent to the Chicago and Northwestern Railroad by building its own commuter station. When gas rationing hits during the war years, this station will become a vital link between company and employees.* BOTTOM: *A large traveling banner is passed around Department 5 to the section with the best safety record for the month.*

With America now in the war, Abbott concentrates its resources on the needs of the armed forces. First of the "miracle" drugs, sulfanilamide, has been produced by Abbott for several years. Now it is distributed in war zones as *Sterilope* Envelopes. The unique package is sealed on the outside and has an inner sterile envelope with a sifter top containing the sulfa powder. When the powder is dusted evenly over a wound, danger of infection is radically reduced.

Pentothal proves its worth as the ideal battlefield anesthetic. It saves innumerable lives by allowing the severely wounded to be treated near combat zones before being moved to better operating conditions. By war's end, use of *Pentothal* by America's armed forces will reach 62 percent of cases in forward hospitals, with a mortality rate of only .018 percent. And in the years that follow, the drug will help heal war-shattered minds in postwar psychotherapy.

Halazone tablets, adapted from the original *Chlorazene* that purified tainted water in World War I, are shipped by the millions to every fighting front. One infantry battalion cut off from its regiment is supplied for a week when Halazone tablets, wrapped in heavy cloth and inserted into the hollow head of a 105-millimeter shell, are shot into the area occupied by the besieged troops.

Dried blood plasma, processed by Abbott from blood donated by American civilians, will save the lives of thousands of wounded men. As a surgeon from Sicily writes: "Plasma is quite the wonder treatment of this war. A patient goes sour as you watch. You are seeing him die. Beads of perspiration appear, pallor develops, the face becomes pinched, pulse rapid, weak, and thready. Plasma is administered and, presto, in a few minutes the harbingers of death disappear."

123

As the year goes on, the tide of war begins to turn against the Axis on all fronts — in North Africa, Italy, the U.S.S.R., and the Pacific.

In February, Allied forces storm the beaches to take Guadalcanal in the Solomon Islands. In March, a major victory is gained by the U.S. in the Battle of Bismarck Sea when an entire convoy of 16 Japanese transports and destroyers is sunk by American bombers. In May, the North African campaign ends as American and British troops mop up Bizerte and Tunis. In July, Rome is bombed by more than 500 Allied planes, and Benito Mussolini and his entire cabinet resign. In September, the "toe" of the Italian mainland is invaded. Italy surrenders five days later and within a month declares war on Germany.

Back in the Pacific, the island-by-island drive up the chain of Japanese-held territories gains momentum as Marcus Island, then New Guinea are attacked. Japan suffers its worst naval defeat at Rabaul when General MacArthur, suspecting an attack, orders an all-out bombing mission. The Americans quickly follow with landings at Bougainville in the Solomons and Tarawa and Makin in the Gilbert Islands. In Russia, the first breach is made in the Leningrad siege, and Soviet troops go on to recapture Kharkov, Smolensk, and Kiev. The turnaround is now obvious.

For all of 1943, penicillin production in the entire country comes to only 28 pounds. As the war grows in virulence, Abbott works feverishly to improve the productivity of yields. Larger tanks and faster fermentation techniques will certainly be the eventual answer. But how to achieve them? The process at this beginning stage is heartbreakingly slow.

First, bacteriologists must determine the most productive strain of the *Penicillium* mold from a family of over 100 types. Then they must figure out the one culture medium that will give the maximum drug yield. Fat-bellied glass bottles are used to hold the sugary liquid into which the spores of *Penicillium* mold are introduced. After the mold grows for 7 to 12 days in its original bottle, it is transferred to another container. After another week, the mold is discarded and the remaining broth refrigerated and dehydrated. The end product is a powdery penicillin, which is then sealed into a small glass container for later dilution with a saline solution. "Two gallons of the broth," reports the *Chicago Tribune,* "produce a tiny mound of powder which would fit nicely on the thumbnail."

From slow growth in row upon row of bottles comes swifter cultivation in flat pans. Then it's on to 30-liter fermenters that are constantly agitated and supplied with sterilized air. Next, newly designed 5,000-gallon tanks, along with refrigerating units, pumps, and filters for isolation, are added for still-faster fermentation. This new submerged method of mold cultivation reduces the cycle of growth from six to three days, saves labor, and cuts costs sharply. This year, the cost of manufacturing 100,000 units of penicillin is $20. Within two years, Abbott will bring that cost down to less than $2.

TOP: *Abbott's introduction of a new submerged cultivation process contributes to the large-scale production of penicillin. By 1945, penicillin will be manufactured in quantities large enough for domestic distribution through pharmacies.* BOTTOM: *For its contribution of dried blood plasma, Halazone,* Pentothal, *and other products critical to the war effort, Abbott receives no fewer than five Army-Navy "E" Awards for wartime production excellence (DeWitt Clough, front left).*

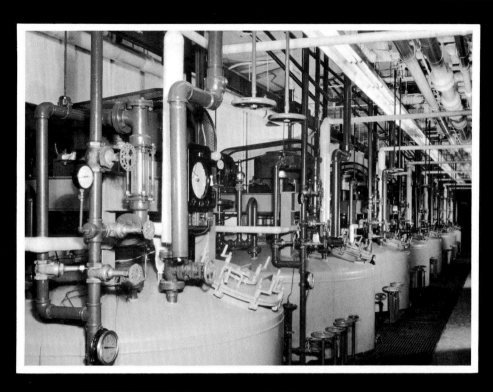

Even though Allied battlefront successes are becoming more frequent, larger and larger casualty lists are published as last-gasp attempts by both Germany and Japan make 1944 one of the grimmest years in history.

Early in the year, the British and Americans land at Anzio, Italy, with Rome only 30 miles away. But they are soon stalemated at Cassino, where the Germans throw all their strength into their mountaintop monastery stronghold. It takes three months of incessant bombings and artillery barrages before the Nazis evacuate their position. By June 4, the Germans are pushed out of Rome. Two days later is the long-awaited D-Day as the Allies establish their beachheads in Normandy.

In the Pacific, Allied forces in February take Kwajalein and Eniwetok and go on to attack the main Japanese naval base at Truk. By June, B-29 bombers are attacking Japan, and the Battle of the Philippine Sea ends with a loss of 400 Japanese planes while only 130 U.S. aircraft are lost. Saipan falls in July, Guam in August.

In the U.S., President Roosevelt wins reelection to a fourth term, defeating New York Governor Thomas E. Dewey. Roosevelt dumps his vice president, Henry A. Wallace, bypasses two other logical candidates for the job, and selects a little-known senator from Missouri named Harry S Truman.

Abbott's use of fine art for advertising illustration, a project of ad manager Charles Downs, triggers a much bigger idea for the company.

On the day Pearl Harbor was attacked by the Japanese, Thomas Hart Benton, an outspoken Missouri artist, was lecturing in Los Angeles. So shaken was he by the news that he stopped speaking and walked off the stage. Canceling all lecture dates, he worked in his studio for nine weeks. When he emerged, he had created seven paintings depicting the devastations of war. He called his series "The Year of Peril." Spotting a newspaper clipping on Benton's work, Downs promptly called him with the idea that Abbott purchase all seven paintings for a portfolio of War Bond posters.

With this as a starter, Downs now recruits a stable of important artists that includes John Steuart Curry, Franklin Boggs, Georges Schreiber, Howard Baer, and Kerr Eby. They produce hundreds of drawings, oils, and watercolors of U.S. Army, Navy, and Marine forces in action. One painting by Lawrence Beall Smith, showing three terrified children cowering under the shadow of a Nazi swastika, becomes the first of the Abbott War Bond posters. Other familiar themes are the gaunt soldier in "Remember Me? I Was at Bataan" and Joseph Hirsch's "Till We Meet Again," depicting a soldier waving from the porthole of a transport. Over 50 million copies of Abbott posters are distributed by the U.S. Treasury Department; all are used in bond drives and adapted as posters for civilian defense, recruiting, and war production. One bond drive in Brooklyn alone nets $800 million in pledges. Perhaps that's one reason the U.S. Army Surgeon General will cite the Abbott series as "an eloquent contribution to the war effort that will be far reaching and everlasting."

TOP: *One in a series of seven paintings called "The Year of Peril,"* The Sowers *was painted by Thomas Hart Benton. Abbott purchases all seven from Benton and features them in* What's New. BOTTOM: *U.S. Army General Dwight Eisenhower peps up the troops shortly before launch of the greatest invasion fleet in history on June 6, 1944 — D-Day.*

It is a monumental year, both the end and the beginning of an era. Germany and Japan collapse and are forced to accept unconditional surrender. The end comes also for three of the world's five leading heads of state.

The beginning? One is a mighty new instrument for everlasting peace, as the United Nations is optimistically launched in San Francisco. The other, also a mighty new instrument, poses the threat of everlasting damnation as the world's first atomic bomb bursts on Hiroshima.

The chronology of war's end has almost a drumbeat staccato. In February, General MacArthur returns to Manila, while across the globe 1,000 U.S. bombers blast Berlin to rubble. In March, U.S. Marines take Iwo Jima after a month of heavy fighting, as the U.S. First Army secures the Remagen bridgehead and sweeps across Germany. In April, President Roosevelt dies of a cerebral hemorrhage. Two weeks later, Benito Mussolini is executed, and the following day Adolf Hitler commits suicide in his Reichschancellery bunker. German forces in Italy surrender two days later, and Germany surrenders within a week. On August 6, an atomic bomb is dropped on Hiroshima, killing 100,000 Japanese outright. On August 9, a plutonium-core bomb is dropped on Nagasaki, killing 75,000. On August 14, Japan sues for peace.

Thus ends World War II, after nearly six traumatic years in which almost 45 million people have died, most of them civilians.

The final year of World War II is also the last year as chief executive for S. DeWitt Clough, the Abbott advertising copywriter turned president. Next year, he will move to the chairmanship and turn over the reins to Rolly M. Cain. Clough's 12-year record is impressive: annual sales of only $4.1 million when he took office in 1933 now are $37.9 million, an 833 percent increase. The number of shareholders is up from 1,084 to more than 6,000, and an investment of $1,000 in Abbott stock in 1933 is now worth $8,774.

Impressive as well are the research gains Abbott is making in one of the knottiest areas of medicine: the search for a drug to treat children who have *petit mal* epilepsy. This form of the disease is characterized by quick twitchings or convulsions or a few moments of unconsciousness after a sudden slump to the floor. While children often outgrow the disease, it seriously affects their social and educational development.

After five years of intensive work, Abbott appears to have an answer. Laboratory tests indicate the drug, which is named *Tridione*, prevents convulsions in mice. When tests are eventually expanded into the clinical area, results are even more conclusive. Used on 150 patients at Children's Hospital in Chicago, *Tridione* completely wipes out attacks in 30 percent and markedly reduces the frequency of seizures in the rest. One young girl, who suffered 40 seizures every day for six years, was subjected to only 1 attack a week after two months' treatment, and none at all after four. Before long, the drug will bring a brighter future to children around the world.

Even though public demand is modest and the profit margin slim, *Tridione* will remain for years one of Abbott's most rewarding drugs.

Expanding on a plan originated by Charles Downs, manager of advertising, Abbott commissions a number of paintings by nationally known artists for use as posters to stimulate the sale of War Bonds. "Till We Meet Again" may be among the best-remembered of the series.

This, the first of the postwar years, finds the U.S. caught up in runaway prices and wage demands as most wartime controls are lifted ... a desperate shortage of housing as servicemen return ... the most bitter labor disputes since 1919 as a series of strikes idles five million workers ... and the menace of East-West conflict and Communism with what Winston Churchill describes as "the iron curtain [which] has descended across the continent."

It seems odd less than a year after the Hiroshima and Nagasaki bombings that the U.S. finds it necessary to conduct the first Bikini Atoll atomic bomb tests in the Pacific. Leave it to the French to put it in perspective when a "bikini" swimsuit is modeled at a Paris fashion show the same week.

President Truman proclaims independence for the Philippines, keeping the promise the U.S. made on acquiring the islands from Cuba in 1898. The French recognize Vietnamese independence, but fighting against the Communists goes on as Ho Chi Minh tries to drive out the French and unite Indochina. In Argentina, Juan Perón wins election as president, a rule that will last until 1955. And John D. Rockefeller, Jr., gives property worth $8.5 million along New York's East River as a permanent site for the United Nations.

Americans are talking about Kathleen Winsor's racy new novel, *Forever Amber.* It avoids the expected Boston banning when a Massachusetts judge rules it "more of a soporific than an aphrodisiac."

The immensely inquisitive Abbott scientist Dr. Donalee Tabern has the first inkling of their potential. But he has no idea, in the beginning, how to use what he envisions — radioactive drugs. The thought itself is perplexing enough, coming only months after the horror of atomic bombings in Japan. Yet this year, the same year the Atomic Energy Commission's experimental plant in Oak Ridge, Tennessee, turns out its first batch of raw radioisotopes, a special laboratory is set up at Abbott to develop radioactive materials for use in biology and medicine. That step is a first for the pharmaceutical industry.

The only way to tell Dr. Tabern's laboratory from any other is by the warning sign on the door and the film badges and pocket meters his people wear. "Radiation Hazard" is quite enough to keep the curious away. Inside, a whole new medical jargon is coming into existence. "Hot" pharmaceuticals, as they are called, include Gold-198, Iodine-131, and Carbon-14. In Dr. Tabern's lab, radioactive materials are handled very deliberately, very carefully, and from a distance. The investigators wear hoods and heavy gloves. Rube Goldberg-like mechanical tongs are used to grasp the containers, which are shielded by thick blocks of lead. Investigators view their work indirectly, by mirror reflection.

At first, the radioactive substances are used as tracers to tag the progress of a drug after it is administered to a patient. Later, localized rays from radio-gold injected directly into growths will be capable of destroying cancerous tissues with relatively little effect on surrounding tissues. Still later, this small laboratory will spawn the first "atomic drugstore" and eventually will lead to entire new dimensions in medical diagnosis and technology.

TOP: *Toward the end of the war, a race begins in the pharmaceutical industry to discover and produce more antibiotics like penicillin. Here Building F-1 is under construction, as Abbott responds quickly to the challenge.* BOTTOM LEFT: *These heavy filtering devices are used in the extraction of streptomycin, Abbott's next antibiotic development.* BOTTOM RIGHT: *A young couple admire their new son, as returning servicemen give birth to America's "baby boom."*

130

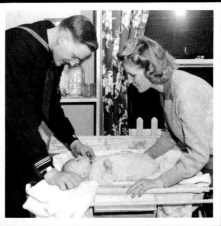

The intensity of the East-West conflict steps up with several different anti-Communist actions in the U.S. First, the government bans all Communist party members and sympathizers from holding office in its executive branch. Next, President Truman creates the Central Intelligence Agency to counter Soviet espionage activities and Moscow's attempts to establish Communist governments in many countries.

Hollywood gets into the act when 10 screenwriters and producers who refuse to tell whether they are card-carrying members are exiled from their jobs. All will receive short prison sentences. Even passage of the widely debated Taft-Hartley Act has anti-Communist overtones. Not only does it erase many of labor's former advantages, such as the closed shop and the right to strike, but it prohibits the use of union funds for political purposes, forces unions to publish financial statements, and insists that all union leaders attest they are non-Communists.

America's most dramatic success of the year comes in foreign policy when the "Marshall Plan" — proposed at Harvard commencement exercises by Secretary of State George C. Marshall — is instituted. It will spend over $12 billion in American aid to restore economic health to free Europe and to halt the spread of Communism. Meanwhile, Britain's Prime Minister Clement Attlee proposes a program of austerity and longer working hours to see the country through an economic "Battle of Britain" brought on by a worldwide dollar famine. And the Truman Doctrine takes effect, with the aim of protecting Greece and Turkey from Communist domination.

Only 11 months after he becomes president of Abbott, Rolly Cain is dead of a heart attack. His successor is Raymond E. Horn, whose campaigns as director of sales have been instrumental in moving the company to revenues of nearly $60 million.

The tragically brief reign of Rolly Cain comes at a time when Abbott appears ready to break away from wartime restrictions and move well up in the ranks of the pharmaceutical industry. Research productivity is coming into its own, with 61 new products introduced this year. Some are new drugs, others improved preparations of drugs already in use. Penicillin is a prime example. From a prewar laboratory curiosity, penicillin has become a big business, with national sales of over $100 million. But even with vastly increased production, there's not enough penicillin to meet physicians' demands. Nor are there enough dosage forms of the wondrous drug. Injectable penicillin is the physician's staple, but now Abbott adds a procaine penicillin for easier injection and longer action, tablets for oral use, troches for dissolving in the mouth, a pleasant-tasting *Dulcet* for children, a penicillin ophthalmic ointment, and even a veterinary form.

But the real sleeper among the year's new products is called *Aminosol*. This is a radical new development for supplying protein to surgical patients by intravenous feeding. I.V. feeding is nothing new; Abbott originated the business in 1936 when it began supplying dextrose and saline solutions to hospitals, and the company has become the country's largest supplier. But now, for the first time, a nearly complete diet — amino acids, vitamins, minerals, and dextrose — can be fed by tube to the hospital patient.

TOP: *Money and machinery are pumped into France as part of the "Marshall Plan" to help put a fallen postwar European economy back on its feet.* BOTTOM: *During the late 1940s, Abbott employees are very familiar with this end-of-the-day scene outside the main gate of the North Chicago plant.*

132

The year starts in violence when a Hindu extremist assassinates Mahatma Gandhi because he agrees to the partition of India, and conflict continues as Communists take over Czechoslovakia in a coup d'état. A new State of Israel is proclaimed with David Ben-Gurion as prime minister, and Soviet forces in Germany set up a blockade to cut off rail and highway traffic between West Germany and Berlin, leading the U.S. and Britain to airlift 4,500 tons of food and supplies a day for over a year. The phrase "Cold War" is introduced by Bernard Baruch in a speech before the South Carolina legislature. "Let us not be deceived," Baruch says. "We are today in the midst of a Cold War."

President Truman wins reelection over both Thomas E. Dewey and the *Chicago Tribune,* which hits the streets early with a headline proclaiming Dewey the winner. State Department official Alger Hiss is accused by *Time* senior editor Whittaker Chambers of supplying Soviet agents with secret U.S. documents. Quick to get in the act is young Representative Richard M. Nixon. Hiss finally goes to prison three years later, convicted of perjury for concealing his membership in the Communist party.

A Streetcar Named Desire tops off its second year on Broadway by winning the New York Drama Critics Circle Award for best original American play, and a Pulitzer prize for playwright Tennessee Williams. In Bloomington, Indiana, a zoologist named Alfred Kinsey publishes a controversial book, *Sexual Behavior in the Human Male,* better known as the "Kinsey Report." It would not have caused a blush 2,000 years earlier in Rome.

TOP: *Abbott further serves the community by supplying the Midwest's hay fever sufferers with daily pollen counts, taken here by Oren C. Durham (left) at the North Chicago plant.* BOTTOM LEFT: *Lydia Oelschlaeger, DeWitt Clough's secretary for 43 years, is among the first to enjoy the benefits of Abbott's new retirement plan.* BOTTOM RIGHT: *Blanche, Stella, and Stanley (Vivien Leigh, Kim Hunter, and Marlon Brando) share a cramped, depressing flat in the 1948 production of Tennessee Williams' A Streetcar Named Desire.*

Those who don't suffer from hay fever might not have heard of the man or the service he performs. But for the past 17 years, a quiet Abbott scientist named Oren C. Durham has been tracking pollen densities throughout the Midwest to help hay fever sufferers breathe a little easier.

Probably the nation's foremost authority on ragweed pollen, Durham started out in 1931 by amassing thousands of spore specimens collected from more than 100 cities. With the approach of each hay fever season, he prepares detailed graphs showing pollen density in the major population centers. Each year he flies thousands of miles to check pollen concentrations and to gather specimens. He has even developed his own "sky hook" to capture the spores. A small streamlined bracket attached to the side of his open-cockpit biplane catches pollen on a greased microscope slide. After landing, Durham can tabulate precisely the potential pollen density for each area. His daily newspaper reports soon become the hay fever sufferer's bible.

In later years, Abbott will use Durham's idea, minus the biplane, to report daily pollen counts. From early August until first frost, an Abbott technician will begin each day by climbing to the roof of a research building to remove a biological slide from a device resembling a spinning birdhouse. Results will be reported in a recorded telephone message.

This year, the 25 Year Club, started in 1944, gets a new name — the Quarter Century Club. Many retirees plan a trip from the Sun Belt each year to attend the annual banquet. One member of the club's founding committee, Lydia Oelschlaeger, was S. DeWitt Clough's secretary for 43 of her 45 years at Abbott.

135

THE ABBOTT **Pharmagraph**

VOL. 8 NO. 1 • MAY, 1949

A number of nations change face. First, China's Chiang Kai-shek resigns his presidency and moves his Nationalist forces to Taiwan after suffering mainland reverses from the Communists. Within months, a new People's Republic of China is proclaimed with Mao Tse-tung as chairman and Chou En-lai as premier and foreign minister. On the other side of the world, the Republic of Éire is founded. England recognizes Irish independence but keeps Northern Ireland within the United Kingdom. A new organization called the North Atlantic Treaty Organization (NATO) is created when 12 nations join to pledge mutual assistance against aggression.

The British pound is devalued from $4.03 to $2.80, while in the United States the Dow-Jones average falls to 161 at midyear. Americans can still get a loaf of bread for 15¢, a gallon of gasoline for 25¢, and a 10-inch TV for $250.

In the world of medicine, the big news surrounds the synthesis of ACTH from liver bile acids by Merck scientists and the astounding news that blood pressure can be lowered by the powdered root of a tropical plant called rauwolfia. Meanwhile, the rapid-fire introduction of a wave of new antibiotics continues: Terramycin from Pfizer, Aureomycin from Lederle, and Chloromycetin from Parke, Davis. It is beginning to be a Golden Age.

By year's end, 74 new Abbott products have been announced. Some are new drugs, some medical devices, others improved variations of products already in use. This outpouring comprises the most products ever introduced in one year by Abbott. To put it in perspective, with over 70 percent of Abbott sales coming from products less than 10 years old, this year's volume of more than $67 million would have been only about $20 million without the decade's new products.

With price cuts of as much as 55 percent on many of the company's penicillin products, the search for new drugs has become the lifeblood of the business. In this decade alone, Abbott has brought out 519 new products, an average of more than 50 a year. Sixteen are new forms of penicillin.

Prolific as it may be, research is hardly a series of spur-of-the-moment discoveries. As any investigator at his lab bench can attest, it is almost endless, day-after-day drudgery . . . a discipline that demands infinite patience, incessant tabulations, and incalculable disappointments. A new antibiotic, for example, is not necessarily a new wonder drug. The vast majority are worthless for human therapy. Either they don't work at all against a virulent organism or else they work too well, destroying useful bacteria. Conducting antibiotic research is like playing a slot machine, with each new antibiotic a coin. Any one may hit the jackpot, but the most common reward is a lemon.

The bottom line? Abbott has isolated more than 3,000 antibiotic-producing organisms and is finding 15 to 20 new ones each month. So far, not one has shown the promise of the mold spore that Alexander Fleming discovered in his laboratory.

TOP: *Introduced in 1942 to replace* Abbograms, *the* Pharmagraph *will serve as the company's major employee publication until 1962, when* Abbottopics *is born. The cover of this 1949 issue of the* Pharmagraph *features a painting done for the company by James Chapin.* BOTTOM: *Initial signatories of the North Atlantic Pact establishing NATO are depicted by this cartoon from the early Cold War years.*

138

This year, the midcentury mark, finds Americans deeply concerned about two major issues: the growth of Communism and a foreign policy that never seems to bring a lasting stability.

In June, North Korean troops cross the 38th Parallel and invade South Korea. The United Nations determines an international "police force" shall be sent to end the hostilities. Thus begins the Korean War, which will last for more than three years. In September, UN forces under the command of General Douglas MacArthur land at Inchon and go on to recapture Seoul. The action seesaws across the 38th Parallel until UN troops reach the Manchurian border at the Yalu River, where a mass of Chinese Communists counterattack, forcing the possibility of a war between China and the West.

Back in the States, a Communist "witch-hunt" begins when Senator Joseph McCarthy starts four years of hearings on alleged Communist infiltration. Meanwhile, another presidential hopeful, Senator Estes Kefauver from Tennessee, begins his own televised investigation of organized crime. Organized labor presses for better working conditions and higher wages. Finally, the Brink's robbery in Boston, almost perfectly executed, puts the entire year somewhat in perspective. The robbers make off with about $3 million; the FBI will spend $25 million investigating the crime.

Thirty-six months after becoming president of Abbott, Raymond E. Horn is forced to step down because of illness. This means the company will have its third president in only four years. The new head is Dr. Ernest H. Volwiler, first president since Dr. Burdick to come from the world of science.

Dr. Volwiler's management style is in night-and-day contrast to some of his predecessors. He blends a quiet, modest manner with a scientist's insatiable curiosity. He is not an advocate of bold risks, and there is nothing fiery or intemperate in his decisions. Dr. Volwiler brings a precise, pragmatic approach to the job. One of his first moves, after a contemplative study of the company's catalog of 1,000 products, is to lop off 300 that are no longer profitable and are duplicated by many other companies.

A month after Dr. Volwiler becomes president, Abbott launches a drug that later will become one of the nation's most controversial and politically battered products. This is *Sucaryl,* the cyclamate compound that is 30 times sweeter than sugar. It was discovered in 1937 when a young graduate chemist at the University of Illinois lit a cigarette, laid it on a lab bench heavily stained with salts of sulfamic acid, and, on his next puff, noticed a sweet taste. Testing samples of every compound on his bench, he found the one responsible and jotted down his report.

Three years later, Dr. Volwiler, then director of research at Abbott, was looking for a better product than saccharin for diabetic diets and worked out an arrangement for Abbott to test the compound. For the next 12 years, Abbott and then the FDA subjected it to intensive pharmacological and clinical studies. In 1950 it is finally approved — to the immense relief of the nation's diabetics and dieters.

TOP: *Strikes and lockouts shatter the U.S. auto industry, as union workers press for wage increases and better working conditions.* BOTTOM: *Development of disposable I.V. administration sets, such as* Venopak *(shown being assembled), accompany Abbott's growth into a major supplier of bulk intravenous solutions.*

This must be the "Catch 22" of all years. UN troops fighting in Korea know that victory cannot be won until the strategic Chinese Communist positions above the Yalu River are destroyed. This, however, would be tantamount to declaring war on China, which has a military alliance with the U.S.S.R. It seems to be a "no-win" situation. General MacArthur has a solution: he wants to make all-out air attacks on the People's Republic of China. President Truman is horrified and quickly relieves MacArthur of his command. MacArthur's farewell address quotes a popular barracks ballad when he says, "Old soldiers never die; they just fade away."

Britain's Labour government falls after six years in power and Winston Churchill, now 77, returns as prime minister. British intelligence officer and Soviet double agent H. A. R. "Kim" Philby is working in Washington and transmitting classified information about the CIA to the Communists. He will eventually seek asylum in the Soviet Union. In the U.S., Ethel and Julius Rosenberg are found guilty of giving atomic secrets to Soviet agents. They will be executed two years later. Former Secretary of State George C. Marshall, now 70, is called a Communist agent by Senator Joe McCarthy who, so far, has been unable to show evidence that anyone he's named is guilty of subversive activity.

In baseball, two living legends begin their centerfield careers in New York when Willie Mays joins the Giants and Mickey Mantle becomes a Yankee.

The advent of *Sucaryl* marks a perplexing departure for Abbott. It is the first real consumer product to hit the prescription-oriented company. The first marketing approach is predictable: it is ethically advertised to the medical profession and promoted only through drugstores.

Almost by osmosis, news of the remarkable sweetener gravitates to the brand-new world of dietetic beverages. An aggressive Brooklyn-based firm, Kirsch Beverages, ventures that 100,000 cases of *Sucaryl*-sweetened soft drinks just might be sold by year's end. The entire batch is gone in 60 days. By next year, no fewer than 400 food manufacturers will have invaded grocery stores with canned fruits, jellies and jams, frozen desserts, and baked goods — all saving precious calories because of *Sucaryl*. But the real market lies with low-calorie soft drinks. By 1952, the number of *Sucaryl*-containing soft drinks will have soared to 10 million cases. And that's only the beginning of the boom. The honeymoon for *Sucaryl* will last 18 more years.

Strangely, this year also sees the introduction of a second Abbott consumer product, although it will take 22 years to become one. This is *Selsun* Suspension, a dandruff remedy based on selenium, the rare metal that makes electric eyes open doors. This product, too, comes to Abbott from another company. Twenty-five years earlier, a General Electric chemist, looking for ways to detect mercury vapors in laboratory air, had developed stable selenium sulfide. Knowing the compound had good medical prospects, since sulfur had long been used in the treatment of skin diseases, the company tried it in soap, salve, and even shaving cream. But GE has no interest in entering the drug field, so Abbott acquires the rights and immediately turns *Selsun* into a prescription-only dandruff remedy.

TOP: *The Korean War moves into its second year. American infantry pose in a Victory V, but the war will drag on two more years, before reaching a stalemate in 1953.* CENTER: *Sodium cyclamate is perhaps better known to consumers as Abbott's new sugar substitute,* Sucaryl. BOTTOM: *Easily a favorite social event at the company, annual spring variety shows often involve hundreds of employees in acting and production casts. This scene is from the production of* Harmony House.

141

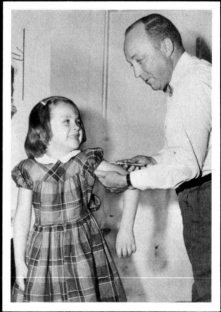

In a year fraught with the spreading danger of Communist domination, how can it be that flying saucers and panty raids take such precedence? Unidentified objects of all kinds are reported flying through the night skies and outside sorority dormitories, but most people refuse to believe there's anything unfriendly in either event.

The U.S. policy to arm Western Europe to make it more costly for the U.S.S.R. to start a war has many foes, but both presidential candidates — Adlai E. Stevenson and Dwight D. Eisenhower — support the NATO idea. Eisenhower and his running mate, Richard M. Nixon, easily defeat the Stevenson-Sparkman Democratic ticket with an electoral majority of 442-89. The one-sided victory is partly the result of "Ike's" enormous popularity and partly a personal rebuke to the Truman regime. Elsewhere in the U.S., a polio epidemic strikes more than 50,000 Americans at the same time that microbiologist Jonas Salk is investigating the different strains of polio virus. The first successful mass inoculations of the Salk vaccine will be given to schoolchildren in Pittsburgh two years later.

Three of the world's leaders are lost when Britain's King George VI, long a heavy smoker, dies of lung cancer, Israel's President Chaim Weizmann also dies, and Egypt's King Farouk is deposed.

The remarkable wartime success of penicillin has paved the way for an entire new generation of antimicrobial agents. That the drug industry has been so productive in such a short span of time is a testament to competitive incentives. Aureomycin from Lederle Laboratories, Terramycin from Pfizer, and Chloromycetin from Parke, Davis all carve out sudden and significant sales successes as the search for new antibiotics becomes top priority around the world. Thousands upon thousands of soil samples will be tested in the nation's labs — almost all with virtually zero practical results.

Abbott research on antibiotics, which has come up desert-dry the last four years, unearths two new antibiotics from opposite sides of the world within a period of a few months. One is isolated from a soil sample an Abbott scientist finds at Illinois Beach State Park, only a few miles north of the laboratory. It shows exceptional promise against amoebic dysentery and is the first antibiotic ever to be aimed specifically against one disease. It is called *Fumidil*.

The other comes from 6,000 miles away, from a soil sample found in the Philippine Islands. It results from the shared research efforts of three companies — Eli Lilly, Upjohn, and Abbott. Lilly will name its drug Ilotycin, Upjohn will prefer the generic erythromycin, and Abbott will call its product *Erythrocin*. The new drug seems to show good promise against certain organisms which have developed immunity to penicillin and do not respond to other antibiotics. Because of this unique characteristic, *Erythrocin* will become a "shelf" antibiotic, saved for use after all others have failed. The designation will muffle sales for several years.

TOP: *Abbott's rail crew from Department 890 replaces track on the 30-year-old spur to the shipping room.* **BOTTOM:** *For two years, the U.S. will suffer from one of its worst epidemics of poliomyelitis — infantile paralysis. Beginning in 1954, mass immunization made possible by a new vaccine developed by Dr. Jonas Salk will prevent further spread of the disease.*

143

In the U.S., this year sees the end of all wage and salary controls, the lifting of price controls on many consumer items and services, and the removal of rent ceilings as, for the first time in 24 years, a Republican administration takes over the White House. Around the nation, the most frequent topics of conversation: the explosive McCarthy investigations, the end of hostilities in Korea when an armistice is signed in July at Panmunjom near the 38th Parallel, and the conquest of Mt. Everest by New Zealand climber Sir Edmund Hillary and Nepalese Sherpa tribesman Tensing Norkay.

Joseph Stalin dies at 73 after ruling the U.S.S.R. for the past 29 years. He is succeeded as premier by Georgi Malenkov, who will head Russia until 1955, while Nikita Khrushchev is named first secretary of the Communist party. Marshal Tito is elected first president of the Yugoslav Republic, and Swedish diplomat Dag Hammarskjöld is elected secretary-general of the UN.

Back in the U.S., the Boston Braves shift their franchise to Milwaukee, which immediately becomes the most baseball-happy town in the country when it leads both leagues with an attendance of 1.8 million. The beloved and bedraggled St. Louis Browns get the message and move east to become the Baltimore Orioles. None of this perturbs the New York Yankees as they roll to their fifth consecutive World Series victory, beating the Brooklyn Dodgers.

On Wall Street, a new exchange is created when the old New York Curb Exchange (whose members have not traded from curbs since 1921) becomes the American Stock Exchange.

Because of its leadership and experience in nuclear medicine, Abbott was encouraged by the Atomic Energy Commission to set up its own facilities in Oak Ridge, Tennessee, for on-the-spot conversion of radioisotopes to finished pharmaceuticals. The site the company chose turned out to be an abandoned funeral home. Fortunately, that has not turned out to be an omen.

By 1953, the tiny lab's output ranges from radioactive gold used in medical research to radioiodinated serum albumin for locating brain tumors. Most intriguing of all are the "empty capsules" called Radiocaps. To the eye, the capsules appear to contain nothing at all. But inside is an accurately controlled, invisible, and unweighable film of radioiodine that clings to the inner wall. This capsule greatly simplifies the diagnosis and treatment of thyroid disorders. The patient swallows one capsule and, on the following day, is measured for the amount of iodine absorbed in the thyroid, with the amount gauged by the clatter set up from a scintillation counter 100 times more sensitive than a Geiger counter. This marks the first time any radioactive pharmaceutical is available in a form safe enough for doctors and patients to handle without the usual precautions. It is a breakaway from the "atomic cocktail" that has to be administered in heavily shielded hospital rooms.

In another 10 years, Abbott will announce an even simpler thyroid test with its *Triosorb* diagnostic kit. The patient swallows no radioactive substance; all that is needed is a blood sample in a test tube, inoculated with a radioactive form of a thyroid hormone.

TOP: *Due in part to the work of researchers such as this one, Abbott Laboratories numbers among its accomplishments of the early 1950s a very clear leadership in the field of radioactive drugs and diagnostic products.* CENTER: *The rapid entry into international markets makes a large contribution to Abbott's growth during this period.* BOTTOM: *Because of his tremendous personal popularity, Dwight Eisenhower (shown here during his inaugural parade) easily rolls over Adlai Stevenson to capture the U.S. presidency.*

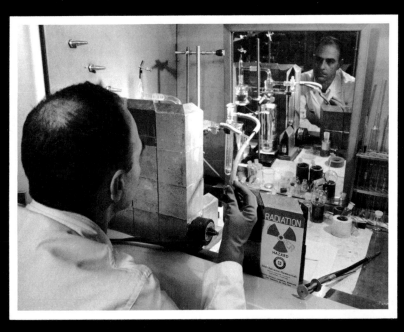

145

France desperately pleads for American aid to relieve her troops surrounded at Dienbienphu in Indochina. "France has arrived at a favorable turn in the war," says Admiral Arthur Radford, chairman of the U.S. Joint Chiefs of Staff. He hints broadly to the chief of the French armed forces that the U.S. might consider committing American airpower. But he forgets to check first with President Eisenhower, who declines to order armed intervention without the approval of Congress, the support of America's allies, and reforms in the government of Prime Minister Ngo Dinh Diem. The president overrules Radford, Vice President Richard Nixon, and Secretary of State John Foster Dulles, all of whom want to send U.S. troops to Vietnam.

Eisenhower officially acknowledges the 1952 detonation of the first hydrogen bomb, and the power of a second nuclear test explosion, in the Marshall Islands, exceeds all estimates.

Closer to home, Americans are worried about a mild business recession and rising unemployment that reaches the 2.9 million mark — nearly twice as high as in 1953. One sign of the times: only 154 Americans will have incomes reaching $1 million or more this year, down from 513 in 1929. Howard Hughes doesn't feel the pinch as he writes a personal check for $23.5 million to buy all the stock of RKO Radio Pictures. Hughes has held a controlling interest in RKO since 1948, and his capricious management has seen the company lose $22 million while other studios have made money. A 19-year-old rock and roll singer named Elvis Aron Presley makes his first commercial recording. RCA introduces its first color television, and, by coincidence, Omaha's C. A. Swanson Company picks this time to introduce frozen TV dinners.

TOP: America conducts its second large-scale atomic test. CENTER: High technology apparently has not yet found its way into the counting, filling, and labeling of Iberol, an anti-anemia iron supplement. BOTTOM: Spring shows and annual sales meetings are graced with the familiar harmony of the Abbott Medicine Men — Bill Ehnert, Herman Schaefer, Roy Truelsen, and Les Biere.

As with any business, not all years are good years for Abbott. Sales of slightly more than $88 million are actually lower than the previous year's. It is only the seventh time since Dr. Abbott founded the company in 1888 that the volume of business has declined. Net earnings are lower this year than in any of the past eight years and dividends are cut back to 1949 levels. Worse yet, in an era of explosive growth for the pharmaceutical industry — coming mainly from the rapid-fire introduction of new antibiotics — Abbott seems to be struggling. For the past three years, sales increases have averaged about one percent a year, while both net earnings and dividends have dropped. In essence, 1954 is the type of year when the annual report stresses manufacturing efficiencies, not new products and financial gains.

In a diagnosis of drug companies, *Forbes* magazine states that "some Wall Streeters thought they had Abbott neatly tabbed as a prairie drugmaker which achieved a drowsy kind of stability by somehow avoiding the more sensational drugs." Few things get more under Dr. Volwiler's skin than this kind of hasty generalization. He sees the world of drug discovery and drug-making as one of constant change and challenge, with frustrations aplenty but a horizon that is virtually unlimited. And he well knows that a major part of the Abbott research program is pledged to the fast-growing field of antibiotics. What he has no way of knowing at the time, however, is that *Erythrocin*, after a slow start, will go on to become one of the largest-selling antibiotics in the world.

147

🌐 It is a year of major political shuffle as Premier Georgi Malenkov of the U.S.S.R. resigns and is succeeded by Marshal Nikolai Bulganin. Prime Minister Winston Churchill of Great Britain, 81, also resigns and Foreign Minister Anthony Eden takes over. Peronist power in Argentina ends when a military coup quietly overthrows Juan Perón after nine years.

The Cold War eases remarkably with President Eisenhower's dramatic proposal for an exchange of military blueprints and aerial inspections with Russia. Indochina, however, remains a sorely troubled area. Under the terms of the 1954 Geneva Accords, Vietnam is temporarily partitioned along the 17th Parallel, with the Communist Viet Minh, under President Ho Chi Minh, to the north, and the French and the Vietnamese fighting under their command moving to the south. French forces begin a final withdrawal from Vietnam, and the U.S. assumes responsibility for the difficult task of organizing and training the South Vietnamese army. South Vietnam is proclaimed a republic in October, with Ngo Dinh Diem its first president.

At home, Americans are enjoying a fresh burst of prosperity with full employment and peak production as business income climbs 33 percent over last year's levels. Even the AFL and CIO make peace and merge as George Meany begins a 23-year term as president of the AFL-CIO. The New York Stock Exchange suffers a $14 billion loss, the heaviest since 1929, two days after President Eisenhower suffers a heart attack in Denver. Both, fortunately, will recover rapidly.

ⓐ Ebullient James F. Stiles, Jr., who is known around Abbott offices as "Sunny Jim," is now chairman of the board. He is even better known as the godfather of the Abbott benefits program. Beginning in 1933, he has worked out the myriad details of benefits of all kinds. First came a health and accident insurance program that paid from $15 to $40 a week at a cost to employees ranging from 52¢ to $2 a month. Next he added accidental death and dismemberment coverage. Then, in 1938, hospital payments for treatment or surgery were offered to employees and, in the following year, to their dependents. Abbott was the first company of its kind in the nation to provide such coverage. Later, a "blessed event" plan provided a $50 check for each newborn. One newspaper writer summed it up this way: "For about $60 a year, an Abbott employee can get himself insured against practically everything except being divorced or getting drafted in the army!"

Stiles' most innovative effort was the 1951 employee contributory stock purchase plan. Within two years, 95 percent of eligible employees were enrolled. With the growth and stock splits of later years, the plan will end up hatching a tidy nest egg for thousands of Abbott retirees.

The annual picnic for employees and their families follows the tradition established by Dr. Abbott many years before. In the early days, the ladies wore long dresses, men had suspenders and vests, and cars had soft tops. Children enjoyed the races, games, and food, and a day at the lake. Now more than 5,000 people attend the annual affair held at Foss Park in North Chicago, decked out in more modern garb than their predecessors, but having just as much fun.

TOP: *Provision for future expansion of the North Chicago plant is made when Abbott purchases property (outlined in aerial photo) from the American Can Company, which has recently discontinued operations at its North Chicago facility.* **BOTTOM LEFT:** *Picnics and company fairs are sponsored on a regular basis, giving Abbott employees and their families a chance to socialize with fellow workers.* **BOTTOM RIGHT:** *Chairman James F. Stiles, Jr., initiated Abbott's first employee benefits program.*

President Eisenhower easily wins reelection against a second challenge by Democratic hopeful Adlai Stevenson, despite Ike's illness and warnings that he might be succeeded in office by controversial Vice President Richard M. Nixon.

In Europe, Polish workers riot in protest against economic conditions under the Communist regime. In Hungary, more than 100,000 revolt, demanding a democratic government, the return of former Premier Imre Nagy, who was ousted in 1955, and withdrawal of Soviet troops. Over 200,000 Hungarians, including some of the nation's best minds, leave the country. The revolution is all in vain as 16 Soviet divisions and 2,000 tanks move in and quickly quell the uprisings. It does, however, result in the release of Jozsef Cardinal Mindszenty, who has been in solitary confinement since 1948. The Chinese people are equally frustrated at trying to repel communization. From 1949 to 1960, under Mao Tse-tung, almost 26 million Chinese will be liquidated, the largest massacre in world history.

The Italian passenger liner SS *Andrea Doria* sinks after colliding in heavy fog off Nantucket Island, Massachusetts, with the Swedish liner SS *Stockholm*. Lost are 51 passengers plus a $100,000 advanced-design prototype automobile handmade in Italy for Chrysler.

The musical *My Fair Lady* opens at New York's Mark Hellinger Theatre with Julie Andrews as Eliza Doolittle and Rex Harrison as Professor Henry Higgins. It will play there for 2,717 performances, a run of almost seven years. Don Larsen pitches the first perfect game in World Series history as the New York Yankees beat the Brooklyn Dodgers with a 4-3 series score.

Abbott acquires a 207-acre farm in Long Grove, Illinois. Stocked with chickens, turkeys, swine, sheep, cattle, horses, and ponies, the farm soon becomes an invaluable workshop for scientific research on feed additives and drugs useful to farm animals and household pets. The greenhouse and small field plots at the farm are also used for research on new plant growth regulators and insecticides.

Development of veterinary products follows much the same path as that of medicinals for humans. New compounds from company research programs are given experimental trials at the farm to determine dosages and the best method of administration. Those that pass the early tests go on to more exhaustive clinical trials at veterinary and agricultural colleges and other research farms. After that, they'll await FDA approval before they can be marketed.

Primary emphasis in the agricultural product area is on naturally occurring insecticides and growth promotants that are environmentally safe. One product is a microorganism, *Bacillus thuringiensis,* a fermentation product that kills the larvae of plant pests without leaving a harmful residue. A new strain developed in the early 1980s will control the common mosquito and blackfly. Gibberellic acid, also a fermentation product, will be developed in later years to produce better table grapes, oranges, grapefruit, and cherries. Another growth regulator to come from agricultural research will be *Promalin,* an "apple-stretcher" that makes Red Delicious apples look even better.

TOP: *Abbott acquires a 207-acre farm in Long Grove, Illinois, 17 miles southwest of the North Chicago plant. The farm is still used today, as it was then, as a center for agricultural research.* **CENTER:** *Abbott employees are engaged in sterile solutions finishing.* **BOTTOM:** *Freedom fighters pull down a giant statue of Stalin in Budapest, fueling the fires of the Hungarian revolution.*

Britain's Sir Anthony Eden resigns under a cloud early in the year and is replaced by 62-year-old publisher and statesman Harold Macmillan. Within two months, President Eisenhower and Prime Minister Macmillan meet at Bermuda's Mid-Ocean Club to mend the fences strained by last year's Suez crisis.

The U.S.S.R. launches *Sputnik I,* a 184-pound sphere that is the world's first man-made Earth satellite. One month later, it launches *Sputnik II,* which weighs more than 1,000 pounds and carries a live dog. A giant stride is taken toward promoting the economy of Europe and making it a stronger competitor with the U.S. and Britain as France, Belgium, West Germany, Italy, Luxembourg, and the Netherlands remove mutual tariff barriers and form the Common Market. Britain will try to gain entry in 1963 but will be vetoed by France's President De Gaulle and will have to wait until 1973 when the powerful trading block will expand to include the United Kingdom, Denmark, and Ireland. In China, Mao Tse-tung conceives what he calls a "Great Leap Forward" for half a billion peasants. He guarantees food, clothing, and shelter for them in 24,000 communes, but the "Great Leap" also deprives them of all personal property and causes much hardship and suffering. It will set the country back many years.

In America, former *Collier's* magazine writer Vance Packard projects the insidious idea of subliminal selling in his book *The Hidden Persuaders.* Even that idea isn't enough to help Ford Motor when it launches the Edsel. The product will be discontinued in 1959, at an estimated loss of $350 million, the greatest single-product financial loss in business history.

TOP: *The historic Avre River provides a moment of relaxation for this employee at Abbott's plant in St. Remy, France. Along with new overseas operations in Buenos Aires and Manila, St. Remy helps set the tone for Abbott's new program of worldwide expansion in the late 1950s.* **BOTTOM:** *Mao Tse-tung initiates a program of socioeconomic development known as the "Great Leap Forward." This painting depicts him leading the Chinese peasantry out of poverty.*

This becomes a landmark year for Abbott when sales pass the $100 million mark. Even more remarkable is the sales increase of almost $15 million over last year's total. It is larger than the total increases of the previous five years combined. There is, however, still much room for progress. Of the eight leading drug-making companies — which account for about half the industry's sales — Abbott ranks fifth in volume and sixth in earnings.

Even so, Abbott is truly becoming a worldwide company. With products available in 116 countries through manufacturing plants or sales subsidiaries in 37 key nations, business abroad now accounts for almost one-third of the company's sales. Most significant and largest of the overseas plants is the new facility near Buenos Aires, Argentina, with more than two acres of floor space. Close in importance are new sites in the Philippines; Bogotá, Colombia; and St. Remy, France. The Latin American expansion opens a promising new market for Abbott. Not only is the region relatively untouched by the European pharmaceutical firms, but there is strong evidence that Latin American medical practice is becoming more and more closely integrated with that of the United States.

Closer to home, David M. Kennedy, president of Continental Illinois National Bank and later to be named secretary of the treasury by President Johnson, shatters tradition by becoming the first business leader from outside the company to join the Abbott board.

Christmas dinner in the cafeteria sets another record with more than 3,000 served. This year the menu includes 3,486 pounds of turkey, 900 pounds of potatoes, and 54 gallons of green beans. Employees may wonder why the dinners are always on a Monday, but not so the kitchen staff, who need the weekend to prepare.

The Kremlin's game of musical chairs continues as Nikita Khrushchev replaces Nikolai Bulganin as chairman of the Soviet council only three years after Bulganin replaced Georgi Malenkov, who served only two. The odds on Khrushchev are for a slightly longer term. Egyptian President Gamal Abdal Nasser puts together a union of Egypt and Syria that he calls the United Arab Republic. After a series of UAR-provoked riots in Lebanon, U.S. troops move into Beirut as President Eisenhower vows to protect American lives and property and to defend Lebanese independence. It is an uncanny preview of the action President Reagan will take 24 years later.

In America, a right-wing candy manufacturer named Robert Welch forms a new political group in Massachusetts. He names it in honor of a U.S. Army officer killed by Chinese Communists a week after the end of World War II. It is the John Birch Society. Its first, and most unlikely, target is President Eisenhower, whom it calls a Communist agent. As a first move, it isn't exactly a masterstroke in establishing credibility.

Meanwhile, the median American income is now $5,100, which is almost $2,000 higher than 10 years earlier. But, as usually happens, prices are up, too. A family-size Chevrolet that sold for $1,255 in 1948 is now $2,081. The *New York Times* is up to 5¢, the cost of a year's tuition at Harvard climbs from $455 to $1,250, and the hospital room that used to be $13.09 per day now costs $28.17.

Dr. Volwiler, at age 64, moves up to chairman, and George R. Cain, son of the Abbott president of 11 years earlier, is elected president and general manager. Dr. Volwiler started his 40-year career at Abbott as a senior chemist on a laboratory staff of 6, a staff that has now grown to more than 700. He has become a scientific legend, being awarded the coveted Priestley Medal (the highest award in American chemistry) by the American Chemical Society, the presidency of that same society as well as of the American Drug Manufacturers Association, and eventual appointment by President Eisenhower to the board of the National Science Foundation.

George Cain, on the other hand, comes from a nonscientific background. Educated at Williams College in Massachusetts, he worked half a dozen years as an insurance salesman and a broker before coming up through the ranks of sales and marketing at Abbott. Cain is regarded by his colleagues in the pharmaceutical field as confident, resourceful, and good-humored. He needs every one of those traits in his first year as president. Primarily because of a flu epidemic, Abbott sales nudge up 4.8 percent, but net earnings show only a 1.5 percent gain. Part of the reason for the low return is some gutsy decision-making on Cain's part. He expands the company's research budget by a whopping 18 percent to a record high of $5.6 million, bolsters the research staff by more than 100 people, and awards grants of $300,000 to universities and medical schools to support basic scientific studies. They will prove to be wise moves.

TOP: *A year rich with honors for Dr. Volwiler: soon after receiving the coveted Priestley Medal of the American Chemical Society, he moves from the Abbott presidency to board chairman.* BOTTOM LEFT: *As successor to Dr. Volwiler, George R. Cain brings to the presidency a commitment to maintaining the health of the company and the people it serves.* BOTTOM RIGHT: *Nikita Khrushchev visits England shortly after becoming head of the Soviet Communist state and party.*

Cuba's dictator Fulgencio Batista flees the country after seven years in power as rebel leader Fidel Castro, 32, storms into office. He calls his revolution humanistic, not Communistic. In China, Mao Tse-tung steps down as the country's chairman but remains head of the Chinese Communist party.

The strange birth defect known as phocomelia, in which babies are born with flipperlike stubs instead of normal arms or legs, suddenly appears in a few cases in West Germany. It will later be traced to women's use of thalidomide during pregnancy. In the U.S., the Food and Drug Administration takes two abrupt actions. First, it ruins Thanksgiving for many when it claims that part of the nation's cranberry crop has been contaminated. Then it announces that the poultry industry has voluntarily stopped selling chickens treated with the growth stimulant diethylstilbestrol (DES) after studies have indicated that the hormone causes cancer in test animals. The most promising dietary news of the year comes when the Mead Johnson Company turns a ho-hum hospital product into a tasty weight-reducing agent called Metrecal. It becomes an all-time marketing success.

South Africa decides to ban television, and the decision will remain in effect for the next 16 years. In India, villagers travel hundreds of miles to New Delhi to get their first glimpse of TV. By 1966, television stations will have been built in five of India's major cities, but the populace will be hard-pressed to afford the $425 sets when per capita income is less than $80 per year.

Abbott packaging, letterheads, invoices, and signs are outdated. It is sometimes difficult to tell that they are from the same company. The label design has evolved from the early 1900s when "Abbott" was written in Dr. Abbott's script and a round "Purity-Accuracy Guaranteed" motto was glued atop the cork. In 1932, a new gray-blue label was introduced. It featured an octagon containing the word "Abbott" in a more modern script.

A new Abbott logo is adopted this year. It is inspired by the snake on the staff of Aesculapius, the ancient symbol of medicine, which the designers twist into something resembling a lowercase *A*. The new logo soon appears on stationery, product packaging from labels to corrugate, business cards, annual reports, and paychecks. Employees like the logo, especially when it comes on a bracelet or tiepin with a diamond marking their 25th anniversary with the company.

In a few years, the new logo will have its largest incarnation when the new corporate headquarters at Abbott Park is developed and four nine-foot-high logos are mounted atop a 100-foot pylon that marks the main entrance.

In Columbus, Ohio, M & R Dietetic Laboratories introduces *Similac* with Iron, another significant advance in infant nutrition. It solves the common problem of anemia in infants not receiving mother's milk. This simple idea becomes a major success.

In an inconspicuous corner of a building at the Abbott North Chicago plant, there is another development of great import for the future — the company installs its first mainframe computer, a Burroughs 200.

TOP: *As shown here in a painting by Hans Moller, entitled* Portrait of a Trademark, *the conception of a new logo coincides with Abbott's announcement of its new corporate identity program.* **BOTTOM:** *For two years, before becoming premier of Cuba, Fidel Castro fights as a guerrilla soldier for the overthrow of the Batista dictatorship.*

157

TWENTY-FIFTH ANNIVERSARY ISSUE NUMBER 220 1960

WHAT'S NEW

East-West tension increases as a Soviet ground-to-air missile downs CIA pilot Francis Gary Powers and his U-2 spy plane flying at 65,000 feet over the U.S.S.R. President Eisenhower admits to sending aerial reconnaissance flights over Soviet territory, and Premier Khrushchev promptly cancels the scheduled Paris summit meeting.

Domestic tensions grow in the U.S. as blacks begin a series of sit-downs to protest segregation and voting obstructions. Congress finally passes a Civil Rights Act, but only after a Southern filibuster sets a record of 125½ hours. The power of television is never more evident as debates between Massachusetts Senator John F. Kennedy and Vice President Richard M. Nixon give an edge to Kennedy more by his appearance and manner than by the substance of his logic. Kennedy goes on to defeat Nixon, with a scant margin of 119,000 popular votes out of a total of 69 million.

Two "pills" of immense significance make news as the G. D. Searle company changes America's birth control habits when it introduces Enovid, the first commercially available oral contraceptive. The second pill never quite gets to market as FDA researcher Frances Kelsey delays approval of The Wm. S. Merrell Company's thalidomide. Although the drug is widely used in Britain and West Germany for sleeplessness, tension, and nausea, Kelsey points out that British patients are complaining of numbness in their fingers and toes and that severe birth defects are being reported in West Germany. The thalidomide tragedy will lead to passage of the 1962 Kefauver-Harris amendments to the Food, Drug and Cosmetic Act of 1938.

TOP: *Chicago Convention. Scenes like this are common in the 1960s, as Abbott continues to bolster its sales force.* BOTTOM LEFT: What's New, *the Abbott advertising department's monthly journal for physicians, celebrates its 25th anniversary.* BOTTOM RIGHT: *Primarily because of bad makeup and poor lighting, U.S. Vice President Richard Nixon makes a less favorable impression on the American people than does Senator John F. Kennedy during the nation's first televised presidential debates.*

The rumblings of government intrusion become louder and more pronounced as Senator Estes Kefauver continues his hearings on the pharmaceutical industry. Abbott, as an industry leader, is subpoenaed to submit its records, but the company is never called upon to testify. Even so, Abbott takes a vigorous role in defending the industry against charges that range from price-fixing and profiteering to the claim that "detail men brainwash physicians."

For a start, the company publishes a series of pamphlets that correct allegations made by the Kefauver committee. Then Abbott takes exception to a seven-page feature in *Life* magazine titled "Big Pill Bill to Swallow." The feature cites a product, Temaril, made by an Abbott competitor, Smith, Kline & French Laboratories. George Cain officially protests the inaccuracies, but *Life* refuses to correct them. When S-K-F opts not to become involved, Abbott decides to act. Over a weekend, company officials write a point-by-point refutation of 13 different misstatements in the article, then Abbott spends $32,000 to buy a full-page "paid editorial" in *Life.* The company mails reprints to the nation's physicians and pharmacists, to shareholders, and to members of Congress.

Some druggists pay to reproduce the ad in their local newspapers; others include copies in their billing. George Cain is well pleased with the favorable reception given the editorial, though he terms it "the world's most expensive letter to the editor."

A sad note comes as Abbott loses two former leaders. S. DeWitt Clough, president from 1933 to 1946 and chairman until 1952, dies in January, and six months later he is followed by Raymond E. Horn, president from 1947 to 1950.

159

After Castro seizes American-owned property and business interests, the U.S. imposes an embargo on all Cuban exports and sends a note to the Organization of American States (OAS) charging that Cuba has received substantial arms shipments from the Soviet bloc. Castro then demands that the U.S. embassy staff in Havana be reduced, and Washington closes the embassy and severs all relations. Three months later, the CIA-sponsored Bay of Pigs invasion ends in disaster and embarrassment as 1,600 Cuban exiles are repelled by Castro forces, with heavy loss of life.

Meanwhile, East Germany seals the border as the Berlin Wall stops all movement from East Berlin to West Berlin.

On a more peaceful note, the first manned spaceship circles the earth in April as Soviet cosmonaut Yuri Gagarin makes the orbit in 89 minutes. Three weeks later, Alan B. Shepard, Jr., makes the first U.S. manned space expedition. FCC Chairman Newton Minow calls television "a procession of game shows, violence, formula comedies about totally unbelievable families, blood and thunder, . . . cartoons, and, endlessly, commercials — many screaming, cajoling, and offending." In other words, a "vast wasteland." Finally, a man named Ray Kroc borrows $2.7 million to buy out the McDonald brothers. Over his lifetime, he will parlay his venture into a worldwide hamburger enterprise of more than 7,500 outlets.

This year Abbott repeats the pattern it set the year before: new sales records yet lower earnings. In 1960, competitive reductions in antibiotic prices and higher operating costs squeezed earnings. This year's three percent sales gain is offset by a three percent decrease in earnings — chiefly because of lower vitamin prices and higher administrative costs, including a 12 percent boost in research expenditures.

George Cain decides that it is time to set up a new senior management structure. He wisely perceives that while management's objective in day-to-day decisions is profitable operation, the more important longer-term objective is profitable growth. Cain scraps countless committees, streamlines managerial functions, and cuts the cumbersome relationship that has had nine senior officers reporting to him. He delegates specific and broadened assignments to five vice presidents. Dr. Charles S. Brown, noted as a chemical engineer and production chief, gains added responsibility when he takes charge of all domestic and Canadian operations. Frederick J. Kirchmeyer, whose 22 years with Abbott have encompassed duties ranging from pharmaceutical research to director of new products, heads an expanded product planning and development area. Charles S. Downs, former director of advertising, is put in command of public relations. Paul Gerden, general counsel, is appointed head of administration. And lone newcomer Albert R. Wayne, previously president of Mead Johnson's international division, is charged with strengthening and integrating Abbott International operations.

In another bet on the future, Cain purchases 420 acres of farmland five miles southwest of the North Chicago plant. Through the years, Abbott Park, as the new site is called, will become the company's world headquarters, and the investment there will far exceed that at North Chicago.

TOP: *Alan B. Shepard, Jr., is "packed in" Freedom 7, in preparation for America's first manned suborbital flight.* CENTER: *Abbott President George R. Cain (head of table, right) sets a modern precedent by recruiting board members from outside the company.* BOTTOM: *With the addition of this new research building at North Chicago, Abbott doubles its available research space.*

161

The New York Times.

LATE CITY EDITION

U. S. Weather Bureau Report (Page 91) forecast:
Partly cloudy, breezy, and today.
Fair and cool tonight and tomorrow.
Temp. range: 54—45; yesterday: 66—44.

VOL. CXII.. No. 38,258. © 1962 by The New York Times Company. Times Square, New York 36, N. Y. NEW YORK, TUESDAY, OCTOBER 23, 1962. FIVE CENTS

U.S. IMPOSES ARMS BLOCKADE ON CUBA ON FINDING OFFENSIVE-MISSILE SITES; KENNEDY READY FOR SOVIET SHOWDOWN

U. S. JUDGES GIVEN POWER TO REQUIRE VOTE FOR NEGROES

High Court Upholds Order Forcing the Registration of 54 in Alabama County

Special to The New York Times

WASHINGTON, Oct. 22 — The Supreme Court held today that Federal judges have the power to make state registrars put specific Negroes on the voting rolls.

Alabama had challenged an order by Federal District Judge Frank M. Johnson Jr. requiring the registration of 54 specific Negroes in Macon County, Ala.

Chinese Open New Front; Use Tanks Against Indians

Nehru Warns of Peril to Independence —Reds Attack Near Burmese Border and Press Two Other Drives

NEW DELHI, Oct. 22 — Prime Minister Jawaharlal Nehru told the people of India tonight that the time has come for us to realize fully this grave warning followed word that the advancing Chinese had opened a third front in the Himalayas, near the Burma border, and had used tanks for the first time. Five more Indian posts fell to the Chinese.

"The time has come," he said "for us to realize fully this menace that threatens the freedom of our people and the independence of our country."

Prime Minister Nehru said India would not abandon her economic development program and policy of nonalignment with international blocs, but rallied the nation to switch "from peacetime to those which prospering the slow-moving methods."

Excerpts from Nehru's speech will be found on Page 2.

SHIPS MUST STOP

Other Action Planned If Big Rockets Are Not Dismantled

By JAMES RESTON
Special to The New York Times

WASHINGTON, Oct. 22 — President Kennedy drew the line tonight, not with Cuba, but with the Soviet Union. After almost a generation of trying to keep the "cold war" from reaching a direct confrontation between United States and Soviet power, a decision has been made to force Soviet missile bases from this hemisphere at the risk of war.

This is the official interpretation of President Kennedy's speech tonight, and the orders

PRESIDENT GRAVE

Asserts Russians Lied and Put Hemisphere in Great Danger

Text of the President's address is printed on Page 6.

By ANTHONY LEWIS
Special to The New York Times

WASHINGTON, Oct. 22 — President Kennedy imposed a naval and air "quarantine" tonight on the movement of offensive military equipment to Cuba.

In a speech of extraordinary gravity, he told the American people that the Soviet Union, contrary to promises, was building offensive missile and bomber bases in Cuba. He said the

The Cold War heats up to the boiling point when U.S. air surveillance discovers a string of Soviet offensive missile and bomber bases in Cuba. President Kennedy immediately orders an air and sea blockade, sealing off the island to prevent further arms shipments to Castro. The tension eases one week later when Khrushchev agrees to dismantle and remove the Cuban missile sites and the U.S. reciprocates by lifting the quarantine and quietly removing its missiles from Turkey.

Half a world away, America sends money, arms, and the first ground forces to help South Vietnamese forces launch Operation Sunrise, which is intended to deprive Vietcong guerrillas of the support of the peasantry. The move becomes the first step in escalating an Asian civil war into a full-fledged American military action. The International Control Commission, established in 1954 to supervise implementation of the Geneva Accords, accuses North Vietnam, South Vietnam, and the U.S. of violating the agreement.

Back in the United States, former Vice President Richard Nixon, losing his bid to unseat California Governor Edmund G. Brown, tells the press, "Just think how much you're going to be missing; you won't have Nixon to kick around anymore because, gentlemen, this is my last press conference."

Elsewhere in the country, a pudgy former Ohio State golfer named Jack William Nicklaus draws boos when he defeats America's idol, Arnold Palmer, in a playoff for the U.S. Open. And three baseball teams — the New York Mets, Houston Colts, and Los Angeles Dodgers — all play their first season in new homes.

Cain's series of strategic moves in 1961 pay off handsomely in 1962. Sales increase over $14 million to top $144 million, and earnings per share rise 22 percent, the largest gain in the last 16 years.

Heartening as the financial news is, it is tempered by the thought that tougher times lie ahead with Congressional passage of the new, more restrictive drug regulations. A result of the Kefauver hearings, the legislation is a mixed bag for pharmaceutical firms. Abbott, for one, applauds those parts of the amendments that tighten controls to assure safe and effective drugs. Other parts, however, already indicate they could slow the pace, multiply the paperwork, and increase the costs of drug discovery. The overall concern is that the regulations, under the guise of public interest, will stifle rather than aid medical progress.

The *Value Line,* an independent investment analysis service, weighs the effect of this new legislation on industry and comes out with a bullish report on Abbott. Its survey ranks company shares as "above average" for year-ahead market performance and "highest" for five-year growth potential. "Heavy research outlays of recent years are on the verge of bearing fruit in immediate and long-term growth for Abbott," says *Value Line.* "By any reasonable criteria most drug equities are priced much too high. The thesis that they are all growth stocks in perpetuity has been punctured by competition, the Kefauver hearings, and a slowdown in earnings growth. Only one issue, Abbott Laboratories, is ranked favorably — both for probable market performance in the coming 12 months and for appreciation potential over the 3-to-5-year pull."

TOP: *Abbott Laboratories, Ltd., of England, begins operations at its new plant in Queenborough, Kent. Containing a quarter million square feet of manufacturing space, this plant will help Abbott compete intensively in the English market and will pave the way for participation in the fast-growing European market.* BOTTOM: *Headlines of the* New York Times *set the scene for the tense Cuban missile crisis.*

The November assassination of President John F. Kennedy in Dallas shocks the nation and the world and ends an administration of 34 months that has pledged many domestic programs. Kennedy's assassin is 24-year-old Lee Harvey Oswald, a former Marine sharpshooter who has spent time in the U.S.S.R. and is married to a Russian citizen. Oswald is gunned down two days later in the Dallas jail by nightclub operator Jack Ruby, who is sentenced to death but will live until 1967, when he dies of natural causes.

In June, NAACP leader Medgar Evers is murdered. Shortly thereafter, 200,000 blacks march on Washington to demonstrate support for civil rights, where Martin Luther King, Jr., commemorates the centennial of the Emancipation Proclamation by saying, "I have a dream . . . a dream that one day, on the red hills of Georgia, sons of former slaves and sons of former slaveowners will be able to sit down together at the table of brotherhood."

Britain also has its problems. British journalist H. A. R. Philby disappears from Beirut and the Soviet Union gives him asylum. But this is nothing compared to the scandal created by War Secretary John Profumo and call girl Christine Keeler, who, it is discovered, is passing along nuclear secrets to a Soviet spy. The English are only slightly cheered when a long-haired Liverpool rock group called The Beatles introduces its first worldwide success, something called "I Want to Hold Your Hand."

It may have begun on the golf course at Old Elm Club when George Cain asked his close friend, Jack Searle, what he might think of the idea of putting their two companies together. Startling as it sounds, the idea of merging Abbott Laboratories and G. D. Searle & Co. has intriguing possibilities. For one thing, the fit is almost perfect. Both began in the same year, 1888. Searle had bought the old Abbott plant in Ravenswood in 1925. Both went on to become eminently successful and, more recently, both bought adjacent tracts of land for expansion in Lake County. Their one point of departure: while both companies had offered a pre-World War I catalog of several hundred products, the Searle line was slashed mercilessly during the Great Depression to eliminate everything but specialties developed in its own laboratories — leaving one of the shortest, but most profitable, product lines in the industry. Searle's best-known products are Enovid, an oral contraceptive; Pro-Banthine for stomach ulcers; and Dramamine for motion sickness.

In late July, boards of the two companies agree on a financial plan for merger. The new name is to be Abbott-Searle, Inc., with Jack Searle as chairman and George Cain as president and chief executive officer. Meshing product lines is next and that is no problem; there are few competitive products. Finally comes the jigsaw of trying to fit people from two organizations into one combined operation. After 10 weeks of almost day-to-day negotiations, the problems can't be solved, and the companies break the engagement.

The merger that "might have been" paves the way for another that goes on to become one of the all-time classic success stories in the industry.

TOP LEFT: *The 200,000,000th I.V. bottle rolls off the production line and is preserved for posterity.* TOP RIGHT: *To commemorate the occasion, Herbert S. Wilkinson (right), vice president of pharmaceutical sales, presents the bottle to Abbott President George R. Cain.* BOTTOM: *Amid national and worldwide mourning, the body of President John F. Kennedy lies in state in the rotunda of the U.S. Capitol.*

165

President Johnson wins a landslide re-election with the largest plurality in U.S. history when he gets 61.1 percent of the popular vote and a 486-52 majority in electoral votes over Arizona's ultraconservative Barry Goldwater. Two other world powers change leaders: A Soviet coup d'état strips Nikita Khrushchev of all power and he is succeeded by Leonid Brezhnev as first secretary and Aleksei Kosygin as premier. In Britain, the Labour Party takes over as Harold Wilson replaces Sir Alec Douglas-Home and begins a prime ministry that will last until 1970.

One of the world's worst earthquakes, with a Richter scale rating of 8.6, rocks Alaska and creates devastating seismic tidal waves that hit the coasts of Alaska, Oregon, and California.

The U.S. Congress authorizes President Johnson "to take all necessary measures to repel any armed attack against the forces of the United States and to prevent further aggression" after three North Vietnamese PT boats fire torpedoes at an American destroyer in the international waters of the Gulf of Tonkin. Three days after the attack, American aircraft bomb North Vietnamese installations and naval craft. Further retaliation comes when a vast increase in U.S. aid to South Vietnam is announced. A secret memo from Assistant Secretary of Defense John McNaughton puts it all in perspective. The U.S. objective in Vietnam, he says, is not to "help a friend" but to avoid humiliation.

With the proposed Searle merger off, Abbott resumes negotiations with M & R Dietetic Laboratories of Columbus, Ohio. The two companies had been close to agreement in 1963 when talks were suspended by the Searle situation. A special shareholders' meeting in February approves the exchange of 365,000 Abbott shares worth $42.2 million for M & R. With the merger, Richard M. Ross, president of M & R, becomes the largest individual Abbott shareholder. He is elected to the Abbott board and continues as president of the new Ross Laboratories division of Abbott. For Abbott, the merger is a major diversification in pediatric and grocery products with *Similac,* the nation's best-selling infant formula, and *Pream,* the widely used powdered coffee creamer. For Ross, it deepens leadership in domestic markets and makes possible more widespread distribution overseas through Abbott's worldwide organizations. For shareholders, it seems to be, in baseball parlance, the perfect trade. Everybody wins and nobody loses.

At the end of 1963, Abbott shares hit an all-time high of 124 — a gain of 47½ points over the last 12 months. It is a remarkable market performance for Abbott and leads to a three-for-one stock split in April. This means that the venturesome investor who risked $3,725 for 100 shares of Abbott in 1929 gets enough dividends in 1964 to cover his original investment, plus $288. His total dividends over the span of those years add up to $69,000, and his original 100 shares have now multiplied to 5,016 shares, with a market value of $235,000.

TOP: *This colorful cityscape, entitled* Abbott City *(oil, 36" × 48"), was painted by Franklin McMahon. Depicting more than 50 Abbott buildings from around the world, the painting symbolizes the company's global expansion.* **BOTTOM:** *The mid-1960s mark the beginning of Beatlemania, as a young "mop-haired" rock group emerges from the cellar clubs of Liverpool, England, to take the music world by storm.*

In mid-1965, President Johnson authorizes the first full-scale combat offensive in Vietnam. A month later, 125,000 U.S. troops are there and the president announces a doubling of the draft call. "I have asked the commanding general, General Westmoreland, what more he needs to meet this mounting aggression," he says. "We will meet his needs . . . We will stand in Vietnam."

In the United States, civil rights demonstrations have become more violent. In Selma, Alabama, Martin Luther King, Jr., and 763 others are arrested for protesting discrimination against black voter registration. Former Black Muslim leader Malcolm X is fatally shot as he prepares to address a Sunday afternoon audience in New York City on the need for blacks and whites to coexist peacefully. The Watts section of Los Angeles erupts in bloody race riots as 10,000 blacks burn and loot an area of 150 square blocks, destroying $40 million in property and ruining more than 200 businesses.

Elsewhere in the news, the miniskirt designed by Mary Quant at a provocative two inches above the knee draws whistles at its first appearance in London. And a rock group called The Warlocks experiments in San Francisco with LSD and multimedia electronic events. Next year, under the leadership of guitarist Jerry Garcia, the band will explode on the music scene with a new name, The Grateful Dead.

This is a year of building for Abbott . . . not only in bricks and mortar but in strength of the overseas operation and the management team at home.

A strong harbinger of growth is the work under way at Abbott Park. Now ready to be occupied are three structures for vaccine development as well as a seven-acre warehouse, power plant, and radiopharmaceutical research and production center that replaces the old Oak Ridge plant. Still in the planning stage are a new administration headquarters plus a three-building research complex that includes a three-story unit for pharmacology, pathology, and toxicology; a large single-story animal care building; and a research administrative unit. Eventually, Abbott Park will house over 4,000 employees in more than 2.9 million square feet of floor space. In Columbus, the Ross division begins construction of a $3.25 million technical center with a 60,000-square-foot, five-story laboratory and office building and a two-story pilot plant.

Overseas, Abbott strengthens its position in the huge Japanese market by forming Nippon-Abbott K.K. to market Abbott pharmaceutical products in Japan. It is the company's second joint venture with Dainippon Pharmaceutical Co., Ltd., of Osaka. First was the Dainabot Radioisotope Laboratories, Ltd., formed in 1962 to manufacture radiopharmaceuticals. Abbott bolsters its place in the competitive German market when it forms Deutsche-Abbott GmbH in cooperation with C. H. Boehringer Sohn, a leading German drug manufacturer.

Finally, Abbott strengthens its management structure when Dr. Charles S. Brown is promoted to executive vice president and Edward J. Ledder, vice president of pharmaceutical marketing, is elected to the board and the operations committee. With long, productive Abbott careers already behind them, both will figure even more prominently in the years ahead.

TOP: *By 1965, construction of Abbott Park is well under way, as seen in this aerial photo looking northeast.* BOTTOM LEFT: *In the early 1960s,* What's New, *long touted by critics as a first in medical journalism, gives way to* Abbottempo, *whose focus as an international medical quarterly accommodates a growing trend toward a worldwide exchange of ideas.* BOTTOM RIGHT: *Black activist Malcolm X predicts in his autobiography that he won't live to see the book published. Ironically,* The Autobiography of Malcolm X *appears in print not long after his assassination in New York City.*

ABBOTTEMPO

a 1965/3

Targets in the Hanoi area of North Vietnam are being bombed incessantly by U.S. planes, and by year's end, nearly 280,000 U.S. troops are stationed in South Vietnam. The buildup continues as President Johnson tours New Zealand, Australia, Malaysia, and South Korea, and attends a seven-nation Vietnam conference in the Philippines. Pope Paul VI issues an encyclical asking for an end to hostilities, and Senator J. W. Fulbright challenges the legality of American intervention in Vietnam.

The worst famine in 22 years sweeps across India. The U.S. sends 8.3 million tons of food grains to the hunger-ridden nation. The airlift is the brainchild of North Carolina Democratic Representative Harold Cooley, who says it will "show to the world the great heart of America."

In the U.S., Massachusetts voters elect the first black senator since Reconstruction, Edward Brooke. Within a year, Thurgood Marshall will be sworn in as the first black Supreme Court justice and Carl Stokes (Cleveland) and Richard Hatcher (Gary, Indiana) will be elected the first black mayors of major cities. Finally, five years after TWA boss Howard Hughes lost control of his own airline, he sells off his stock at an inflated $86 a share, pockets the $546 million profit, and moves on to Las Vegas to become the world's richest recluse.

With Abbott expanding rapidly, George Cain continues to juggle the lineup of his top management team. Much like a baseball manager trying to find the right combination, he shuffles different men to different positions. He names three new executive vice presidents to join Chuck Brown, who becomes head of scientific and manufacturing operations, as his four-man cabinet. Ted Ledder draws the heaviest responsibility: the Ross division, grocery products, and a reorganized radiopharmaceutical operation, as well as pharmaceuticals. Albert R. Wayne is named executive vice president for Abbott International and Paul Gerden is put in charge of administrative activities. With these moves, Cain believes he has the management he needs to give close direction to all areas of the changing company.

Abbott business is now concentrated in five distinct areas — professional pharmaceuticals, hospital products and services, pediatric products, consumer and industrial brands, and the international division. Pharmaceuticals and hospital products continue to be the cornerstone, but the fastest-growing segment is international, up 76 percent over the last five years. The "sleeper" is the radiopharmaceutical business, which will eventually develop into the dynamic, market-leading diagnostics division.

Before the year is out, one more division will be added to Ledder's charge. Abbott acquires the Faultless Rubber Company of Ashland, Ohio, in exchange for 110,000 Abbott shares worth about $4 million. Faultless makes a broad line of drugstore and hospital products, including household gloves, hot water bottles, ice caps, ostomy appliances, surgical gloves, catheters, and disposable surgical supplies. Virtually ignored as a throw-in to the deal is an idea that's ahead of its time: a cutproof golf ball.

TOP: *Richard M. Ross (right), president of the Ross Laboratories division of Abbott, looks on as Governor James A. Rhodes snips the ribbon to officially open the new $3.3 million technical center (*BOTTOM LEFT*) in Columbus, Ohio.* BOTTOM RIGHT: *Tactical transport helicopters shuttle troops of the 2nd Battalion during an assault near Bong Son, South Vietnam.*

U.S. public sentiment grows stronger against the war in Vietnam and the draft at home as more troops are shipped overseas and casualties mount alarmingly. Demonstrations across the country bring out college students, women's groups, and scientists in protest against the use of napalm and the escalating U.S. involvement.

In South America, Ernesto "Che" Guevara, who helped Fidel and Raúl Castro oust the Batista regime from Cuba in the 1950s, is killed by Bolivian troops. In the Middle East, the six-day Arab-Israeli war finds Israel wiping out Syrian and Egyptian forces and expanding its territory by occupying Arab Jerusalem and claiming the strategic Golan Heights and the West Bank of the Jordan. The UN asks Israel to rescind its claims and the Soviet Union severs diplomatic relations, but neither action is enough to persuade the Israelis.

The Doctor's Quick Weight Loss Diet by Brooklyn physician Irwin Stillman urges readers to drink eight 10-ounce glasses of water a day in combination with a high-protein diet to lose 7 to 15 pounds a week, while another doctor faces fraud charges for claiming that safflower oil softens and helps eliminate body fat. One legitimate breakthrough comes in Capetown, South Africa, as surgeon Christiaan Barnard performs the first human heart transplant. His patient survives 18 days.

George Cain phrased it well when he said: "This company must be built around the individual. Ideas must come from individuals who refuse to be discouraged by corporate size and organizational bric-a-brac. The contributions of the scientific man, the uncommon man, the man with a sense of urgency — these are the keystones of our future."

Cain completes his search for "the uncommon man, the man with a sense of urgency" when he names Ted Ledder president, while Cain continues on as chairman and chief executive. Ledder is a kind of modern-day Horatio Alger at Abbott, having started in 1939 as a 47¢-an-hour wage worker on a production line and then scaling virtually every rung in the corporate ladder. On his return from sea duty in World War II, Ledder became an assistant manager of pricing. His next move was to rotation training in production planning. By 1954, his talents were recognized by Herb Wilkinson, sales vice president, who moved him into sales to head up all sample programs. From there, Ledder rose rapidly and was named assistant director of sales in 1960. He became first director of Abbott pharmaceutical marketing a year later, was named vice president of pharmaceutical marketing in 1963, was elected to the board in 1965, and became an executive VP in 1966.

The company celebrates a parallel climb when sales top $300 million this year. Looking back, it took Abbott 69 years to become a $100 million company, 7 more years to hit the $200 million mark, and then only 3 more years to make the $300 million level. For Abbott, as well as its new president, the start was slow but the rate of acceleration fast.

Products are donated by Abbott to help relieve pain and suffering during the Vietnam War. Here a corpsman dresses burns with Butesin *for a Vietnamese villager left homeless after fire destroys her refugee camp.*

The massive Communist Tet offensive comes to South Vietnam in late January as North Vietnamese army and Vietcong forces attack Saigon, Hué, and more than 100 other cities and towns. The bad news will continue into next year when word finally leaks out of the My Lai village massacre that takes place this March. North Korea seizes the spy ship USS *Pueblo* and interns Commander Lloyd Bucher and his 83-man crew for 11 months.

Growing opposition to the Vietnam War enables Senator Eugene McCarthy of Minnesota to make such a strong showing in the New Hampshire primary that President Johnson announces he will not seek reelection. Senator Robert Kennedy jumps into the presidential race and wins several primaries before he is assassinated in a Los Angeles hotel by Jordanian Sirhan Sirhan. In April, Martin Luther King, Jr., steps out on the balcony of his Memphis motel and is slain by a sniper. In Chicago, Mayor Richard Daley gives police "shoot to kill" orders to put down the resulting rioting. The Democratic party convention in Chicago is marked by bloody police confrontations with 10,000 antiwar demonstrators.

The Democrats nominate Hubert Humphrey to succeed President Johnson, and former Vice President Richard Nixon wins a first-ballot Republican nomination over New York's Governor Nelson Rockefeller. Nixon wins the election by a margin only slightly greater than in his 1960 loss to John Kennedy — 510,000 votes out of 70 million cast.

TOP LEFT: *Following this demonstration by black sanitation workers in Memphis, Tennessee, Martin Luther King, Jr. (front right), is assassinated on the balcony of his Memphis motel.* TOP RIGHT: *Looking down into a 35,000 gallon fermenter gives one a unique feel for its enormous capacity and size. Fermenters like this are used for producing such Abbott products as* Erythrocin, Pro-Gibb, *and* Dipel. BOTTOM: *The entire R&D staff gathers for a group photo outside the old research building at North Chicago.*

The metamorphosis of Abbott becomes complete this year. From a traditional ethical pharmaceutical house, the company has broadened its focus to a much wider view of health care. The "new" Abbott emerges as a diversified company with six distinct operating divisions: pharmaceuticals, hospital products, international, Ross Laboratories, group operations, and consumer products. Each division operates as a separate profit center, with its own staff for research, manufacturing, and marketing. More deliberate than unique is the simple fact that each division can now be gauged precisely for its contribution to the bottom line.

For the financial community, there is little question that the portfolio of businesses that make up Abbott make good sense. "We are carving out a new direction," says Chairman George Cain, "and already investment firms are beginning to recognize and reassess Abbott in a different light."

One fascinating new direction comes when Abbott enters the golf business. As far back as 1923, T. W. Miller, Sr., founder of Faultless Rubber, filed specifications for a one-piece golf ball compounded of rubber, zinc oxide, sulfur, and glue. After vulcanizing his golf ball in registering molds to form the dimples, Miller would remove the selvage at the equator of the ball, boil it clean, dip it in a solvent of balata and gutta-percha, and then lacquer it. Thus was born a solid golf ball that, in the early days, might break into chunks on impact. Now, 45 years later, endless laboratory refinements have made the Faultless ball a playable property. That fact is amply illustrated when U.S. Open golf champion Lee Trevino, signing his first professional contract with Faultless, says: "Endorse it? Hell, man, I *play* it!" The golf business will be sold in 1972 as part of a strategy to concentrate on health-care products.

175

Expanded Vietnam peace talks begin early in the year as U.S. troop strength in South Vietnam peaks at 539,000 by February. In June, President Nixon meets with South Vietnam's President Thieu at Midway Island and announces the start of U.S. troop withdrawal, but the last American soldiers won't leave until the cease-fire in 1973. North Vietnamese leader Ho Chi Minh dies in September at age 79 after 15 years as president.

In the United States, headlines of startling significance come within a two-day period in late July. First the bad news: A car driven by Senator Edward Kennedy plunges off a bridge into a tidal pond on Chappaquiddick Island off Martha's Vineyard, Massachusetts. The body of Mary Jo Kopechne, a 28-year-old secretary, is found drowned in the car the next day. Kennedy fails to report the accident to police for 10 hours. More heartening is the news that man walks on the moon for the first time when U.S. astronaut Neil Armstrong steps out of the lunar module from *Apollo 11* and is joined by Edwin "Buzz" Aldrin. "It's one small step for a man, one giant leap for mankind" is the message that signals their historic landing.

"Sesame Street" raises the learning curve of American preschool children when its first program begins on public television, and "Doonesbury," by cartoonist Garry Trudeau, does the same thing for adults when it appears in the *Yale Daily News.* Six years later, it will go on to win the Pulitzer prize. Throughout America, the economy struggles through the worst inflation in 19 years as consumer prices register their sharpest annual increase since the Korean War year of 1951.

TOP LEFT: *An Abbott production worker inspects a tray of* Butterfly *infusion sets. The lightweight, disposable infusion sets replace the older, more cumbersome infusion apparatus.* TOP RIGHT: *Abbott expresses its strong commitment to education by sending personnel into local schools to lecture on drug use, careers, and other important topics.* BOTTOM: *The crew of America's* Apollo 11 *set up shop during the world's first lunar landing.*

Late in the year, Abbott acquires the Murine Company of Chicago and its three well-established products: *Murine* eye drops, *Lensine* contact lens solution, and *Clear Eyes* decongestant. The deal is consummated for 171,000 Abbott shares worth $13.2 million.

Dick Ross retires as president of the Ross Laboratories division, although he stays on as a member of the Abbott board of directors. He started with M & R Dietetic Laboratories in 1938, became general manager in 1946 and president in 1963, and was named president of the new Ross division upon M & R's merger with Abbott in 1964. The new president of Ross is the dynamic Dave Cox, who joined M & R in 1938 as a salesman in Detroit. Cox worked in sales in Cleveland before being brought into the home office as sales manager in 1948.

In October, a study being conducted for Abbott in New York detects an abnormal incidence of bladder tumors in rats being experimentally fed massive doses of cyclamate sweetener over a long term. The dosage used on the rats is so large that it would be equivalent to an average-sized person swallowing 3,500 *Sucaryl* tablets a day for life. Abbott immediately shows the findings to officials at the FDA, HEW, and the National Cancer Institute. Government authorities announce, "We have absolutely no evidence at this point that cyclamates can cause cancer in humans, or that there is any connection between this laboratory experiment and bladder tumors in humans. Even so, we have no recourse but to restrict their use." So, cyclamate-sweetened *Sucaryl* stays on the market as a drug, to be used only by those with a medical need or on the advice of a physician. The situation will go on to become a bureaucratic nightmare for Abbott.

177

In the Middle East, Israeli jets raid Cairo suburbs in January and commandos strike within 40 miles of the Egyptian capital. The Soviet press agency Tass issues a statement pledging "necessary support" to the Arab nations, five of which meet in Cairo and vow to continue fighting to recover the territory occupied by Israel since the 1967 conflict. A fragile cease-fire between Egypt and Israel goes into effect in early August and will be more or less observed from then until Yom Kippur 1973. In September, Egypt's President Nasser dies and is replaced by his good friend Anwar al-Sadat.

In the U.S., the turbulence of campus protests against the war in Vietnam reaches its zenith when University of Wisconsin students, protesting the university's participation in war research, blow up a campus laboratory, killing a graduate student and injuring four others. In Ohio, 1,000 Kent State University students rally and are fired upon by National Guardsmen. Four students are killed and 11 others are wounded. As a result, more than 400 colleges and universities across the nation close down in anti-war protest, and in Washington, nearly 100,000 demonstrators mass around the White House and other government buildings in peaceful protest. President Nixon, unable to sleep, drives to the site of one vigil at the Lincoln Memorial before dawn to talk with the dissidents.

Cyclamates are forced into a hiatus when an FDA ruling in August bans the sweetening agent. The FDA action is based on the Delaney Amendment to the Food Additive Laws, which says that any additive implicated with a higher-than-normal incidence of tumors when fed to man or laboratory animal must be withdrawn from the market. The edict is questionable, particularly when it is well known that Abbott has conducted research on the safety of cyclamates for more than 25 years with no adverse effects seen. Also unusual is the report by the *New York Times* that sugar interests have spent more than $500,000 on research over the past five years trying to find something wrong with cyclamates. The research director of the sugar interests' foundation is quoted as saying candidly, "We are funding research on cyclamates because if anyone can undersell you nine cents out of ten, you'd better find some brickbat to throw at him."

Chairman George Cain achieves an almost total restructuring of his board of directors. The "in-house" board that Cain inherited in 1958 had only two people from outside Abbott. Cain adds Alexander Hood, senior director of J. Henry Schroder Wagg, merchant bankers of London; Dr. Emanuel Papper, dean of the School of Medicine at the University of Miami; Boone Powell, vice president of Baylor University; Leo Schoenhofen, president of Marcor; and James Beré, president of Borg-Warner. With carryovers James Allen, chairman of Booz-Allen & Hamilton, Inc.; Donald Graham, chairman of Continental Illinois National Bank; Arthur Rasmussen, president of Household Finance Corporation; Gilbert Scribner, Jr., president of Scribner & Co.; and Irving Seaman, Jr., CEO of National Boulevard Bank, Cain accomplishes a long-time goal: 10 of 14 directors come from outside Abbott, and he has bolstered considerably the advice available to him.

TOP LEFT: *Nearly 100,000 students mass in Washington, D.C., to protest the Vietnam War.* TOP RIGHT: *On America's first "Earth Day" (April 22, 1970), University of Illinois medical and pharmacy students visit Abbott to express their views on pollution.* BOTTOM: *Expansion of the waste treatment plant at North Chicago is a key component in Abbott's ongoing wastewater treatment program.*

179

The year sees "a new economic policy" for the U.S. as President Nixon imposes a 90-day freeze on prices and wages, suspends conversion of dollars into gold, and invokes a 10 percent import surcharge in an effort to put an end to spiraling inflation and unemployment rates. Wall Street responds to the president's message with enthusiasm as the Dow-Jones industrial average leaps 32.93 points, its best one-day gain to date.

The Pentagon Papers become a cause célèbre by giving inside details of American involvement in Vietnam. The highly classified 47-volume Defense Department study was leaked to the *New York Times* by former defense employee Daniel Ellsberg, who is later indicted for theft of government property. The John F. Kennedy Center for the Performing Arts opens in Washington, D.C., with a performance of Leonard Bernstein's new *Mass.*

Western relations with China improve as the People's Republic is admitted to the UN, Canada and China exchange diplomatic envoys, and Henry Kissinger secretly visits the Asian nation to prepare for President Nixon's upcoming visit.

The U.S. Food and Drug Administration advises Americans to stop eating swordfish because of its high mercury content. While the FDA says 87 percent of the samples it's tested have levels above safe limits, New York State researchers counter that mercury levels in preserved 43-year-old fish are twice as high as current levels. Another cause for concern comes when botulism in a can of Bon Vivant vichyssoise kills a New York man. The FDA shuts down the plant, and the company files for reorganization under Chapter 11 of the Bankruptcy Act.

TOP: *Abbott announces plans for expanding its two plants in Rocky Mount, North Carolina. The plant shown here went into production late in 1968.* **BOTTOM LEFT:** *Abbott employees raise the flag for ecology, marking completion of the company's multimillion-dollar antipollution program.* **BOTTOM RIGHT:** *Zero Mostel plays the charming character of Tevye in* Fiddler on the Roof, *Broadway's longest-running musical to date.*

Some of the traumas of earlier years pale by comparison in mid-March when Abbott suspends all shipments of I.V. solutions and begins a massive recall from the nation's hospitals. Earlier in the month, eight hospitals had reported cases of septicemic blood infections believed to have come from contamination of the cap liner on solutions bottles. Although government agencies stress that the unopened solutions are sterile, they believe the possibility exists of transfer of bacteria from the cap into the solution when the cap is opened, then put back on. Virtually overnight, the company's share of the nation's solutions business drops from 45 percent to zero.

As the largest producer of vital hospital solutions, Abbott recognizes the need to reenter the market as quickly as possible. Within two weeks, President Ted Ledder negotiates an agreement with Cutter Laboratories of Berkeley, California, to convert Abbott production facilities from the screw-cap closure used for more than 35 years to Cutter's vacuum rubber stopper. By mid-April, developmental production using the new closure begins at Abbott plants at North Chicago and Rocky Mount, North Carolina. In June, the FDA approves the Rocky Mount plant, and by the end of July, both plants are back in production. Recalling the start-up toward producing a full line of products again, President Ledder says, "We started distribution with a limited line of key products, but we're now producing a line which meets more than 90 percent of a hospital's needs."

The impact of the I.V. problem on 1971 earnings amounts to a whopping $19 million before taxes, or 70¢ per common share after taxes. But by year's end, Abbott signs contracts and makes shipments to hospitals that equal 57 percent of the company's former volume, with a production of more than 15 million bottles. It is a tremendously costly but incredibly strong start toward recovery.

181

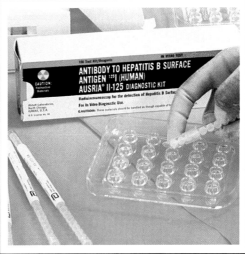

Early in the year, President Nixon, on what he calls "a journey for peace," meets with Chairman Mao Tse-tung and Premier Chou En-lai in Peking, ending a U.S. hostility toward the People's Republic of China that has persisted since 1949. A few months later, Nixon confers with General Secretary Leonid Brezhnev in the first visit of a U.S. president to the Soviet Union. The week of summit talks with Kremlin leaders culminates in a landmark strategic arms pact.

The greatest constitutional crisis in U.S. history has its beginnings in the postmidnight hours of June 17 when five men are arrested inside the Democratic national headquarters in Washington's Watergate office complex. John Mitchell, President Nixon's campaign manager, says the men were not "operating either on our behalf or with our consent." But *Washington Post* reporters Carl Bernstein and Bob Woodward, working 12 hours a day and seven days a week, begin to crack the Watergate affair. In October they report that the Watergate break-in was just one incident in an extensive espionage and sabotage campaign to promote President Nixon's reelection.

Senator George McGovern of South Dakota gets the Democratic nomination for the presidency over Maine Senator Edmund Muskie, who earlier had been even with President Nixon in opinion polls. President Nixon, despite gossip about Watergate, gives the Democrats one of their worst defeats in history when he carries every state except Massachusetts.

At midyear, Abbott and the industry are shocked by the untimely death of George Cain, who has been chairman of the board for the past 10 years. Cain served as president from 1958 to 1967 and saw Abbott sales almost triple to $303 million during his tenure. His proudest accomplishment probably came from the task he completed in 1970, strengthening the Abbott board with a group of professional and scientific leaders to help guide the company through its surging growth.

Two other key decisions of Cain's also have had long-lasting effects for Abbott. When he became president in 1958, Abbott expenditures for research and development were $5.6 million — a somewhat slim 4.8 percent of sales. Through each of the following years, Cain prodded the R&D budget to higher and higher levels, until it reached $31.2 million this year — almost six times the earlier rate.

His other key move demonstrated Cain's canny and consistent knack for picking the right man for the job. This time it was choosing his own successor as president in 1967. The combination of Cain and Ted Ledder became one of those rare managerial parlays that combine the vision and foresight of one man with the other's hardworking, shirt-sleeved pragmatism. It brought a remarkable synergism, and outstanding operating results, to Abbott.

The months that follow George Cain's death are demanding for Ledder, who is caught up in the uphill climb of the I.V. recovery. It is a time for belt-tightening, a time for controlling every facet of costs, and Ledder does this with vigor. Early proof of his leadership comes as Abbott sales break the half-billion-dollar mark and three major new products are introduced: *Tranxene,* a tranquilizer; *Ausria,* a radioimmunoassay test to detect serum hepatitis; and the *ABA-100* blood chemistry analyzer. The journey on the long road back has begun.

Two new Abbott diagnostic systems are introduced — ABA-100 (TOP) and Ausria (BOTTOM RIGHT). Both are cornerstones in the company's effort to become a major factor in the diagnostics business. BOTTOM LEFT: While making diplomatic history with visits to Moscow and China, President Nixon gets a firsthand look at China's Great Wall.

183

For Americans, 1973 is a year of upsets and upheavals. Oil-producing Arab nations cut off shipments, and the energy crisis and soaring grain prices precipitate the worst economic recession paired with the worst inflation in many years. President Nixon announces "major developments" in the Watergate case as his aides, H. R. Haldeman and John Ehrlichman, resign under pressure. Presidential counsel John Dean implicates other Nixon intimates in testimony before a Senate investigating committee. Vice President Spiro Agnew pleads no contest to charges of income tax evasion and is replaced by House Republican leader Gerald Ford.

Attorney General-Designate Elliott Richardson appoints Harvard Law School professor Archibald Cox as special Watergate prosecutor, but President Nixon fires Cox when he insists that the president turn over tape recordings of his White House conversations with his aides relevant to the Watergate break-in. Richardson resigns rather than discharge Cox, and Nixon appeases some of the public and press outcry when he approves Acting Attorney General Robert Bork's appointment of Leon Jaworski to succeed Cox and releases a number of subpoenaed tapes, gaps and all.

A cease-fire agreement in Vietnam finally ends direct involvement of U.S. troops, but only after the death toll reaches 46,000 Americans. The U.S. bombing of North Vietnamese military targets in Cambodia continues another seven months. The Yom Kippur War in the Middle East is the fourth and fiercest Arab-Israeli conflict since 1948.

In the U.S., a footnote of importance: former Wimbledon champion Bobby Riggs loses his "battle of the sexes" to Billie Jean King in straight sets.

TOP: *Chemical manufacturing facilities and technologies have evolved into a multiplant operation, producing a wide variety of pharmaceutical, chemical, and agricultural products. Here, small-scale recovery equipment provides for efficient isolation of fermentation products.* BOTTOM: *Billie Jean King stretches to return volley to Bobby Riggs (not shown) in the heavily publicized "battle of the sexes."*

The pace quickens this year as Abbott works steadily to rebuild its share of the intravenous solutions market. By the end of 1972, unit volume from prerecall days has been recaptured, and the recovery accelerates even more with each passing month of 1973. Now plans are under way to introduce a technologically superior and highly competitive plastic container system for I.V. solutions by next year.

But the big news around Abbott is the exciting growth prospects of an entirely new division, one that has been created to promote disease *prevention* instead of treatment. This is the new Diagnostics Division. "We are bringing together all our activities in diagnostic products and services, including biologicals, radiopharmaceuticals, and clinical instrumentation," says President Ledder. "In other words, all the technologies within Abbott that can help physicians turn the art of diagnosis into the science of diagnosis. The next few years are going to see an exploding market worldwide for diagnostic systems and Abbott is lighting the fuse."

Directly responsible for the new division is 35-year-old James L. Vincent, with Abbott for less than a year. Before joining the company, Vincent was president of Texas Instruments, Asia, Ltd. Now his charge is to produce diagnostics and instruments that are simple, specific, sensitive, automated, and have a low cost per test. Even newer to Abbott is his boss, Robert A. Schoellhorn, who has the newly created position of executive vice president of the hospital group. Schoellhorn had formerly been president of the Lederle Laboratories division of American Cyanamid, and he is exactly the heavyweight Ted Ledder has been looking for to head up this vital part of the Abbott business.

The "long national nightmare" of Watergate, as Gerald Ford calls it, continues. Early in the year, President Nixon steadfastly rejects Watergate committee subpoenas for 500 tapes and documents. He partially relents four months later in reply to a House Judiciary Committee subpoena and submits 1,200 pages of edited transcripts, but the committee says they are inaccurate and unacceptable. The Supreme Court finally gets in the act and rules that Nixon must comply with the order. In late July, the House Judiciary Committee approves three articles of impeachment: for Nixon's blocking of the investigation into the Watergate scandal, abuse of presidential powers, and defiance of its subpoenas. Newly released tape transcripts reveal that, shortly after the Watergate break-in, Nixon had ordered an FBI probe of the incident halted. On August 9, Richard M. Nixon becomes the first United States president to resign from office.

Gerald Ford is sworn in as 38th president and one month later is sharply criticized when he grants Nixon an unconditional pardon. New York's former Governor Nelson Rockefeller is confirmed by Congress for vice president, making this the first time in history that the U.S. has an unelected president and vice president.

In other news around the world, Emperor Haile Selassie of Ethiopia is peacefully overthrown and arrested, and Soviet author Aleksandr Solzhenitsyn is stripped of his citizenship and deported to the West. In California, Patty Hearst, granddaughter of William Randolph Hearst and daughter of *San Francisco Examiner* publisher Randolph Hearst, is kidnapped from her Berkeley apartment.

Despite nationwide energy and material shortages, plus a deepening recession, Abbott sales this year surpass the $750 million mark. Even more rewarding is the after-tax performance. With higher costs for fuel and raw materials, Abbott invokes strict productivity measures, and the year's earnings rise 19 percent.

In the diagnostics area, the company edges closer to solving the problem of detecting serum hepatitis with two new products: *Auscell*, a nonradioactive test that is economical for even the smallest blood bank, and *Ausria II*, a third-generation radioimmunoassay test that reduces the incubation time of blood tests by 15 hours. Formerly, if blood was needed within a few hours, a less sensitive test had to be used. With *Ausria II*, hospitals and blood banks can supply blood for transfusions the same day the blood is drawn. The two tests are considered such a significant improvement that the Bureau of Biologics announces that all donor blood in the U.S. must be tested using only these advanced procedures.

One other aspect of Abbott research offers mind-boggling possibilities as company scientists adapt earthbound biology to outer space. Their experiment, selected by NASA officials over all other entries, will be conducted aboard the *Apollo* spacecraft during next year's joint American-Russian docking mission. It is designed to isolate, under the gravity-free conditions of space, the cells that produce the enzyme urokinase, a therapeutic substance used to dissolve blood clots.

TOP: *With the opening of a new facility in County Sligo, Ireland grows in importance as a manufacturing site for Abbott International. By 1981, two more Irish plants will be in operation.* BOTTOM LEFT: *Back stage, Senator Hubert Humphrey (center left) speaks with William D. Pratt, Abbott vice president of public affairs (center right), shortly before taking part in an Abbott-sponsored television panel on nutrition.* BOTTOM RIGHT: *Gerald R. Ford takes the oath of office as the 38th U.S. president.*

187

In February, four key aides of ex-President Nixon are found guilty of conspiring to obstruct justice in the Watergate case: H. R. Haldeman, John Mitchell, John Ehrlichman, and Robert Mardian. Haldeman, Mitchell, and Ehrlichman are sentenced to two and a half to eight years in prison and Mardian gets ten months to three years at the same time that four other Watergate convicts, John Dean, Jeb Magruder, Charles Colson, and Herb Kalmbach, are released from prison.

One of the most tightly guarded secrets of the Nixon and Ford administrations, "Project Jennifer," is revealed this year. It was a 1974 CIA-sponsored deep-sea salvage operation to raise a Soviet sub that sank in 1968 in 16,000 feet of water off the Hawaiian coast. The vessel, a diesel-powered submarine carrying ballistic missiles, was racked by interior explosions and sank so fast the Russians couldn't pinpoint its location, but the more sophisticated equipment of the U.S. Navy finds it.

In other news, Senator George McGovern visits Cuba at the invitation of Fidel Castro, who seeks an end to the U.S. embargo on food and medicine. In a televised news conference, Castro denies any Cuban role in the assassination of President John Kennedy, charges that the CIA has been behind a number of attempts on his own life, and requests an end to the U.S. trade embargo. His message must be persuasive; in July, the U.S. and 15 Latin American countries vote to lift the sanctions.

The war in Vietnam ends in April as the South Vietnamese government surrenders to the Communists. The longest war in America's history cost the lives of 57,939 Americans, four million killed or wounded Vietnamese on both sides, and $150 billion in U.S. military spending.

The recovery from 1971's I.V. problems seems complete as sales increase 23 percent to $941 million and earnings are up 28 percent. This year's sales are more than three times the total of 1967's and double those of 1971. The excellent operating results bring two dividend increases totaling 21 percent and a two-for-one stock split.

Good as the year is, the stock market hasn't caught on to the Abbott turnaround yet. The company's price-earnings ratio lags behind those of other health-care companies. Some investment analysts are wary of Abbott research and marketing capabilities, while others are critical of the company's product recalls and ongoing disputes with the Food and Drug Administration. The air begins to clear after Abbott invites 100 of the nation's top health-care financial analysts to a full-day investors' seminar at company headquarters. "Abbott did a splendid job in its presentation," says David MacCallum, of Faulkner, Dawkins and Sullivan. "I now have a much more favorable attitude toward them. The company has clearly come a long way since the dark days of 1971. After five years of disappointing performance, Abbott is emerging as a stronger company." Another New York analyst says, "Although Abbott is still in the process of recovering from the intravenous setback, they changed some minds and overcame some worries on the part of investors."

To Executive Vice President of Finance Bernard Semler and Vice President and Treasurer James Hanley, the success of this first seminar dictates a regular series of return engagements.

TOP: *Women across America continue to campaign and lobby for ratification of the Equal Rights Amendment.* BOTTOM: *Abbott strengthens its position in the intravenous solutions market with the introduction of a convenient flexible container. Here two employees inspect the new I.V. solutions bag at the North Chicago plant.*

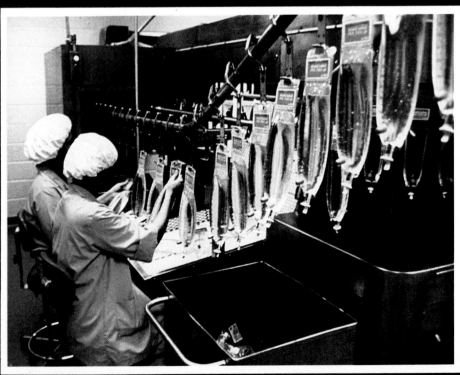

The U.S. bicentennial reaches its zenith on Independence Day as ceremonies begin with a flag-raising atop a mountain in Maine — where dawn first lights the continent — and end nearly a day later as dusk settles over American Samoa in the South Pacific. In between, the 200th anniversary is celebrated with pageantry and prayer, parades and picnics, and, of course, the usual protests. Queen Elizabeth II, starting her East Coast tour in Philadelphia, graciously says that the Fourth of July should be celebrated as much in Britain as in America, because it had "taught Britain a very valuable lesson: 'To know the right time, and the manner of yielding what is impossible to keep.' "

In August, incumbent President Gerald Ford barely edges out former California Governor Ronald Reagan for the Republican nomination, while Georgia Governor Jimmy Carter wins the first-ballot Democratic nomination. The soft-spoken Carter's success in three TV debates contributes substantially to his election victory.

Fellow Chicagoans Milton Friedman and Saul Bellow are Nobel prize winners in economics and literature as, for the first time, winners in all categories come from the United States. In Philadelphia, 29 die and 151 become ill from mysterious "Legionnaire's Disease" during the American Legion convention.

Elsewhere in the world: The U.S. and U.S.S.R. sign a treaty limiting the size of underground nuclear test explosions conducted for peaceful purposes; the treaty includes the first provisions for on-site inspections. North and South Vietnam are reunited after 22 years apart; the new country's capital is Hanoi, and Saigon is renamed Ho Chi Minh City.

In April, the ninth Abbott president is installed as Bob Schoellhorn takes over as chief operating officer and Ted Ledder moves up to chairman. In Ledder's nine years as president, Abbott sales increased from $303 million to exceed, this year, $1 billion for the first time.

Controversy over infant formula is the keynote this year, as Abbott comes under criticism because its *Similac* products are available in some Third World countries. The major point of contention is the widespread use by some formula manufacturers of radio, television, newspapers, sampling, and personal selling to persuade the mother to "be modern" and feed her baby an infant formula rather than breast-feed. Critics point out that mothers who cannot afford to purchase infant formula elect to bottle-feed their babies anyway. To make formula last longer, they overdilute it with water, and the baby becomes undernourished. In other cases, lack of clean water or failure to sterilize the bottles results in a contaminated feeding. The baby then is vulnerable to infectious diarrhea, which is a leading cause of infant deaths in underdeveloped areas.

The chief target is not Abbott at all but international market leader Nestlé. Even so, Abbott, with a team headed by Ross President David Cox, takes the industry initiative with an active program to prevent misuse of *Similac* products. Cox urges all companies to adopt a code of marketing ethics similar to the code Abbott has had for years. This specifically prohibits advertising to mothers and recommends supervision of the infant's nutrition by trained medical personnel. Abbott revises *Similac* labels used throughout the world to include a statement that breast-feeding is preferred, and prints the labels in the language of each country.

TOP: *An Abbott employee uses a microscope to conduct drug safety studies.* BOTTOM LEFT: *Abbott converts to high-speed technology for canning Ross nutritional products and increases line speed by 35 percent.* BOTTOM RIGHT: *Scenes such as this in Washington, D.C., occur in every town and city across the country, as America rejoices during its bicentennial celebration.*

Jimmy Carter, inaugurated as the 39th president of the United States, breaks tradition when he and wife Rosalynn forsake the presidential limousine to trudge 1½ miles from the Capitol to the White House. In world news, Leonid Brezhnev is elected president of the Soviet Union to replace Nikolai Podgorny . . . Indira Gandhi quits as India's prime minister after her ruling party suffers a surprising defeat . . . Menachem Begin becomes Israeli prime minister, upsetting the Labor Party, which has ruled since 1948 . . . and Egyptian President Anwar al-Sadat changes the course of modern Middle Eastern history by becoming the first Arab head of state to visit Israel since the creation of the Jewish state in 1948.

A new Panama Canal treaty is signed by the U.S. this year, giving Panama increasing control over the international waterway. The U.S. agrees to withdraw completely from operating the canal by the year 2000. The Trans-Alaska pipeline finally opens with oil from Prudhoe Bay on Alaska's North Slope flowing 789 miles to the ice-free port of Valdez. Within a few months, 1.2 million barrels a day will be delivered.

The worst disaster in aviation history occurs in March when a KLM 747 jumbo jet collides at takeoff with a Pan Am 747 crossing the runway at Tenerife, Canary Islands. Within moments, nearly 600 people on the two charter vacation flights are dead. In mid-July, lightning bolts strike New York's Con Ed transmission lines, paralyzing the city with a 25-hour power failure. Brazilian soccer great Pelé announces his retirement and plays his last professional game. And the North American Soccer League championship is won by the Cosmos, who defeat the Seattle Sounders 2-1.

The difference between Abbott and its competitors in the health-care category becomes apparent when *Forbes* magazine publishes comparative stock market performances for the five-year period 1973-77. While shares of other major health-care companies have declined 23 percent, the value of Abbott stock has increased 61 percent. It is a fitting tribute to the aggressive management styles of Chairman Ted Ledder and President Bob Schoellhorn. Together, they have doubled sales in just four years and net income in three.

Two keys to the company's growth come from a radical but well-reasoned departure in thinking. Forsaking the industry's timeworn total dependence upon research to provide new, patentable pharmaceuticals, Abbott determines that: first, with rising inflation and almost runaway health-care costs, the correct long-term strategy is to concentrate on cost-effectiveness in the hospital marketplace; and second, with new diagnostic techniques and products coming by leaps and bounds, the next decades will stress the early detection and prevention of disease, rather than after-the-fact therapy.

Both ideas are workable and worthwhile. An excellent example is the *VP* clinical analyzer, one Abbott entry in the clinical chemistry market. With this diagnostic instrument, Abbott participation in the laboratory field will substantially expand. The *VP* performs tests on blood samples with greater speed (400 per hour), more accuracy, and at a lower cost than previous generations of single-channel analyzers.

TOP: *U.S. President Jimmy Carter and his wife, Rosalynn, touch the heart of the country by walking from the Capitol to the White House on inauguration day.* CENTER: *The* VP *clinical analyzer is Abbott's most successful new diagnostic instrument to date.* BOTTOM: *Main entrance to the Montreal, Canada, plant. The first Abbott subsidiary was formed in Canada in 1931.*

With the U.S. economy already faltering, a 110-day strike by soft-coal miners riddles corporate profits and payrolls, forces a rise in the price of steel, and creates fuel shortages, power cutbacks, and record losses for railroads. It is a time for drastic measures. Howard Jarvis, a retired California industrialist, starts his own crusade for overburdened taxpayers when he introduces Proposition 13, a ballot initiative to slash state property taxes by 57 percent. It soon becomes a battlecry for the nation as 23 states call for tax reforms and Congress reduces income taxes, raises the personal exemption, and trims capital gains taxes. President Carter fails, however, in his own call for tax reforms, including abolition of tax deductions for the "three-martini lunch."

The president makes a far better move when he invites Egyptian President Anwar al-Sadat and Israeli Prime Minister Menachem Begin to meet with him in Maryland. When it's over, the statesmen have signed the Camp David Accords, a historic agreement which is hailed as a prelude to a Mideast peace treaty between the old rivals. In Nicaragua, Sandinista rebels launch a full-scale uprising against President Anastasio Somoza Debayle.

Three different Popes occupy the throne at St. Peter's this year. In August, Pope Paul VI dies of a heart attack at age 80. His successor, Albino Cardinal Luciani of Venice, takes the name of John Paul I but dies only 34 days after his election. In a surprise move, cardinals of the church select Karol Cardinal Wojtyla of Poland, the first non-Italian in more than four centuries to be named pontiff. He becomes John Paul II.

TOP: *The Abbott management team of Edward J. Ledder (left), chairman, and Robert A. Schoellhorn, president, plan the company's strategy for long-term growth, a key element of which involves expanding Abbott's overseas operations.* BOTTOM: *Egyptian President Anwar al-Sadat (left), U.S. President Carter (center), and Israeli Prime Minister Menachem Begin seal their agreement reached during the Camp David summit.*

One unusual new venture is negotiated by Chairman Ted Ledder — an agreement with the Soviet Union for Abbott to supply equipment, engineering support, and product know-how to start up a *Similac* infant formula plant in the U.S.S.R. According to Georgi Konoplev, chairman of VO/Technopromimport, the Russians already manufacture two kinds of baby formula. "But *Similac*," he says, "with its high nutritional properties, is considered a particularly good substitute for mother's milk soon after birth."

Last year, Bob Schoellhorn expanded Abbott's overseas reach in a joint venture with Takeda Chemical Industries, Japan's largest pharmaceutical company. The move is seen as a long-term supplement to Abbott research, since the Japanese firm has several interesting compounds under development which Abbott may eventually market in the U.S. and Canada. The joint venture will give Abbott rights to all human pharmaceutical products that come from Takeda research.

Domestically, an exciting new Abbott drug is *Depakene*, an anticonvulsant used for *petit mal* seizures, which usually strike children between the ages of 3 and 15. Chemically unlike other antiepileptic drugs, *Depakene* shows real promise for patients whose seizures cannot be controlled by existing agents.

All of the above are considered at the second Abbott investors' seminar. A comment by Robert Benezra, of Alex Brown & Sons, capsules the opinion of attendees: "The company's past record of operating results, by almost any measurement, is among the best compiled in American business. Ten years ago we viewed Abbott as a second-tier pharmaceutical concern; today we view the company as one of the best-structured and well-positioned entities to garner, on a selective basis, an increasing share of the $350 billion currently spent by the Free World for health care."

Tensions and traumas dominate the early months of 1979. In the U.S., the cooling system on a nuclear reactor at Pennsylvania's Three Mile Island malfunctions, and the plant spews forth low levels of radiation. In Iran, Shah Muhammad Reza Pahlevi is ousted from the throne he has occupied since 1941 and his arch-foe, the Moslem religious leader Ayatollah Ruhollah Khomeini, returns from exile in Paris to take over. In November, hundreds of Moslem militants storm the U.S. Embassy in Tehran and seize 66 Americans as hostages. The 13 women and blacks are released at the end of the month, a 14th hostage is sent home after eight months because of his serious illness, and 52 will be held a total of 444 days.

British voters return the Conservative party to power and a precedent is set when Margaret Thatcher becomes the country's first female prime minister. Thatcher promises to rescue Britain from "the slither and slide to the socialist state." The 30-year state of war between Israel and Egypt officially ends when Anwar al-Sadat and Menachem Begin sign a formal peace treaty before 1,600 invited guests in Washington. Both men credit President Carter with leading the negotiations to a successful conclusion. Another 30-year estrangement ends as the U.S. and the People's Republic of China resume formal diplomatic relations.

Back in the U.S., President Carter is besieged by the sticky issues of inflation, nuclear plant safety, Soviet troops in Cuba, and the big one — American hostages in Iran. His disposition doesn't improve when he reads the results of the latest Gallup Poll, which gives him an approval rating of only 29 percent. This is just a shade better than Nixon received on the day he resigned the presidency.

TOP LEFT: *Pope John Paul II celebrates Mass on the Mall in America's capital.* TOP RIGHT: *In response to a growing demand for nonradioactive early disease detection systems, Abbott introduces* Quantum. BOTTOM: *In addition to its ever-popular infant formula Similac, the Ross division of Abbott manufactures this wide line of medical nutritional products.*

In a year of growing generic competition, increasing government regulation, and rapidly escalating inflation, the company's outstanding record for increased productivity deserves mention.

To some, productivity is no more than a corporate catchword, a cliché invented by business schools. But to Abbott, it is a vital commodity, measured in many ways. This year, for example, the average number of people employed by the company increases by 2 percent, yet sales per employee, measured in constant dollars, are up 10 percent. This comes on top of an 8 percent increase in 1978 and 6 percent in 1977 — all much higher than the national average, which is only 1.8 percent in 1979. Cost controls? Over the past five years, with only minimal price increases, the Abbott ratio of selling and administrative expenses to total sales has been reduced from 27.4 percent to 22.6 percent — which translates to a savings of over $80 million a year. And consider lost time from accidents. The hospital division plant at Laurinburg, North Carolina, this year passes five million hours, almost three years, without a single lost-time accident. There's extra productivity in sales, too. When each Abbott representative adds only one more physician call per week, it is the equivalent of adding 19 more sales representatives at no extra cost.

Add to that: containing the paper blizzard of office work . . . unplugging bottlenecks on filling lines . . . energy conservation . . . and stringent control of capital requirements. Such are the increments of productivity at Abbott — not all heroic, but all eminently workable and all good reasons why earnings increases continue to be higher than sales increases at Abbott.

Shortly before the start of the new year, Soviet armored divisions roll into Afghanistan. But instead of a quick takeover, they find it won't be long before experts begin talking about the Russians' own "Vietnam quagmire" and the likelihood of prolonged war. America's lowest moment comes in April when a daring commando-style raid to rescue the hostages ends in failure and death in a remote desert in eastern Iran. The mission is aborted when three of eight helicopters malfunction. During the pullout, one helicopter collides with a C-130 transport, killing eight and injuring five.

At home, the U.S. ice hockey team wins the hearts of Americans in the Winter Olympics in Lake Placid, New York, when it beats the heavily favored Soviets to win the gold medal. Later, when President Carter's deadline for the Soviet Union to pull out of Afghanistan goes unheeded, the U.S. pulls out of the Summer Olympic games in Moscow. In May, 9,700-foot Mt. St. Helens in Washington blows its top. By the end of the year, eight more eruptions will have left more than 34 people dead, 32 missing, and 150 square miles of prime woodland obliterated.

Inflation in the U.S. bounces around in double-digit figures that reach 12.4 percent by year's end, with food and housing costs leading the way. During the presidential campaign, the major issue is the economy. In a landslide electoral vote, California's former Governor Ronald Reagan makes Jimmy Carter a one-term president as, for the first time since 1954, Republicans win the Senate.

In April, Ted Ledder retires, although he will continue as a director and chairman of the board. In Ledder's 41 years at Abbott, he has seen company sales grow from $11 million to this year's $2 billion. The Abbott track record, particularly in recent years, has been only slightly short of phenomenal. From the time Dr. Wallace Calvin Abbott started the company in 1888, it took 70 years to reach $100 million in sales. Fifteen years later, in 1972, sales topped $500 million. In only four more years, sales bettered $1 billion, and now, four years later, sales have doubled again to top $2 billion.

It's admittedly a tough act to follow, but Ledder's successor, Bob Schoellhorn, seems a likely candidate to continue the strong trend. No stranger to the chemical and health-care businesses, Schoellhorn came to Abbott in 1973 after a 26-year career with American Cyanamid, where he served his last years as president of the Lederle Laboratories division. He joined Abbott, making what he describes as "the best decision of my career," as executive vice president of the hospital group, and was elected to the board in 1974. He became president and chief operating officer of Abbott in 1976 and took over the reins as chief executive officer in 1979. Schoellhorn, like Ledder, is a strong advocate of the shirt-sleeve school of management.

This year Abbott expands two overseas markets when it acquires full ownership of Deutsche-Abbott GmbH in Wiesbaden, West Germany, and the Pravaz Recordati Laboratorios, S.A., of São Paulo, Brazil, and bolsters its hospital entry with the acquisition of Sorenson Research of Salt Lake City, Utah, which makes innovative medical disposables used primarily in hospital critical-care areas.

TOP LEFT: *Eric Heiden (left) of Madison, Wisconsin, prepares for the 10,000 meter Winter Olympic speed skating event in Lake Placid, New York. Heiden will win the event and take a total of five Olympic gold medals.* **TOP RIGHT:** *Abbott Chairman Edward J. Ledder, who retires this year, can look back on 41 years of service to a company he has helped develop into a major worldwide health-care provider.* **BOTTOM:** *Production lines are becoming increasingly automated to improve accuracy and output. Here an Abbott employee operates a vial inspection unit in the hospital products plant in Rocky Mount, North Carolina.*

199

The year begins with a collective sigh of relief. The 444-day siege of spirit ends as the American hostages return from captivity in Iran. President Reagan takes the inaugural vow and promises Americans a "new beginning," but he has barely begun his term when he is struck down by gunfire outside a Washington hotel. Two months later, Pope John Paul II is hit by two bullets in St. Peter's Square, and in Egypt, Anwar al-Sadat is murdered as he watches a parade commemorating his country's 1973 war with Israel.

World leaders are shuffled as Hosni Mubarak succeeds Sadat . . . Deng Xiaoping takes over as China's senior deputy party chairman . . . Socialist party leader François Mitterand defeats incumbent French President Valéry Giscard d'Estaing . . . and Wojciech Jaruzelski becomes Poland's new prime minister. But what really interests the public, it seems, are the trappings of royal romance — an estimated 700 million viewers worldwide turn their TV dials to the resplendent wedding of Charles, Prince of Wales, and Lady Diana Spencer.

After a long and arduous battle with the U.S. Congress, President Reagan wins approval of his economic program, which includes a 25 percent tax cut spread over three years as well as $36 billion in spending cuts.

It's a dazzling year for space science as the shuttle *Columbia* makes two trips, in April and November, with perfect landings each time on a dry lake bed in California. The *Voyager 2,* after a four-year trip in outer space, sweeps past Saturn in August and continues on to a 1986 rendezvous with Uranus.

TOP: *Employees at the Abbott manufacturing plant in Argentina work on a finishing line.* BOTTOM LEFT: *Robert A. Schoellhorn advances from president to Abbott chairman, bringing to his new position a proven record for strong leadership and creative long-range planning.* BOTTOM RIGHT: *Iranian hostages Victor Tomseth, Barry Rosen, and Ann Swift (left to right) wave to the crowd at Rhein-Main Air Base, West Germany, as they board* Freedom One *for a joyous flight home to the United States.*

For the third time in less than six years, shareholders receive a two-for-one stock split. The investor who risked $3,725 to buy 100 shares of Abbott in 1929 has by now received a total of $235,000 in dividends. Even more remarkable, his original 100 shares have grown to 40,128 with a market value of nearly $1.1 million. In the last seven years alone — since 1974 — the market value of the stock has increased eightfold.

At midyear, Bob Schoellhorn moves up to chairman as the Abbott board elects G. Kirk Raab the company's 10th president. Raab has come up through the international ranks after joining Abbott in 1975 as area vice president, Latin American operations. The experience has given him good involvement across many of the key segments of Abbott business: pharmaceutical, hospital, consumer, and nutritional.

One of the year's highlights comes from a unique joint effort among three different Abbott divisions — hospital products, diagnostics, and Ross. They pool their products and techniques to come up with a combined plan for improved nutritional support in hospitals. Physicians are quick to accept the concept because it can shorten hospital stays, prevent complications, and reduce mortality. More than selling a single product, this united effort is part of a carefully charted strategy that continues to draw Abbott away from its competitors.

The Diagnostics Division introduces its *TDx* therapeutic drug monitoring system, which will become its most successful product. The *TDx* permits physicians to measure the level of medication in a patient's blood and adjust future doses. It fills the need for an easy-to-use system that provides fast, reliable results.

201

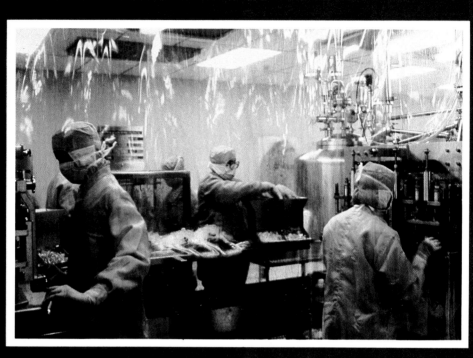

As far as the U.S. economy is concerned, 1982 is a year to forget. Unemployment crashes the double-digit barrier to reach its highest level since 1941, and bankruptcies reach their highest rate since the Great Depression.

News from around the world is similarly bleak. British and Argentine military forces go to war over the Falklands, a tiny chain of islands populated predominantly by sheep. After the fighting, the islands remain under British control. The two-year Iran-Iraq war drags on with no clear-cut victories or defeats, and Israel invades southern Lebanon, declaring it will stop the Palestine Liberation Organization attacks for all time by destroying PLO strongholds. Poland remains under martial law as the Solidarity union, as expected, is banned. And a power shift occurs in the Kremlin when Soviet President Leonid Brezhnev dies at 75 and is quickly replaced by Yuri Andropov, the former KGB chief.

The Italians are jubilant as more than 90,000 fans watch Italy defeat West Germany for the 12th World Cup soccer championship. Many American women are less ecstatic — a June deadline passes, leaving the Equal Rights Amendment three states short of the majority needed for ratification. The year ends as two masked gunmen cut a hole in the roof of an armored car company in New York City and carry off $9.8 million, the biggest heist in U.S. history. Left behind: millions more, and a message scrawled on a dusty mirror — "Robbers was here."

TOP: In the rarefied atmosphere of a "clean room," employees at the Austin, Texas, plant produce intravenous solutions. BOTTOM LEFT: Research and development expenditures increase dramatically in the early 1980s, making research one of Abbott's highest priorities. BOTTOM RIGHT: Prince Charles and Lady Diana add a new son to the British royal family.

With growing concern over the increasing costs of health care, Abbott continues to concentrate on products and services that are designed to reduce the cost of caring for patients. In this effort, the company has a built-in edge over others in the field; none can offer a spectrum of product lines that includes a battery of accurate diagnostic tests, a broad line of effective pharmaceutical and hospital products, as well as a range of nutritionals to sustain health and accelerate recovery from illness. Individually, each contributes to cost-effective health care. Offered together, they give Abbott a tough-to-beat level of diversified health-care management.

One prime example is CAPD, which stands for continuous ambulatory peritoneal dialysis, a system used for patients who suffer from kidney failure, usually as a result of hypertension or diabetes. Instead of having to be hooked up to hemodialysis equipment in a hospital, the patient using the Abbott *Inpersol* line has a small tube implanted in his abdomen and uses this to infuse, and later to drain, dialysis fluid. The process is called an "exchange," and patients do the procedure on their own four times a day. The advantages are many: no hospitalization is required, and the patient can work, travel, and live a fairly normal life.

Another example is PAP, the company's first diagnostic product to use monoclonal antibodies. PAP, a test to monitor prostatic cancer therapy, is among 15 tests in the Abbott enzyme immunoassay (EIA) system which use the *Quantum,* a programmed spectrophotometer that measures enzyme reactions rather than radioactivity to get results. The advantages of nonradioactive testing with *Quantum* are numerous: laboratories don't need special radioactivity licenses and equipment, the shelf life of tests is longer, and the tests can be done in smaller labs.

203

This is the year the Great Recession ends in the U.S. By year's end, the statistics for almost everything — unemployment, corporate profits, production — are much brighter than they were the year before. There is no question that, on the whole, recovery has arrived.

A series of events focus the attention of Americans on foreign affairs, including the Soviet Union's shooting down of a Korean Air Lines jumbo jet; terrorist bombings of the U.S. embassy and Marine compound in Beirut, Lebanon; the U.S. invasion of the tiny island of Grenada; and turmoil in Central America where the Reagan administration tries to stop leftist guerrillas in El Salvador while it finances the "contras" fighting the left-wing Sandinista government of Nicaragua. These controversies, plus American placement of Pershing II and cruise missiles in Western Europe, further chill relations between the United States and the Soviet Union.

In June, Sally K. Ride, a 32-year-old physicist, becomes the first American woman to fly in space when the shuttle *Challenger* lifts off from Cape Canaveral on a five-day mission. Two months later, Lieutenant Colonel Guion S. Bluford, Jr., becomes the first black American to travel in space. And in Salt Lake City, a valiant fight ends when Barney Clark, the 62-year-old Seattle dentist who received the world's first permanently implanted artificial heart, dies 112 days after surgery with his mechanical heart still beating.

A surge of organizational activity hallmarks the year as Abbott adds marketing muscle both overseas and in the U.S. In Japan, Abbott merges three facilities into one unified health-care company called Dainabot, K.K. An offspring of the original alliance between Abbott and Dainippon Pharmaceutical Co., Ltd., the new company, according to Bob Schoellhorn, "will substantially increase our position in the important Japanese health-care market." Abbott increases its majority interest and will have overall management responsibility for marketing in Japan new products that come from Abbott research.

Depakote, an improved patented drug for the treatment of epilepsy is introduced. The drug has the same active ingredient and offers the same degree of seizure control as *Depakene*, introduced in 1978. However, it has a special coating to minimize possible gastric irritation. The FDA announces approval of *Chlamydiazyme*, an enzyme immunoassay test used for the detection of chlamydia, the most prevalent sexually transmitted disease in the U.S.

In the U.S., Abbott develops a new business unit called Abbott HomeCare to serve the rapidly expanding home health-care market. At midyear, Abbott invests $7 million to establish a working relationship with Boston Scientific Corporation, a leader in what are known as "less invasive" surgical products, which eliminate or reduce the trauma of surgery. Those products include catheters and endoscopes that allow, for example, the dilation of an artery using a balloon catheter, a process that replaces bypass surgery, and the nonsurgical removal of kidney stones and gallstones.

TOP: *This 1983 ad, marking the 25th anniversary of* Similac *with Iron, presents a pictorial history of the product whose name has become synonymous with infant formula.* BOTTOM: *A happy and excited Sally K. Ride, America's first woman in space, talks with NASA ground control during her flight on the shuttle* Challenger.

Despite George Orwell's gloomy prophecy for 1984, the year does not bring the world one step closer to the "Big Brother" totalitarian regime he envisioned. It is, instead, the year that sees Geraldine Ferraro as the first female vice presidential nominee of a major party and the Reverend Jesse Jackson as the first black man to make a serious bid for the presidency. It's the year when Walter Mondale, who preached caution and self-denial, is buried in a 49-state landslide vote for President Ronald Reagan. It's the year when the young urban professionals, or "Yuppies," of the baby-boom generation come into their own. And it is the year when America's optimism, patriotism, and self-confidence seem to surge with each of the 83 gold medals the U.S. athletes win at the Los Angeles Summer Olympics.

Overseas, the year is stained by the murder of a priest in Poland and a prime minister in India, and the attempted murder of another prime minister in Britain. It sees the death of a Soviet leader and the birth of an English prince. It is a year of tragedy as 300,000 people die of starvation in Ethiopia . . . as the world's worst industrial accident occurs when a cloud of deadly methyl isocyanate gas escapes from a Union Carbide plant in Bhopal, India, killing 2,500 and injuring 100,000 others . . . and as a truck loaded with explosives races past Lebanese guards and blows up the United States embassy in Beirut, killing 9 people.

"The winds of change are blowing in health care," says Chairman Bob Schoellhorn, "and as they increase in velocity those companies whose products and services don't offer clear-cut financial benefits will find themselves fighting a head wind strong enough to make any progress difficult."

There is no question that fundamental changes are occurring in the delivery of health care. For those less fast on their feet — particularly, this year, in the hospital supply field — the times are troubling. But for Abbott, long-term planning is based on the assumption that pressure on health-care costs will continue to grow. *Business Week* magazine recognizes the success of this strategy "to become less vulnerable to cost-containment pressures in traditional hospital products" when it reports in its September 17 issue that "Abbott won a leading share of the diagnostics market through acquisitions and internal development and built a highly profitable dietary supplement business." In diagnostics, Abbott has successfully jumped past 20 competitors over the last decade to become number one in a $4 billion market, and in medical nutritionals, the company leads the U.S. market.

But Schoellhorn likes a different proof — the kind that shows up on the balance sheet. By year's end, Abbott's vital signs are far healthier than at any time in the company's history. Not only do sales pass the $3 billion mark, but productivity gains continue. While the number of employees has increased 15 percent over the past five years, sales per employee have moved up 57 percent and earnings per employee, 92 percent. As Schoellhorn says, "No single company anywhere in the world is stronger in as many health-care markets as Abbott." The winds, apparently, are squarely at Abbott's back.

TOP: *An employee produces* Abbokinase, *a therapeutic substance that dissolves blood clots.* CENTER: *The completion of this attractive plant near Wiesbaden, West Germany, strengthens Abbott's foothold in the world's third-largest pharmaceutical market in the early 1980s.* BOTTOM: *U.S. President Ronald Reagan (left) and Vice President George Bush team up for a second term, following their landslide victory over Democratic opponents Walter Mondale and Geraldine Ferraro.*

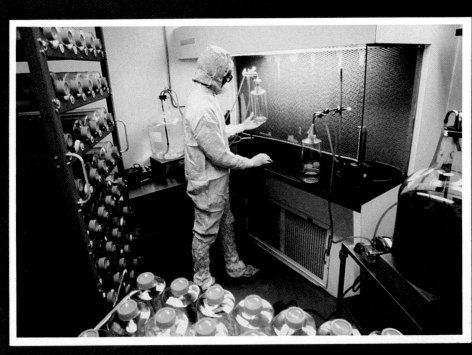

The year that was supposed to edge the world closer to peace ends in a hail of bullets as terrorism and vengeance paralyze the Middle East. Good news comes as Mikhail Gorbachev, the new Soviet leader described as having "a nice smile but ... iron teeth," brings charisma, wit, and vigor to East-West relations. His summit meeting with President Reagan cools heated rhetoric and moves nuclear talks off dead center.

But autumn sees the beginning of a cycle of violence as planes and ships are hijacked and innocent blood is spilled at the Rome and Vienna airports. Shiite Muslims hijack TWA flight 847 in June, and in October, four Palestinians hijack the Italian cruise liner *Achille Lauro,* murdering an elderly American and dumping him overboard in his wheelchair. U.S. warplanes intercept the hijackers' getaway plane and force it down, causing a crisis in U.S.-Egyptian relations. And so the game of Middle East brinksmanship spins on and on.

But not all the news is bad. Africa's hunger cries are heard around the world, and a gush of fundraising follows. Rockers in London and Philadelphia give 17 nonstop hours of "Live Aid" for 162,000 concertgoers, raising $82 million for famine relief, and "USA for Africa" produces another $70 million from sales of its "We Are The World" recordings. In Chicago, emotionally starved sports fans finally get a season of smiles as William "The Refrigerator" Perry and the Chicago Bears plunge toward their first Super Bowl trophy.

TOP: *The hub of Abbott's diverse operations as a worldwide health-care products manufacturer is Abbott Park, its corporate headquarters.* BOTTOM LEFT: *Health and Human Services Secretary Margaret Heckler and FDA Commissioner Frank Young hold a press conference to announce the approval of HTLV III EIA, Abbott's new diagnostic test for detecting the presence of the antibody to the AIDS virus. It is the first such test approved in the U.S.* BOTTOM RIGHT: *Chicago Bears running back Walter Payton moves his team a few yards closer to its first Super Bowl championship.*

208

A series of important breakthroughs dot the Abbott research calendar this year. In March the company is awarded the first government license to produce a diagnostic test to screen blood for the antibody to the AIDS virus. The Abbott test is considered to be more than 99 percent accurate in testing blood samples. With a special task force of 40 employees working around the clock, it takes Abbott only eight months to develop the test and produce enough to begin to satisfy world demand.

In April the FDA approves *Lupron,* a promising new injectable drug for the treatment of advanced prostatic cancer. It is the first product to be marketed by TAP, the joint venture between Abbott and Takeda Chemical Industries. With 86,000 new cases of prostatic cancer diagnosed each year, the disease is the third most common cause of death among older men. *Lupron* represents the first new hormonal therapy in more than 40 years and avoids the side effects associated with estrogen therapy.

June sees the Abbott introduction of *Vision,* a desk-top whole blood analyzer for physicians' offices. About the size of a microwave oven, the new machine provides results for glucose, cholesterol, and other common blood tests in just eight minutes. It allows doctors to test blood in their offices and begin treatment on the spot if a problem exists. Without *Vision,* doctors and patients have to wait 24 to 72 hours for blood test results from a laboratory.

In September the FDA approves Abbott *ADD-Vantage,* a unique intravenous drug delivery system. With *ADD-Vantage,* potent drugs that do not have long-term stability in solution can be mixed just before they are administered. Within four months, 12 major pharmaceutical companies have signed up to use the system.

USA Today captures the contrasts and contradictions of 1986 when it says, "It was a difficult year to keep the faith, since so many things we had faith in failed so publicly, so unmistakably."

In January stunned Americans watch as the space shuttle *Challenger* explodes in the sky barely a minute after blasting off, killing six astronauts and Christa McAuliffe, the New Hampshire teacher who is aboard as part of a campaign to rekindle public interest in the space program.

The April explosion of the Soviet Union's Chernobyl nuclear-power plant showers clouds of radiation upon Russia's neighbors, and kills 31 people while displacing 135,000 others. The disaster, the worst in 35 years of commercial atomic power production, proves that even when used for peaceful purposes, the atom is capable of global damage.

In the Philippines, Corazon Aquino replaces Ferdinand Marcos as president. A volcanic eruption in Colombia kills an estimated 25,000 people, destroys 14 towns, and leaves more than 19,000 homeless. The U.S. Congress passes the Tax Reform Law, which is designed to simplify the federal taxation system. Late in the year the Iran-"contra" affair erupts into the headlines.

On a more positive note, the United States stretches "Hands Across America" to help the hungry, then celebrates the Statue of Liberty's 100th birthday on July 4th with a four-day party filled with fireworks, tall ships, and torchlight parades. Finally, the crazy quilt of 1986 brings on a rampaging bull as Wall Street propels its longest, strongest postwar stock market rally into its 53d month as the Dow-Jones closes the year at 1895.95, up 22.6 percent.

TOP LEFT: *Following a face-lift and general reconditioning, the Statue of Liberty celebrates her 100th birthday.* TOP RIGHT: *A researcher at work at Dainabot, K. K., Abbott's only diagnostics research facility outside the U.S.* BOTTOM: *Representatives of Abbott's 2000-member Puerto Rican workforce ride a float during their island's Constitution Day parade.*

210

Abbott will long remember 1986 for its flood of corporate honors as well as for significant rewards to its shareholders.

Financially, the company reports sales totaling $3.8 billion, an increase of almost $450 million. This single-year gain looks even more impressive in perspective, since it exceeds total Abbott sales for the first 61 years of company history. During the year, dividends are increased for the 14th consecutive year. The 20 percent increase puts dividends at double their rate of just four years earlier. At the same time, the company authorizes a two-for-one stock split — for the fourth time in the past 11 years. All in all, it's another winning year for Abbott shareholders.

Chairman Bob Schoellhorn receives twin awards when *Crain's Chicago Business* names him "Executive of the Year" and the *Wall Street Transcript* gives him its gold award as "the best chief executive in the health/hospital supply industry for the past year." The final touch comes late in the year when *Dun's Business Month* labels Abbott one of the five best-managed companies in America. They point out that Schoellhorn has taken the internal growth route to make Abbott one of the most diversified and profitable companies in the health-care industry.

Now the world leader in diagnostics, Abbott enters the growing market for the detection of abused drugs with a family of accurate, flexible, and cost-effective tests. These tests are among 70 new diagnostic products introduced this year. The company further solidifies its number-one position in the worldwide market for the antibiotic erythromycin with the introduction of *PCE*, a new polymer-coated form that provides fast, consistent absorption while it minimizes the potential for gastrointestinal side effects.

One of the year's more prominent headlines comes from the trading pits of Wall Street. On Black Monday, October 19, the Dow-Jones industrial average drops a record 508 points — a 22.6 percent loss in value. Record one-day declines in markets around the world follow, and weeks later analysts are still assessing the damage and debating the long-term repercussions. But the huge drop reverses rising interest rates and intensifies efforts by the President and Congress to reduce the massive federal deficit.

Two Democratic presidential candidates drop out of the race after unprecedented scrutiny by the media reveals events involving their "character." And the continuing investigation of the Iran-"contra" affair wends its way through tedious summer-long Congressional hearings.

In England, Margaret Thatcher wins again, to become the first British leader in 160 years to be elected to three consecutive terms as prime minister. But the nail-biting Persian Gulf situation, with Kuwaiti oil tankers carrying U.S. flags, continues to muddy international waters.

The U.S. and Soviet Union sign an agreement on arms reduction. Even the glowering Russian attitude seems to be softening as General Secretary Mikhail Gorbachev calls for a "democratization" of the political process and introduces a new word — *glasnost*, which means "openness" — into the world lexicon.

Chairman Schoellhorn strengthens his top management team early in the year when the board names Duane L. Burnham to the new post of vice chairman and chief financial officer and installs Jack W. Schuler as president and chief operating officer.

As Abbott moves through its 100th year, the company's balanced diversity — in pharmaceuticals, nutritionals, hospital products, and diagnostics — flexes a muscle power no competitor can claim and forms a solid foundation for future growth. In pharmaceuticals the new alpha-blocker *Hytrin* receives FDA approval as a major drug to treat high blood pressure. In nutritionals the company widens its lead in the U.S. market for both pediatric and medical nutritionals. In hospital products the unique *ADD-Vantage* drug delivery system attracts 15 pharmaceutical companies to market their I.V. products as part of the Abbott system. And in diagnostics Abbott continues its leadership with its rapid growth in tests for AIDS, hepatitis, and abused drugs.

From a financial standpoint the results are impressive. Sales top $4 billion. Since 1975, under the leadership of Ted Ledder and Bob Schoellhorn, the number of Abbott shares has multiplied 16-fold and market value has increased 19 times compared to the value at the end of 1974. The *Fortune* 500 listing now shows Abbott among its top 100 companies. And in October, Abbott is listed on the Tokyo Stock Exchange.

It is clear that the company's decision to develop technologies that not only improve health care but also reduce costs is paying off.

"All in all," as Dr. Abbott might have said, "it's not a bad beginning. Now we'll see what the second century brings."

TOP: *An Abbott research scientist works with DNA samples in the development of new diagnostic technologies.* BOTTOM LEFT: *As Abbott moves confidently into its second century, it will be guided by (from left) Duane L. Burnham, vice chairman; Robert A. Schoellhorn, chairman; and Jack W. Schuler, president.* BOTTOM RIGHT: *U.S. President Ronald Reagan plays host to Britain's Prime Minister Margaret Thatcher.*

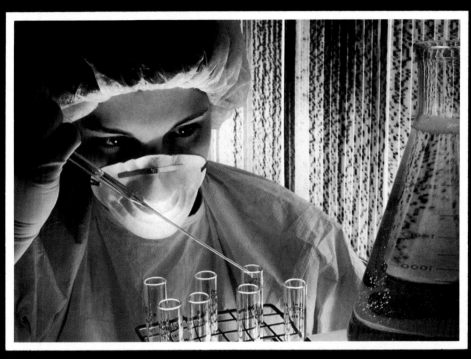

Index

215

Bulganin, Nikolai, 148, 155
Bulgaria, 64
Burdick, Alfred S., 63, 77, 79, 88, 103, 104
  and acquisitions, 83, 90, 95, 104
  and *Alkaloidal Clinic*, 46, 50
  background of, 46
  becomes Abbott president, 81
  and research, 66, 68, 70, 83, 84, 104
Bureau of Biologics, U.S., 186
Burgess, Gelett, 28
Burggraeve, Adolphe, 15
Burnham, Duane L., 212
Burroughs, Edgar Rice, 66
Burroughs 200 computer, 157
Business Week magazine, 206
Butyl alcohol, 84
Butyn (Abbott product), 84, 92

Cain, George R., 159, 163, 164, 175, 183
  background of, 155
  becomes Abbott chairman and CEO, 172
  becomes Abbott president, 155
  and board of directors, 179, 183
  and management structure, 161, 170, 172
  and research, 155, 183
Cain, Rolly M., 112, 132
  background of, 101
  becomes Abbott president, 128
California (U.S. battleship), 121
California Institute of Technology (Cal
  Tech) (Pasadena, California), 21
Cambodia, 184
Camel cigarettes, 64
Camp David Accords, 195
Camp Fire Girls, 59
Canada, 48, 97, 181
  Abbott facilities in, 59, 112
Cannon, Hughie, 43
CAPD (continuous ambulatory peritoneal
  dialysis), 203
Capone, Alphonse, 88, 92, 97, 101
Carbolic acid, 70
Carbon-14, 130
Carlisle Indian School (Pennsylvania), 63
Carlos, King (of Spain), 50
Carnegie, Andrew, 41
Carnegie Steel, 41
Carpentier, Georges, 81
Carrel, Alexis, 83
Carter, Edgar B., 101
Carter, Jimmy, 199
  becomes U.S. president, 190, 192
  and Israeli-Egyptian negotiations, 195,
  197
  and tax reform, 195
Carter, Rosalynn, 192
Cartoons
  "Doonesbury," 177
  "Popeye," 97
  Pulitzer prize, 177
"Casey at the Bat" (poem), 15
Castro, Fidel, 157, 161, 163, 172, 188
Castro, Raúl, 172
CBS (company), 95
Cermak, Anton, 104
Challenger (space shuttle), 204, 210
Chamberlain, Neville, 112, 115
Chambers, Whittaker, 135
Chaplin, Charlie, 17, 59
Charles, Prince (of Wales), 201
Charleston (dance), 88
Chekhov, Anton, 46
Chemical Warfare Service, U.S., 77
Chernobyl nuclear-power plant accident,
  210
Cherokee Strip, 24
Chesterfield cigarettes, 64

Chevrolet automobile, 155
Chiang Kai-shek, 88, 137
Chicago Bears, 208
Chicago Creek (Colorado), 52
Chicago Fire Department, 79
Chicago Health Department, 59
Chicago Stock Exchange, 97. *See also*
  Stock market
Chicago Tribune, 124, 135
Chicago White Sox, 77
Children's Hospital (Chicago, Illinois), 128
Chile, 21
China, People's Republic of, 59, 61, 137
  Boxer Rebellion in, 39
  Communist party in, 137, 150, 152, 157
  international relations of, 141, 181, 183,
  197
  in Korean War, 139, 141
  in Sino-Japanese Wars, 28, 112
Chlamydiazyme (Abbott product), 204
Chlorazene (Abbott product), 70, 123
Chlorine gas, 68
Chloromycetin, 137, 143
Chou En-lai, 137, 183
Christian Endeavor Society, 59
Chrysler automobile, 150
Churchill, Winston, 68, 117, 119, 130, 141,
  148
CIA, 132, 141, 159, 161, 188
Cigarettes, 26, 39, 46, 61, 64
Cigars, La Palina, 95
Cinchophen (Abbott product), 75, 84
Cincinnati Reds, 77
CIO, 148
Civilian Conservation Corps, 108
Civil Rights
  Act, 159
  protests, 159, 164, 168, 175
Clark, Barney, 204
Clear Eyes (Abbott product), 177
Cleveland, Grover, 15, 23, 32, 48
Clinic Publishing Company, 30, 41, 48, 50
Clough, Simeon DeWitt, 48, 55, 57, 112,
  135, 159
  and acquisitions, 83, 101
  background of, 46
  becomes Abbott business manager, 50
  becomes Abbott chairman, 128
  becomes Abbott president, 104, 106
Cocaine, 84
Cod liver oil, 103
"Cold War," 135, 148, 163
Collier's magazine, 152
Colombia, 43
  Abbott facilities in, 152
Colson, Charles, 188
Columbia (space shuttle), 201
Columbia University, 101
Comiskey Park, 104
Commerce and Labor, U.S. Department of,
  44
Common Market, 152
Communist party
  in China, 137, 150, 152, 157
  in Czechoslovakia, 135
  in Hungary, 150
  in Poland, 150
  in Russia/U.S.S.R., 72, 132
  in U.S., 132, 135, 139, 141, 144
  in Vietnam, 148, 188
Concentration camps, 104, 112
Congress, U.S., 52, 159
  Congressional Medal of Honor, U.S., 75
  black senator, first since Reconstruction,
  170
  election statistics, 59, 110
  female member of, first, 72
Continental Illinois National Bank, 152, 179
Cook, Frederick, 57

Cooley, Harold, 170
Coolidge, Calvin, 84, 86
Cooper, Gary, 92
Corbett, "Gentleman Jim," 23
Corfu, 79
Corrigan, Douglas ("Wrong Way"), 115
Cosmos, 192
Cox, Archibald, 184
Cox, David, 177, 190
Cox, James M., 79
Coxey, Jacob, 26
Crain's Chicago Business, 210
Crane, Stephen, 28
Crete, 32
Cromwell, Hobart W., 101
Crump, E. H., 57
Cuba
  Abbott subsidiary in, 112
  and Bay of Pigs, 161
  and Cuban missile crisis, 163
  and Cuban Rebellion, 32, 35
  international relations of, 161, 188, 197
  in Spanish-American War, 32, 35, 41
Curry, John Steuart, 101
Cutter Laboratories, 181
Cyclamates, 139, 177, 179
Czechoslovakia, 115, 117, 135

Dainabot, K.K., 204
Dainabot Radioisotope Laboratories, Ltd.,
  168
Dainippon Pharmaceutical Co., Ltd., 168,
  204
Dakin, Henry D., 70, 77
Daladier, Edouard, 115
Daley, Richard, 175
Dalí, Salvador, 46
Dardanelles, 68
Darrow, Clarence, 86, 88
Darwin, Charles, 88
D-Day, 126
Dean, Daffy, 106
Dean, Dizzy, 106
Dean, John, 184, 188
Death penalty in U.S., 103
Dehn, Adolf, 108
Delaney Amendment to the Food Additive
  Laws, 179
Dempsey, Jack, 81, 84, 99
Deng Xiaoping, 201
Denmark, 43, 119, 152
Depakene (Abbott product), 195, 204
Depakote (Abbott product), 204
Department of Defense, U.S., 181
Dermatological Research Laboratories, 83,
  104, 106
DES (diethylstilbestrol), 157
Deutsche-Abbott GmbH, 168, 199
Dewey, Admiral George, 35
Dewey, Thomas E., 126, 135
Diagnostics Division, 170, 184, 206
  products in, 144, 186, 192, 201-3, 208-12
Diasone (Abbott product), 119
Dicumarol discovered, 70
Diesel, Rudolf, 46
Dillinger, John, 106
Dix, Dorothy, 30
Doblado, Manuel, 112
Doctor's Quick Weight Loss Diet (book),
  172
Dole, Sanford, 39
Domagk, Gerhard, 119
Doolittle, Jimmy, 123
"Doonesbury" (cartoon), 177
Dorais, Charles ("Gus"), 64
Dosimetric Medical Review, 19
Dosimetry, 23
  Abbott ends involvement in, 50, 64, 66,
  68, 77

217

219

Quarter Century Club, 135
Queen Elizabeth (film), 63

Raab, G. Kirk, 201
Radford, Arthur, 146
Radio, 79, 95, 97, 99, 115
Radioactive drugs, 90, 130, 144
Radiocaps (Abbott product), 144
Radioisotopes, 130
RAF (Royal Air Force), 119, 123
Ragged Dick (book), 37
Railroad accidents in U.S., 39, 48, 52
Raiziss, George W., 83
Rand, Sally, 104
Rankin, Jeannette, 72
Ranson, James W., 28, 44
Rasmussen, Arthur, 179
Rauwolfia, 137
Ravenscroft, Edward H., 59, 79
Ravenscroft, Mrs. Edward H. *See* Abbott, Lucy
Ravenswood, Illinois, Abbott facilities in, 15, 19, 41, 79, 88, 164
Ravenswood Exchange Bank, 52
RCA, 146
REA, 108
Reagan, Ronald, 155, 190, 201, 204, 208
  elected U.S. president, 199, 206
Red Badge of Courage (book), 28
Reed, Walter, 39
Reichsbank, 115
Reichstag fire (Germany), 104
Relativity, theory of, announced, 70
"Remember Me? I Was at Bataan" (War Bond poster), 126
R. J. Reynolds Company, 61, 64
Rhodes, Cecil, 43
Rice, Grantland, 86
Rice Institute (Houston, Texas), 21
Richardson, Elliott, 184
Richter, Emily, 28, 63
Richter, Ida, 28, 63
Rickenbacker, Eddie, 75
Ride, Sally K., 204
Riggs, Bobby, 184
Riis, Jacob, 19
RKO Radio Pictures, 146
Rockefeller, John D., 61
Rockefeller, John D., Jr., 130
Rockefeller, Nelson, 175, 186
Rockefeller Foundation, 86
Rockefeller Institute, 83
Rockne, Knute Kenneth, 64, 101
Rocky Mount, North Carolina, Abbott plant in, 181
Roentgen, Wilhelm, 28
Rogers, Buddy, 92
Rolls-Royce Company, 46
Romanov dynasty (Russia), 72
Rommel, Erwin, 123
Roosevelt, Franklin Delano, 59, 104, 128
  and economic recovery, 104, 108, 115
  elected U.S. president, 103, 110, 119, 126
  and World War II, 112, 121
Roosevelt, Theodore, 35, 41-50
  elected U.S. president, 39, 46, 63
Rosenberg, Julius and Ethel, 141
Ross, Richard M., 88, 166, 177
Ross, Stanley, 88
Ross Laboratories, 166, 168, 170, 175, 177, 201
  and *Similac*, 88, 190
Rosten, Leo, 108
"Rough Riders," 35
Royal Ballet company (Great Britain), 101
Royal Infirmary (Great Britain), 101
Ruby, Jack, 164
Rush Medical College (Chicago, Illinois), 46

Russia. *See also* Union of Soviet Socialist Republics (U.S.S.R.)
  in Balkan Wars, 64
  and Russian Revolution, 72, 77
  in Russo-Japanese War, 46, 48
  in World War I, 66, 68, 72

Saccharin, 50, 66, 139
Sadat, Anwar al-, 179, 192, 195, 197, 201
St. Helens, Mt., 199
St. Johnsbury Academy (Vermont), 17
St. Louis Browns, 144
St. Louis Cardinals, 106
St. Mary's Hospital (London, England), 121
St.-Vincent Millay, Edna, 108
Salk, Jonas, 143
Salomé (opera), 52
Salvarsan, 72
Sandburg, Carl, 108
San Francisco, California, Abbott branch office in, 59
San Francisco Examiner, 186
Saroyan, William, 108
Saskatchewan (Canadian province), 48
Schamberg, Jay Frank, 83
Schoellhorn, Robert A., 192, 206, 212
  awards received by, 210
  background of, 199
  becomes Abbott chairman, 201
  becomes Abbott president, 190
  heads hospital group, 184
  and international expansion, 195, 204
Schoenhofen, Leo, 179
Schreiber, Georges, 126
Schuler, Jack W., 212
Scientific theories and discoveries. *See also* Inventions
  ACTH synthesized, 137
  in blood pressure, 137
  Dicumarol discovered, 70
  electrons discovered, 23
  heart implant, first artificial, performed, 204
  heart transplant, first human, performed, 172
  heavy water discovered, 101
  heparin discovered, 70
  insulin discovered, 83
  leukocytes discovered, 83
  penicillin discovered, 95
  quantum theory proposed, 39
  relativity, theory of, announced, 70
  Salk vaccine developed, 143
  uranium split, 117
  in vitamins, 61, 83, 90
  X rays discovered, 28
  yellow fever, cause of, proven, 41
Scopes, John T., 88
Scopes "monkey trial," 88
Scribner, Gilbert, Jr., 179
Scribner & Co., 179
Seaman, Irving, Jr., 179
Searle, Jack, 164
G. D. Searle & Co., 88, 159, 164
Seattle, Washington, Abbott branch office in, 59
Seattle Sounders, 192
SEC, 108
Selden, George B., 28
Selenium, 141
Selfridge, Thomas, 55
Selsun Suspension (Abbott product), 141
Semler, Bernard, 188
Serbia, 64, 66
Serbo-Croat-Slovene Kingdom, 97
"Sesame Street" (TV program), 177
Seven-Up, 97
Sexual Behavior in the Human Male (book), 135

Shahn, Ben, 108
Shattuck, Henry B., 28, 44
Shepard, Alan B., Jr., 161
Sherman, James S., 55
Sherman, John, 19
Sherman Antitrust Act, 19
Shiite Muslims, 208
Ships
  disasters
    Andrea Doria, 150
    Larchmont, 52
    Lusitania, 68
    Mississippi steamboat fires, 15
    Stockholm, 150
    Titanic, 63
Show is On (Abbott employee show), 117
Siciliano, Angelo, 83
"Sidewalks of New York" (song), 26
Similac (Abbott product), 88, 166, 190, 195
  with Iron, 157
Simmons, George H., 55
Simpson, Wallis Warfield, 110
Sinclair, Upton, 50
Singapore, 123
Singer Building, 55
Sino-Japanese Wars, 28, 112
Sir Barton (horse), 77
Sirhan Sirhan, 175
Slavery, 15, 59
Smith, Alfred E., 26, 95
Smith, Kate, 101
Smith, Lawrence Beall, 108, 126
Smith, Kline & French Laboratories, 159
Soccer. *See also* specific team
  North American Soccer League championship, 192
  Pelé, 192
  World Cup championship, 203
Socialist Labor Party, U.S., 55
Social Security, 119
Solidarity union, 203
Solzhenitsyn, Aleksandr, 186
Somoza Debayle, Anastasio, 195
Son of the Sheik (film), 90
Sopwith, Thomas, 63
Sopwith Aviation, 63
Sorenson Research, 199
South Africa, Union of, 59, 157
South Dakota, 17
  University, 37
South Korea, 139
Soviet Union. *See* Union of Soviet Socialist Republics (U.S.S.R.)
Space program
  and Abbott research, 186
  Apollo, 177, 186
  black in space, first American, 204
  manned flights, first, 161
  moon landing, first, 177
  space shuttles, U.S., 201, 204, 210
  Sputnik, 152
  Voyager 2, 201
  woman in space, first American, 204
Spain, 19
  in Spanish-American War, 32, 35, 41
  and Spanish Civil War, 110, 112, 117
Spanish influenza, 75
Sparkman, John J., 143
Spencer, Lady Diana, 201
Spindletop claim (Texas), 41
Spirit of the Border (book), 50
Spirit of St. Louis (plane), 92
Spitfire airplanes, 119
Spring Show (Abbott employee show), 117
Sputnik (spacecrafts), 152
Stalin, Joseph, 72, 86, 90, 144
Standard Oil Company, 61
"Star-Spangled Banner," 101
Statue of Liberty, 210

221